Globalization of Chinese Enterprises

Globalization of Chinese Enterprises

Edited by

Ilan Alon

and

John R. McIntyre

palgrave
macmillan

First published 2008 by
PALGRAVE MACMILLAN
Houndmills, Basingstoke, Hampshire RG21 6XS and
175 Fifth Avenue, New York, N.Y. 10010
Companies and representatives throughout the world

PALGRAVE MACMILLAN is the global academic imprint of the Palgrave
Macmillan division of St. Martin's Press, LLC and of Palgrave Macmillan Ltd.
Macmillan® is a registered trademark in the United States, United Kingdom
and other countries. Palgrave is a registered trademark in the European
Union and other countries.

ISBN-13: 978–0–230–51562–8 hardback
ISBN-10: 0–230–51562–2 hardback

This book is printed on paper suitable for recycling and made from fully
managed and sustained forest sources. Logging, pulping and manufacturing
processes are expected to conform to the environmental regulations of the
country of origin.

A catalogue record for this book is available from the British Library.

A catalog record for this book is available from the Library of Congress.

2007048701

10   9   8   7   6   5   4   3   2
17   16   15   14   13   12   11   10   09   08

Printed and bound in Great Britain by
CPI Antony Rowe, Chippenham and Eastbourne

From Ilan Alon: To Kareen
From John McIntyre: To Sim and Tim

Contents

List of Figures, Tables and Exhibits

Figures

Tables

Exhibits

Foreword

John Child

Even excluding Hong Kong, China has become the largest source of foreign direct investment (FDI) outflows among developing and transition economies. This surging outflow of "China dollars" has been stimulated by the country's huge reserves of foreign currency which by the end of 2006 exceeded US$1000 billion. It clearly indicates that the increasing globalization of China's enterprises is becoming a very significant factor in world business.

The collection of chapters in this book makes an extremely timely contribution to our understanding of an important and relatively new phenomenon. It offers analytical insights into the globalization of Chinese enterprises supported by more specific studies of selected sectors and firms. One fundamental analytical distinction discussed is that between asset-seeking and asset-exploiting internationalization. Much outward FDI from China has been seeking to acquire the oil and other raw material assets required to feed the country's sustained rapid industrial growth. Other outward FDI has had the ultimate aim of exploiting overseas markets, but in the shorter term also reflects the need of Chinese enterprises to acquire the assets necessary to achieve such exploitation – in particular, advanced technology, international brands, and managerial expertise. A further contribution this book offers is the discussion in some chapters of the pattern that Chinese enterprise globalization follows. For example, it is recognized that many Chinese firms undertake a preparatory stage of "internal" internationalization in which they acquire global production and quality competencies through serving as producers for OEMs or through forming joint ventures with multinational corporations. Questions are raised as to whether there are several globalization patterns present among Chinese firms, and whether these conform to the Western experience of firm internationalization rather than the "latercomer" strategy that has been noted for globalizing companies from Korea and Taiwan.

The *Globalization of Chinese Enterprises* surfaces a number of specific issues as well. Do the globally competitive advantages of Chinese firms embrace more than just low production costs? Do Chinese firms, for instance, typically possess a distinctive entrepreneurial advantage through their membership of close-knit networks founded on *guanxi*? Are domestic networks of particular significance for helping to resource smaller enterprises that would otherwise find overseas expansion a daunting challenge? Are there institutional factors peculiar to China supporting the globalization of Chinese enterprises, especially informal assistance in terms of ready and cheap finance? Or is it also the case that some Chinese firms strive to invest abroad in order to escape domestic institutional restrictions such as interference from government officials and limitations on their ability to raise capital in the market?

This book also contains rich insights from studies of internationalizing sectors, notably automobiles and electronics, as well as notable examples of globalizing Chinese enterprises, such as Haier, Huawei, Lenovo, TCL, and Wuliangye. In this way it makes a valuable start to the process of providing firm- and sector-specific information on Chinese globalization, a process that is going to take some time but that is so essential to enable the identification of contextual and other influencing factors.

It has been both an education and a pleasure to read this book and I commend the authors for their efforts in producing it and organizing the focused conference from which it derives. I am sure that you will find it equally rewarding.

John Child
Chair of Commerce
Birmingham Business School
University of Birmingham
Birmingham, UK

Preface: Chinese Firms at the Crossroads

*Shaomin Li**

A question looming large: Where is China going?

For all of us who study China, no matter whether from economic, managerial, or marketing perspectives, there is always a general question looming large over us – "where is China going?" or "is China going to replace the United States as the world leader?" While social scientists tend to study this question directly at the macro level, we, as students of international business, mostly trained in management and marketing, tend to study it indirectly from the firm-level perspective. I will first take the macro approach and then come down to the firm level to discuss the role of firms in China's institutional change and globalization.

China's phenomenal economic growth seems to defy economic theories. Douglass North recently admitted that institutionalists know little about how China's institutional settings have created economic success (North, 2005). He observes:

> None of the standard models of economic and political theory can explain China. After a disastrous era of promoting collective organization, in which approximately thirty million people died of starvation, China gradually fumbled its way out of the economic disaster it had created by instituting the Household Responsibility System which provided peasants with incentives to produce more. This system in turn led to the TVEs (town–village enterprises) and sequential development built on their cultural background. But China still does not have well-specified property rights, town–village enterprises hardly resembled the standard firm of economics, and it remains to this day a Communist dictatorship.

And then North poses a question: "What kind of a model is that for the developing world?" While he does not answer it directly, he does note that "it is not a good model and it is still not clear what the outcome will be."

Sharing his confusion, and with the recent development in and debate on China, I have been thinking about the major issues concerning China's development. Based on my study and exchange with colleagues, I have summarized the following four puzzles on China's development. Addressing them will help us better understand where China is today and how the future holds for it.

Puzzles of China's development

Puzzle 1: How has China achieved record economic growth under an institutional environment that does not seem to be conducive to economic development?

If one describes a country that is under Communist rule, where the government controls what the citizen can say and hear, where the legal system is poor, and corruption is rampant, does that country sound like one that can enjoy phenomenal economic growth? Obviously not. But as we all know, the description fits China.

Take the case of corruption. Why does *not* corruption drag down the Chinese economy? According to the corruption ranking by Transparency International, China's corruption level is high. Most countries with similar corruption levels have low economic growth except China. Why?

Under Mao Zedong, firms (and individuals) were confined in a straight-jacket. They had neither the incentive nor the freedom to perform. When Mao died, Deng's reform was to simply untie the firms, to give them freedom to produce and sell what they produce. With the memory of the absolute poverty under Mao still fresh, and the sudden liberalization from government control, the Chinese firms and workers released tremendous energy and worked very hard, creating the Chinese growth miracle. Corruption was used as a lubricant to make the totally disfunctioning, rigid Communist bureaucracy move, improving efficiency. In this sense, the phenomenal growth is created by reducing the stifling Communist regulations, not by establishing sound political and economic institutions.

By now, many Chinese firms have become powerful, and some individuals have become wealthy. However, the market lacks transparent and fair rules, it is based on personal connections and, as a result, corruption is rampant. It is time for China to go further to establish the rule of law and checks and balances (Li, Park, & Li, 2004). The issue is how can China achieve it and what is the role of the Chinese firms in it?

Puzzle 2: Why do the Chinese seem to be uninterested in democratization?

Of the former Communist countries undergoing rapid transition, all have embarked on democratization except China. The conventional wisdom is that the Chinese are not eager to embrace democratization lest it may precipitate social unrest that halts its economic progress (McGregor, 2006). Is this true or is it a myth?

Opinion surveys in China show that about two-thirds (65–70 percent) of Chinese citizens support the ideas of democracy, comparable to the percentage in mature democratic countries such as the United States (Chen, 2006). The statement that "the Chinese do not want democracy" is a myth. The issue is how can China achieve democracy? There are two schools of thoughts among political scientists: Ronald Inglehart of Michigan University emphasizes the role of the masses (Inglehart, 2003), while Samuel Huntington of Harvard emphasizes the role of elites (Huntington, 1991). China may need the effort of both to have a peaceful democratization.

Another myth is that "democracy slows down economic growth." Research by Adam Przeworski of New York University and associates shows that democracy does not hinder economic growth (Przeworski, Alvarez, Cheibub, & Limongi, 2000). Poor economies have similar probability to develop either under democracy or under dictatorship. However, democracies are more capable of absorbing social shocks such as strikes and demonstrations, whereas dictatorships are more vulnerable to such shocks. Furthermore, for countries with similar income levels, citizens under democracy have much better lives than their counterparts under dictatorship.

Puzzle 3: Is the importing of low-priced Chinese goods the cause of Americans losing jobs? How do we understand the trade imbalance and how long can it last?

Trade disputes between the United States and China are basically that the Chinese government keeps the yuan way undervalued so that it can export goods below cost and take away American jobs. The second part is not quite true – the low and semiskilled Chinese workers are not competing directly against mostly high-skilled American workers yet. However, the first part is true – the Chinese are subsidizing our consumption of goods and capital, but how long can it last?

As long as China's major economic institutions and key economic factors, such as the exchange rate, remain controlled by the Chinese government and as long as US political institutions and economy remain strong, the needed reforms in property rights, currency mechanisms, transparency, among others, will only avail in limited circumstances. The key is further economic liberalization in China, and economic adjustment in the United States. I have great faith in the political and economic institutions of the United States, which have the built-in ability to adjust to maintain US competitiveness.

But unfair competition remains an issue. In this regard, Americans are more principled in their commitment to the doctrine of fair trade than the Chinese under the legacy of Mao's communism. Americans tend to follow fair trade principles even if it means foregoing some business opportunities. Examples abound in a variety of unexpected areas in the United States: some stores are closed on the Sabbath day (e.g., Chick-fil-A). Businesses are urged to "do well by doing good." Business ethics is taking center stage in the business community and business education. Many Chinese executives may lack business ethics education and may be extremely practical to the point of not following any moral principles whatsoever in conducting business. This may result in a type of competition between Chinese and American firms that appears asymmetrical.

Puzzle 4: Why are Chinese firms (or the Chinese economy) so competitive? How long can their competitiveness last?

Based on the literature and anecdotal evidence, I can speculate on the following four possible factors that may have made the Chinese firms and workers competitive:

(a) The horrible memory of absolute poverty under Mao (1949–1976). This gives a strong motivation to the Chinese to work extremely hard and save what they earn. This factor will be relatively quickly weakened as the new generation knows little about Mao and the hardship of the era.

(b) A culture – the Confucian work ethic – that values hard work, personal sacrifice for the family, frugality, and investment in education. Cultural theorist Hofstede quantifies the Confucian work ethic and estimates that its value is about 120 for China and 60 for India (Hofstede & Hofstede, 2005). This culture will be around longer than the memory of Mao, but will be gradually weakened as China becomes wealthy (as has happened in Japan).

(c) A large reservoir of low-cost labor. If we go to any Wal-Mart store in the United States, it is hard to find anything that is *not* made in China. This gives us the impression that the Wal-Marts, the GEs, the Nikes, and the GMs of the world are employing most of the Chinese in the working age group (15–64). But in reality, Chinese manufacturing industry employs only 37 million workers and there are 889 million people in the working age group (NBS, 2005). Most of them are in the rural area with little opportunity to earn a decent wage. This reserve labor force presents a strong pressure to keep the wage level from rising. This factor will take a long time to be fully utilized.

(d) A pro-business government. The Chinese Communist Party's main goal is to develop and grow the economy while maintaining its monopoly on political power. Its policy has been carefully designed to promote economic development by liberalizing trade, privatizing state assets, and removing state subsidies. However, all of these things are done with reservation and under substantial control. This is an uncertain factor, as political change can be rather abrupt.

In the framework of institutional change and its effects on a firm's strategy and performance, there are at least two major issues that need to be examined. The first is *how institutions affect firms*. International business and strategy scholars have accumulated a rich literature on this. The second issue is *how institutions change* in China (Li, Li, & Zhang, 2000). This is more difficult to study and has been largely overlooked. Or maybe this has been viewed as exogenous to firms and thus beyond the scope of international business and strategy studies.

Coming back to the theme of my article – Chinese firms at the crossroads – the reform was not initiated by firms; rather, it was initiated by the state seeking to unleash firms. This liberalization released tremendous energy in the firms to make profits. As a result, market competition in China is perhaps the fiercest in the world.

Now, the initiator of the reform, the government, seems to have run out of new tricks. The reforms seem to have come to a halt to bolster institutions and the rule of law. Political scientists such as Minxin Pei of the Carnegie Endowment for International Peace summarize it this way (Pei, 2006): "Although an initial pioneer in embracing market reforms, China today has fallen behind most former Soviet bloc countries, its large developing country peers (Mexico, Brazil and India) and most of its East Asian neighbours in terms of privatisation, regulation and the rule of law." Pei calls the problem facing China's reform as "trapped transition," characterized by "faltering institutional reforms and political stagnation."

The role of firms in China's institutional change and globalization

For enterprises, what does trapped transition imply? If we view the Chinese firm as a person, he was totally tied up during Mao's era, and then Deng and associates freed him. During the free-reigning reform years, freed firms competed fiercely, some, such as state-owned enterprises (SOEs), had special resources from the state. More than a quarter of century of market competition has turned some of the Chinese firms from weak kids into strong adults – huge powerful enterprises. However, most of them are adult only in body weight and muscle, but not in mentality. They now stumble onto the world market like clumsy giants, with little knowledge of the rules of mature markets.

Thus, the implication of the trapped transition is that the Chinese firms face the task of institutional learning and creation (Hargrave & Van De Ven, 2006; Oliver, 1991; Puffer & McCarthy, 2006). They can no longer be passive recipients of institutional arrangements by the state. They need to become active participants in institutional building in China, and learn the ways of global governance.

So far research on firms in China has viewed the firm as more or less a passive player reacting to the institutional settings and changes in China. The focus has been how institutions affect a firm's strategy and performance (e.g., Park, Li, & Tse, 2006). It is time for us to put the firms on the right-hand side of the equation, namely, as an independent variable to examine the role of firms in China's institutional change.

Anecdotal evidence from China has already illustrated the rising import-ance firms exert in institutional building in China. For example, when the Chinese government planned to increase the income tax rate for for-eign firms in 2004, some 54 foreign firms formed a coalition to voice their concern.

To understand the role of enterprises in institutional change, historical context is relevant. For example, the rise of England as the founder of the modern capitalism – the combination of the free market and liberal demo-cracy – may provide some hint on where China is going and how its enter-prises may play a role. In the past 400 years or so, some 500 city-states in Europe competed to become world powers. Economic historian Daron Acemoglu and associates of MIT (Acemoglu, Johnson, & Robinson, 2002) found that two main conditions were important in the rise and fall of these city-states: cross-Atlantic trade and a not-so-absolute monarch who shared the benefit of the trade with its subjects. Their reasoning is that cross-Atlantic trade would generate wealth and resources; if the king did not monopolize trade and allowed the merchant class to benefit from trade, then the latter would be able to accumulate wealth for political activities. Once the newly rich merchant class had accumulated the resources, it would push for rule of law and eventually democracy.

Spain and Portugal had access to cross-Atlantic trade, but their rulers were absolute and thus the two nations did not rise; Italy's rulers were benevol-ent but Italy did not have access to cross-Atlantic trade, thus it failed to ascend. Only England (and to some extent the Netherlands) had both and rose, which subsequently created the institutions of modern capitalism. The newly rich merchants in England funded the effort to limit the power of the monarch, ushering in pluralism and democracy.

Today's China meets the first condition: having access to a hugely prof-itable international trade; but is the Communist Party "not-so-absolute"? Can enterprises use their newly acquired resources to push for institutional change? These are the most fundamental and urgent issues for students of Chinese enterprise to tackle. The chapters in this book represent a welcome effort in addressing these issues.

Note

* I would like to thank Ilan Alon, Tim Devinney, Bill Judge, Dominick Salvatore, David Selover, Deepak Sethi, and Jun Xia for their comments and suggestions on earlier versions of this article.

References

Acemoglu, D., Johnson, S., & Robinson, J. (2002). The Rise of Europe: Atlantic Trade, institutional change, and economic growth: MIT.

Chen, J. (2006). Personal interview on public opinion polls in China by author (October, Norfolk): Old Dominion University.

Hargrave, T. J. & Van De Ven, A. H. (2006). A Collective Action Model of Institutional innovation. *Academy of Management Review, 31*(4), 864–888.

Hofstede, G. & Hofstede, G. J. (2005). *Cultures and Organizations: Software of the Mind.* New York: McGraw-Hill.

Huntington, S. P. (1991). *The Third Wave: Democratization in the Late 20th Century:* Oklahoma University.

Inglehart, R. (2003). How Solid is Mass Support for Democracy–and How Can We Measure it? *Political Science & Politics, 36*, 51-57.

Li, S., Li, S., & Zhang, W. (2000). The Road to Capitalism: Competition and Institutional Change in China. *Journal of Comparative Economics, 28*, 269–292.

Li, S., Park, S. H., & Li, S. (2004). The Great Leap Forward: The Transition from Relation-based Governance to Rule-based Governance. *Organizational Dynamics, 33*(1), 63–78.

McGregor, J. (2006). No more Chinese Whispers. *Wall Street Journal* (Sept 12).

NBS. (2005). *China Statistical Yearbook (CD version).* Beijing: National Bureau of Statistics of China.

North, D. (2005, 7 April). The Chinese Menu (for development). *Wall Street Journal,* p. A14.

Oliver, C. (1991). Strategic responses to Institutional processes. *Academy of Management Review, 16*, 145–179.

Park, S. H., Li, S., & Tse, D. (2006). Market Liberalization and Firm Performance during China's Economic Transition. *Journal of International Business Studies, 37*(1), 127–147.

Pei, M. (2006). China Is Stagnating in Its "Trapped Transition." *Financial Times* (Feb 24).

Przeworski, A., Alvarez, M., Cheibub, J., & Limongi, F. (2000). *Democracy and Development: Political Institutions and Well-being in the World, 1950–1990.* Cambridge: Cambridge University Press.

Puffer, S. M. & McCarthy, D. J. (2006). Can Russia's State-managed, Network Capitalism be Competitive? Institutional Pull versus Institutional Push. *Journal of World Business, In press.*

Acknowledgements

This book has benefited from the reviews, edits, and discussion of many participants including:

Provost Roger Casey – Rollins College
Dr. Ping Deng – Maryville University
Dr. Gary Dessler – Florida International University
Dr. Yuping Du – Guangdong University of Foreign Studies
President Lewis Duncan – Rollins College
Dr. Chen W. Ferguson – Miami University
Dr. Marc Fetscherin – Rollins College
Jill Gable – Rollins China Center
Dr. Hongmei Gao – Kennesaw State University
Dr. James Gilbert – Crummer Graduate School of Business
Dr. Baiyun Gong – University of Pittsburgh
Dr. Zhao Hao, Cheung Kong Graduate School of Business
Dr. William Jankowiak – University of Nevada, Las Vegas
Dr. Jonatan Jelen – Parsons, The New School for Design & New York University
Dr. James Johnson – Crummer Graduate School of Business
Dr. Theodore T. Herbert – Crummer Graduate School of Business
Onur Kocaoz – Rollins China Center
Jun Kurihara – Harvard University
Professor Allen H. Kupetz – Crummer Graduate School of Business
Dr. Thomas Lairson – Rollins College
Dr. Shaomin Li – Old Dominion University
Dr. Qiang Li – Tsinghua University
Chrissy Leto – Rollins College Special Events
Xiaolin Lu – Rollins College
Dean Udeth Lugo – Rollins College
Dean Craig McAllaster – Crummer Graduate School of Business
Dr. Donald Rogers – Rollins College
Dr. Marc Sardy – Rollins College
Dr. Li Sun – University of Texas – Dallas
Bill Suchy – Orange TV & Vision TV
Dr. Kenna Taylor – Rollins College
Dr. Mark F. Toncar – Youngstown State University
Dr. Louise Tourigny – University of Wisconsin

Dr. Francis M. Ulgado – Georgia Institute of Technology
Dr. Fei Ling Wang – Georgia Tech University
Dr. Kaimei Wang – Cambridge University
Ping Wu – Rollins College
Kenneth Wright, Esquire – Baker Hostetler
Wenni Xiong – Eximuse Global Group
Dr. Monica Yang – Adelphi University
Dr. Wei Yang – Otto-von-Guericke University
Dr. Xiaohua Yang – Queensland University of Technology

We thank the following organization for supporting our efforts to bring together a group of talented scholars that make up the contributions for this book. These organizations include:

Crummer Graduate School of Business www.rollins.edu/crummer
Georgia Tech Center for International Business Education and Research – http://www.ciber.gatech.edu (http://www.ciber.gatech.edu/)
Georgia Tech College of Management – mgt.gatech.edu
Rollins China Center – www.rollins.edu/chinacenter
Rollins College Department of International Business www.rollins.edu/inb

Notes on Contributors

Ilan Alon is the Petters Chair of International Business and Executive Director of Rollins China Center, Rollins College, Winter Park, Florida. He is the author, editor, and co-editor of 10 books and over 100 published articles, chapters, and conference papers. His three recent books on China include *Chinese Culture, Organizational Behavior and International Business Management* (Greenwood, 2003), *Chinese Economic Transition and International Marketing Strategy* (Greenwood, 2003), and *Business and Management Education in China: Transition, Pedagogy and Training* (World Scientific, 2005). Dr Alon is a recipient of the Chinese Marketing Award from the Tripod Marketing Association (China) and the Society for Marketing Advances (USA), and the Rollins College McKean Award for his work on education in China. He has taught courses in top Chinese MBA programs including Shanghai Jiao Tong University, Fudan University, and China Europe International Business School. He is also an international business consultant and a featured speaker in many professional associations. (ialon@rollins.edu)

John Child holds the Chair of Commerce in the Birmingham Business School, University of Birmingham, UK. His MA and PhD are from the University of Cambridge, which also awarded him a higher doctorate (ScD) for his outstanding scholarly work. In 2002, he was elected Fellow of the Academy of Management, and in 2004 received the Distinguished Contribution Award of the International Academy for Chinese Management Research. In 2006 he was made Fellow of the British Academy (FBA). He was Dean and Director of the China-Europe Management Institute in Beijing 1989–1990 and the Diageo Professor of Management at Cambridge University, before taking up his current post at Birmingham. Professor Child was Editor-in-Chief of *Organization Studies* from 1992 to 1996. He is the author or co-author of 18 books and over 130 articles in learned journals. He published two new books in 2005: *Organization: Contemporary Principles and Practice* (Blackwell) and (with David Faulkner and Stephen Tallman) *Cooperative Strategy* (Oxford University Press). j.child@bham.ac.uk

Ping Deng is Associate Professor of Business Administration at John E. Simon School of Business in Maryville University of St. Louis, USA, where he teaches courses mainly in international business and corporate finance for both MBA and undergraduate students. His research interests concentrate on global strategic management and particularly foreign direct investment (FDI) related with Asian–Pacific countries. He has published dozens of articles in peer-reviewed academic journals such as *Business Horizons*, *Asian Survey*, and *Journal of International Management* and also made numerous presentations at leading scholarly conferences including the annual meetings of Academy of Management (AOM) and Academy of International Business (AIB).

Dr Deng has regularly served as paper reviewer for a number of leading journals including *Journal of International Business Studies* and *Journal of World Business*. Also, he has frequently been interviewed by and quoted in influential national media and news magazines such as *Fortune* magazine and India's *Economic Times*. In April 2006, he was invited to Mexico City by the United Nations Conference on Trade and Development (UNCTAD) to critique a draft of the conference's 2006 *World Investment Report* (WIR) and made suggestions to UNCTAD for the report's final version. (pdeng@maryville.edu)

Quek Kia Fatt is an associate professor at the School of Medicine and Health Sciences, Monash University, Malaysia campus, and was formerly at the Faculty of Medicine, University of Malaya. He is a fellow of the Royal Institute of Public Health (FRIPH), UK, and a medical statistics consultant. He has published extensively in leading international refereed journals. His research interests include public health, urology, health psychology, quality of life, and management. He is currently working on several joint research papers with the first author. (quek.kia.fatt@med.monash.edu.my)

Marc Fetscherin is Assistant Professor in the International Business Department at Rollins College. He teaches various courses related to International Business. Dr Fetscherin was Fellow at Harvard University as well as a researcher at the University of California at Berkeley. He received his PhD in Economics and Social Science from the University of Bern, Switzerland. He also holds a master degree in Business Administration (MBA) from the London School of Economics (LSE), UK, as well as a Master in Management (MIM) from the University of Lausanne, Hautes Etudes Commerciales (HEC), Switzerland. Dr Fetscherin has extensive international experience and speaks five languages. From an early age he has lived and traveled internationally. In the last couple of years he has traveled to over 25 countries, and has lived in some of them for several months. He also has international business experience consulting at McKinsey & Company, a global management consulting company. Currently he is also the Chief Executive Officer of Bonfort SA, a Swiss-based luxury refinement company. (mfetscherin@rollins.edu)

Xudong Gao received his PhD degree from Sloan Management School, MIT, in 2003. He is the Associate Professor of Department of Innovation and Entrepreneur Management, School of Economics & Management, and the research scientist of technology innovation center, Tsinghua University. He is the author, editor, and co-editor of 5 books and over 50 published articles, chapters, and conference papers. His current research interests include technology strategies, strategic management, and high-tech entrepreneur management.

James P. Gilbert, Ph.D., is Professor of Quantitative Analysis and Operations Management at the Crummer Graduate School of Rollins College. Jim was Director of Inventory Planning at the DeVilbiss Corporation in Toledo, Ohio. Along with his colleague Richard J. Schonberger, he developed the area of just-in-time purchasing from work originating at the Toyota Manufacturing Company of Japan. These purchasing practices are now used worldwide. His teaching, research, and consulting expertise include just-in-time systems, quality management practices, and quantitative decision support for efficient business systems. Jim was co-general chair and Program Chair for the Production & Operations Management International Conference in Shanghai, China, held at the China–Europe International Business School (CEIBS) in 2006.

Dr Gilbert is Lilly Teaching Fellow, a Richard B. Russell Teaching Award recipient, a past MBA Teacher of the Year, and several times the Department of Management Teacher of the year. Dr Gilbert has taught outside of the United States, teaching Contemporary Quality Management at the Institute d'Administration des Enterprises, Université Jean Moulin, Lyon, France. He is past Division Chair of the Operations Management Division of the Academy of Management. Jim served the Production and Operations Management Society (POMS) from 2002 to 2005 as vice-president for meetings and served as co-general chair for the 2005 operations management conference in Shanghai, China. Dr Gilbert has led consulting projects at Cirent Semiconductors (now Agere Systems), Scholastic Books Fairs, Johnson & Johnson, Scholastic, Inc., PEMCO Aviation Group, Asia Bovea Brown (ABB), HTE, Inc., among others. (jgilbert@rollins.edu)

Ted Herbert is Professor of Management at the Crummer Graduate School of Business at Rollins College in Winter Park, Florida, USA. He is Fellow of the Academy of Management and of the Southern Management Association. He has published 13 editions of textbooks and a reference book on management education and development (named an "Outstanding Academic Book" by *Choice*), more than 80 scholarly articles, and numerous cases. His research has been presented to professional and academic audiences in over 120 papers throughout the United States, Canada, China, Mexico, Australia, France, and Italy. The journals in which he has published his work include *Strategic Management Journal, Academy of Management Review, Journal of Management, Management International Review, International Journal of Entrepreneurship and Innovation, Entrepreneurship Theory and Practice, Organizational Dynamics, Business Quarterly, Decision Sciences,* and *Journal of Business and Entrepreneurship.* Dr Herbert is an active consultant to organizations on strategy and strategy-related issues. (therbert@rollins.edu)

Loi Teck Hui is a fellow of the Association of Chartered Certified Accountants (ACCA), UK, and a member of the Strategic Management Society. He has worked with a Big Four firm, major multinational corporations, Chinese firms, and academic institutions. His research works have appeared in international journals and conferences. He is conducting a sponsored research at the University of Malaya and will be expected to serve a state-related entity. He is the recipient of *outstanding paper reviewer* award from the management consulting division of the Academy of Management in 2006. (Loi.Teck.Hui@accamail.com)

Jim Johnson, a native of London, England, is Associate Professor of International Business and Director of Global Consulting Projects for MBA students at the Crummer Graduate School of Business, Rollins College, Florida. Prior to relocating to the United States in 1987, he lived and worked in the United Kingdom, Spain, Finland, Yugoslavia, and Mexico. He received his PhD in International Business and Strategic Management from the University of South Carolina in 1997. Dr Johnson's research interests focus on cross-cultural management, developing cross-cultural competence, strategic decision making in multinational corporations, and the management of international alliances. His research has been presented at major international conferences and has been published in top journals in strategic management and international business. In 2005, he ranked among the Global Top 100 researchers in international business. He is a member of the Academy of Management and the Academy of International Business. (jpjohnson@rollins.edu)

Jun Kurihara is a senior fellow at Mossavar-Rahmani Center for Business and Government, John F. Kennedy School of Government, Harvard University, Cambridge, Massachusetts. He is the author and co-author of 5 books and about 40 published articles and conference papers. His books and recent articles on China include *Chugouku: Habado karano Kensho* (*China: A Japanese Perspective at Harvard*, Tokyo: Keio University Press, forthcoming), A Difficult Manage Trois in An Incommodious East Asia:

Japan-U.S.-China Relationship in the Early 21st Century (presentation material at Kobe Gakuin University, Kobe, Japan, 2006), The Impact of Knowledge Networks on International Cooperation in the Asia Pacific Region (presentation material at the Harvard-Fudan-Kansai Keizai Doyukai Symposium, Osaka, Japan, 2005), and Economic Development in Northeast China: A Study of Electronic Components Industry (Mimeograph, 2005). Mr Kurihara serves an advisor to the Maureen & Mike Mansfield Center, the University of Montana, with a view to promoting an intellectual dialogue among the three countries: the United States, Japan, and China. Prior to joining the Harvard community in 2003, he was asked by the Chinese Academy of Social Science (CASS) in Beijing to deliver speeches on the Japanese economy and US-Japan relations every quarter between 1998 and 2002. (Jun_Kurihara@ksg.harvard.edu)

Thomas D. Lairson is Gelbman Professor of International Business, Professor of Political Science, and Director of the International Studies Center at Rollins College. He is the co-author of *International Political Economy: The Struggle for Power and Wealth* (Wadsworth, fourth edition forthcoming). Professor Lairson is author of numerous articles on topics ranging from American foreign policy in the early cold war to the political economy of high-technology development. Most recently, he wrote "Supply Chain Management and the Internet," in Hossein Bidgoli (ed.) *The Internet Encyclopedia*, John Wiley, 2004. He has served on the editorial board of the important journal *PS: Political Science and Politics*.

Professor Lairson was the first Ford Foundation Professor of International Relations at the Institute for International Relations in Hanoi in 1994. He is twice winner of the Arthur Vining Davis award for outstanding teaching at Rollins. Dr Lairson's current research includes a book manuscript, "Knowledge, Institutions and Economic Growth in Asia," and "Globalization Compared: Understanding Complex Systems of Development Across the 19th and 20th Centuries." (tlairson@rollins.edu)

Thomas C. Lawton is Director of Joint Honours Programmes and Associate Professor of Strategy and International Business at Tanaka Business School, Imperial College, London. He is a visiting professor at the Tuck School of Business, Dartmouth College (USA), IEDC – Bled School of Management (Slovenia), and Trinity College, Dublin (Ireland). He holds degrees from University College Cork and the London School of Economics and has a PhD in International Political Economy from the European University Institute in Florence, Italy. Dr Lawton's research and consulting expertise focuses on strategic leadership and market breakout, the process and practice of strategy and corporate internationalization.

Dr Lawton is also a leading authority on aviation management and the competitive dynamics of the global airline business. His numerous professional and academic journal papers have been published in reputable international journals such as *Management International Review, European Management Journal, Thunderbird International Business Review, Long Range Planning, Venture Capital, International Business Review, Business and Politics*, and the *Journal of Public Policy*. He is also the author or editor of five books, including *Strange Power* (2000) and *Cleared for Takeoff* (2002). His latest co-authored book, *Breakout Strategy: Meeting the challenge of double-digit growth*, is published by McGraw-Hill, New York, 2007 (http://mcgraw-hill. co.uk/breakoutstrategy/). Dr Lawton can be contacted by telephone at +44 20 7594 9117 or via e-mail (t.lawton@imperial.ac.uk).

Qiang Li is pursuing his master degree in the Department of Innovation and Entrepreneur Management, School of Economics & Management, Tsinghua University. He is the author of six published articles and conference papers. His current research interests include globalization strategies of Chinese enterprises and technology strategies. (liq2.04@em.tsinghua.edu.cn)

Shaomin Li is Professor of Management and International Business at Old Dominion University and Associate Editor of *Corporate Governance: An International Review*. His current research focuses on the business environment in countries undergoing rapid political and economic transitions. He has written and edited 9 books and has published more than 40 academic articles. His articles have appeared in *California Management Review, Demography, Journal of Comparative Economics, Journal of International Business Studies*, and *Journal of Mathematical Sociology*, among others. His commentaries on China appeared in *The New York Times* and *The Wall Street Journal*. In 1990 Professor Li co-founded the Center for Modern China in Princeton and served as the founding editor of *Modern China Studies*. Professor Li has taught in China, Hong Kong, and Korea. Professor Li graduated from Peking University, obtained his PhD from Princeton University, and was a post-doctoral fellow at Harvard University.

Ku-Ho Lin is associate research fellow at Chung Hua Institution for Economic Research (CIER) in Taiwan. He received his PhD in Management Studies from Royal Holloway, University of London, UK, in 2005. Dr Lin's research field focuses on internationalization strategy and international marketing, He has written several papers that have been published or accepted for publication in international journals and conference proceedings. Dr Lin can be contacted by telephone at +886 2 27356006 ext.523 or via e-mail (link@cier.edu.tw).

John R. McIntyre has been Executive Director of the Georgia Tech Center for International Business Education and Research (CIBER), a national center of excellence, since 1993 and a professor of international business management and international relations with joint appointments in the College of Management and the Sam Nunn School of International Affairs of the Georgia Institute of Technology, Atlanta, Georgia. He is also a senior fellow of the Center for Trade and International Security of the University of Georgia, Athens, Georgia. He received his graduate education at McGill, Strasbourg, and Northeastern universities, obtaining his PhD at the University of Georgia. Prior to joining Georgia Tech in September 1981, he was Research Associate for International Management at the Dean Rusk Center, University of Georgia School of Law. Published articles are in journals such as *Osteuropa Wirtschaft* (Munich), *Technology and Society*, *Public Administration Quarterly*, *International Management Review*, *Defence Analysis* (London), *Studies in Comparative and International Development*, *Crossroads* (Oxford), *The Journal of European Marketing*, *Jeune Afrique*, *Le Moci* (Paris), *CCE International* (Paris), *Politique Internationale* (Paris), *International Trade Journal*, *International Executive*, *Fordham International Law Journal*, *Journal of Global Business*, as well as many book chapters. He is author and co-editor of the following books: *Uncertainty in Busines-Government Relations: The Dynamics of International Trade Policy*, *The Political Economy of Technology Transfer*, *National Security* and *Technology Transfer: The Strategic Dimensions of East-West Trade*, *International Space Policy: Legal, Economic, and Strategic Options for the Twentieth Century and Beyond* and *Japan's Technical Standards: Implications for Global Trade and Competitiveness*, as well as *Business and Management Education in Transitioning and Developing Countries: A Handbook* and *Business and Management Education in China: Transition, Pedagogy and Training*. Dr McIntyre has extensive experience in designing and implementing international business education programs at the graduate, executive, and undergraduate levels. He has been the recipient of numerous government, foundation, and private corporate grants to further the internationalization of business education and the integration of foreign language, technology, international affairs into the management curriculum. (John.McIntyre@mgt. gatech.edu)

J. Mark Muñoz is Assistant Professor of International Business at the Millikin University in Decatur, IL. He has published in international journals such as the *Journal of Global Business and Technology*, *International Entrepreneurship and Management Journal*, and *Journal of Developmental Entrepreneurship*. He is the author of two books on globalization entitled *Land of My Birth* (Gyldan, 2005) and *Winning across Borders* with Marios Katsioloudes (ABP, 2006). He is a member of the editorial board of two international business journals, and has been a recipient of two Best Research Awards and a literary award. (jmunoz@mail.milikin.edu)

Mike W. Peng (Ph.D., University of Washington) is Provost's Distinguished Professor of Global Strategy and Executive Director of the Center for Global Business at the University of Texas at Dallas. He is widely regarded as one of the most prolific and most influential scholars in global strategy, and one of the foremost experts on China strategy. He has published over 40 articles in leading academic journals and authored 3 books. His most recent book, *Global Strategy*, is the best-selling textbook in this field in the world and is being translated into Chinese in 2006. He is Editor-in-Chief of the *Asia Pacific Journal of Management*, and has served on the editorial boards of the *Academy of Management Journal, Academy of Management Review, Journal of International Business Studies,* and *Strategic Management Journal.* He has also published his work in leading practitioner journals such as the *Harvard Business Review, Academy of Management Executive,* and *China Business Review.* (mikepeng@utdallas.edu)

Marc Sardy is Assistant Professor in the International Business Department at Rollins College. He teaches various courses related to International Business. Professor Sardy received his PhD in Finance from the University of Cambridge, UK. He also holds a master degree in statistics (MS) from the Zicklin School of Business, Baruch College, CUNY, as well as a Bachelors in Economics from the University of Chicago. He is particularly interested in International Finance, Entrepreneurship, Entertainment economics & Finance, and Complexity in Financial markets. Dr Sardy has extensive international experience. He has lived and worked in the United Kingdom, Australia, Canada, Malaysia, France, and the United States and has visited and worked in over 30 countries in the last 6 years. He also has international business experience working in consulting for Bain & Company, a global management consulting company. His recent research includes studies on equity duration, liquidity management of banking assets, the globalization of Chinese brands through joint venture and acquisition, studies of the Chinese automotive industry, entertainment economics, research on stock price reversals and income sensitive loans. (msardy@rollins.edu)

Matt Simmons is an international business consultant with experience in North America, South America, Europe and Asia, including Greater China. His experience in China began in 1996 in Shanghai and, since then, he has worked throughout the mainland, Hong Kong, and Taiwan, including living in the region from 1997 to 2000. He is currently an Executive MBA student at the Crummer School of Business, Rollins College, Winter Park, Florida. He has spoken and presented papers at several telecommunications industry conferences throughout the Asia–Pacific Region and Greater China, including the first China CDMA International Summit in Beijing in 1998. (mssimmons@rollins.edu)

Clyde D. Stoltenberg is the Barton Distinguished Chair in International Business and Associate Director of the Center for International Business Advancement at Wichita State University. Previously, he served as Professor and CIBER Co-Director at the University of Kansas, Executive Director of the East Asia Business Program at the University of Michigan, and Director of International Business Programs at the University of Texas, San Antonio, and California State University, Long Beach. His publications on Asian law and business have appeared in such journals as *American Journal of Chinese Studies, Asian Survey, Columbia Journal of World Business, Journal of Asian Business, Thunderbird International Business Review,* and the international law journals at Cornell, Michigan and Northwestern. He has been a visiting professor at Nankai University and the University of Hong Kong and an invited speaker on trade in services at conferences organized by the Law Institute of the Chinese Academy of Social Sciences and the Chinese Ministry of Justice. He is on the editorial board of the *Journal of Asian Business* and served as Editor-in-Chief of the *American Business Law Journal.*

Li Sun is a PhD student in the School of Management, University of Texas, at Dallas. He is the author or co-author of 9 books and over 20 published articles in China. His books include *Benchmark Management for High Growth Companies* (China Social Science Press, 2005), *Light Asset Strategy: Designing New Business Models for Creation Value* (China Social Science Press, 2003), *Merger and Acquisition Strategy* (China Industry and Business Press, 1995), and *Entrepreneur* (China Economics Press, 1993). His paper, "Complexity of Channel Evolution in China" (*Journal of Management,* Taiwan, 1999), received the 1999–2000 Best Paper Award from the Chinese Management Association. Prior to joining UTD, he was a senior partner in a leading Chinese consultant firm for financing startup companies. (sunli@yahoo.com)

Weiqiang Tan is a PhD candidate in the School of Business, Sun Yat-sen University, Guangzhou, China. His research fields are corporate finance and MNC activities in China. His recent papers include conference papers "An Analysis on Financing Activities of Foreign Funded Enterprises in China," published papers "Credit Trade: An Empirical Investigation from

View of Corporate Financing Motivate" (*South Economics*, 2006, in Chinese), "On the Consistency of Option Pricing Model with a General Equilibrium Framework" (*Journal of Systems Science and Information*, 2006, in Chinese). He is the co-editor of book *Modern Financial Economics* (Northeast Finance and Economics University Press, 2004, in Chinese). (gdtwq2002@yahoo.com.cn)

Fangcheng Tang received his PhD degree from School of Management, Xi'an Jiaotong University. He is a postdoctor of Department of Innovation and Entrepreneur Management, School of Economics & Management, Tsinghua University. He is the author and co-editor of 2 books and over 30 published articles, chapters, and conference papers. His current research interests include globalization strategies of Chinese enterprises, strategic management and new technology commercialization. (tangfch@em.tsinghua.edu.cn)

Xioahua Yang is Senior Lecturer in International Business in the Faculty of Business, Queensland University of Technology, Australia. She has presented and published in the areas of international R&D strategic alliance, foreign direct investment, international corporate social responsibility, and expatriate management in many international conferences and journals, including *Journal of High Technology Management Research* and *Journal of Emerging Markets*. She has been an invited speaker at a number of forums. She is the co-editor of Asia Pacific Journal of Management Special Issue Conference in November 2006.

Dr Yang has taught in the United States, Australia, and China in the areas of global business strategy and cross-cultural negotiation. In Fall 2006, she was a visiting associate professor in the School of Management at National Sun Yat Sen University in Kaohsiung, Taiwan. Previously, she has directed and conducted overseas study programs in Europe and Asia. She has also been a consultant and advisor to governments and firms. (x3.yang@qut.edu.au)

1
Introduction

Ilan Alon

While the 19th and 20th centuries belonged to Europe and the United States, respectively, many observers of China believe that the 21st century belongs to Asia and, more specifically, China (also called the Middle Kingdom). Oded Shenkar of Ohio State University, in his book *The Chinese Century* (Wharton School Publishing, 2005), shows how China is already dominant in so many industries and claims that the "Chinese economic miracle" resembles more the rise of the United States in the 20th century, rather than the Japanese economic growth after World War II. To the first question, Shenkar shows that China is already the "world's factory," occupying a large share in the total production in many industries:

- Toys: 70 %
- Bicycles: 60 %
- Microwave ovens: 50 %
- Shoes/clothing: 50 %
- Televisions: 33 %
- Air conditioners: 33 %
- Mobile phones: 33 %
- Washing machines: 25 %
- Refrigerators: 20 %

China is the third largest exporter after Germany and the United States, and the fifth largest outward foreign direct investor (Child and Rodrigues, 2005).

China' population is more than 10 times larger than that of Japan. This advantage gives it leverage with trade partners and abundant cheap labor for the foreseeable future. Secondly, China is a permanent member of the Security Council of the UN, with global ambitions for political leadership. Furthermore, the Chinese can import applicable knowledge and technology easily from Hong Kong, Taiwan, and overseas Chinese worldwide, and put these resources together using entrepreneurial ventures. Finally, China's foreign direct investment (FDI) inflows have exceeded those of the United States, and are changing the economic landscape. China is leveraging the FDI inflows to climb up the technology ladder, upgrade its human resources, and expropriate know-how through piracy, counterfeiting, and the like.

Not only is China the most populous nation attracting the most FDI, it is also the world's largest producer of coal and steel, the largest consumer of aluminum, copper, and cement, the largest market for cell phones, and the largest holder of US treasury bills.

What's next for China? Nothing short of global leadership is sought by the government. In the economic sphere, the government has identified global champions that it hopes will become globally competitive. Under the social market economy (SME), the government has a rolling five-year plan that helps direct the economy[1] by ceding to market forces in the management of resources without forfeiting control. State-owned enterprises (SOEs) have sold shares in stock markets in China, Hong Kong, New York, and London, but the Chinese government still controls 50–90% of the shares, and appoints executives and managers.

The next frontier in the economic battlefield is the globalization of Chinese enterprises. Lenovo's purchase of the IBM PC division is a well-known example. Little, however, is known about why and how Chinese firms internationalize. On the one hand, they are governed by the market forces of demand and supply, but, on the other hand, they can be aided and injured by the political agenda of the Chinese government. For example, the government has helped Chalco, an aluminum producer, by shutting down small competitors in China and thus facilitating its quest for resources globally. The Chinese banking industry is still protected. Citigroup and HSBC cannot accept Chinese yuan (also called renminbi or RMB) deposits of more than US$1 million. For the petroleum companies, the government has reduced the downside risks of exploration by developing oil and gas deposits and selling them back to the companies at a discount. The government also charges a lower income tax rate to domestic firms as compared to the rate charged to international oil companies. In the telecom industry, the government has set rates 5–10 times higher for China Mobile as compared to foreign competitors. In the utilities industry, Huaneng Power International gets expedited approvals for new power plants through strong relations in local and national governments (Yan, 2007).

Most studies of internationalization have been grounded in the paradigms of developed countries. However, it is increasingly apparent that the resulting theories may have to be adjusted when applied to China – which is one of a kind even among today's transition economies in terms of the emerging SME, uniquely controlled by market forces, government directives, and institutional constraints.

The globalization of the Chinese enterprises and the economy is a subject not well researched and is at the forefront of increasing attention. While research is scarce, notable articles exist. One such seminal article on examining the motives and patterns of Chinese multinationals was written by Child and Rodrigues (2005) in *Management and Organization Review*. The authors found that to create competitive position in the marketplace, Chinese firms seek technological and brand assets. Firms in China simultaneously draw inward production capabilities through original equipment manufacturing, on the one hand, and seek out acquisition targets and organic growth abroad, on the other hand. Each strategy has its advantages and disadvantages. Original equipment manufacturers (OEMs) provide an opportunity for knowledge and technology transfer but risk the need to balance the powers of the foreign company. Acquisition is the fastest way into a market, but risks of overpaying and the liability of foreignness are high. Finally, organic growth facilitates localization and improves global operations integration, but is slow and requires high investment and a capacity to manage overseas operations.

Filling this gap in the literature, this book represents a selection of peer-reviewed and presented conference papers on the first-ever international conference focused solely on "The Globalization of Chinese Enterprises" held at Rollins College, Winter Park, Florida (November 2006), and cosponsored by Rollins China Center and Georgia Tech CIBER.

This collection of papers makes a singular contribution to a field so scarcely researched. This book divides the topic into four sections:

I. Resources and Outward FDI
II. Institutional Considerations
III. Regional Implications
IV. Case Studies

Section I: Resources and outward FDI: Strategic implications

In Chapter 2, Deng builds on the resource-based view (RBV) theory to develop a framework for understanding outbound Chinese FDI into developed countries. The foundation of the model is that asset-seeking FDI occurs for the purpose of enhancing a firm's competitive advantages. Guided by the theoretical framework and by a critical review of the current Chinese business environments and institutional constraints, the authors have made several hypotheses related to asset-seeking motivations and the absorptive capability of the firm. According to the asset exploration perspective, FDI is viewed as a means to develop firm-specific advantages or acquire necessary strategic assets in host countries. Such asset-seeking FDI emphasizes that establishment of foreign subsidiaries via FDI can help enhance a firm's knowledge base and competitive edge through resource accumulation and capability building.

To validate his hypotheses, the author uses a qualitative, multiple-case-study research method, with three iconic Chinese firms – Haier, TCL, and Lenovo. As leading Chinese firms in their respective industries, they are regarded as the flagships of Chinese companies, thus constituting perhaps "best practices" in outward FDI from China. For the purpose of the research, both primary and secondary sources of data have been collected. The primary data were collected mainly in July and August 2004, and have been updated through numerous other personal communications thereafter. While the primary source was semi-structured interviews, secondary sources were also consulted through the corporate documents and websites. The secondary data enable the author to identify the key issues for the research, design the semi-structured interview questionnaire, and verify the validity of the primary data.

As a latecomer, Chinese firms appear to be in a more urgent position to engage in asset-seeking FDI for the purpose of addressing their competitive disadvantages and catching up with the incumbent global giants. Asset-seeking theories of FDI for Chinese firms must incorporate strategic and capability factors. Failure to incorporate either of the factors will lead to an incomplete picture of international expansion of Chinese firms. The chapter, therefore, makes an important contribution to the RBV theory as it relates to the globalization of Chinese firms and allows scholars of the globalization of China to assess variables of potential importance, for example, the absorptive capacity of the firm in incorporating new knowledge into their global portfolio. This chapter, therefore, supports the need for adapting theories to the Chinese institutional structure.

Chinese firms acquire knowledge and accumulate experience by increasing the involvement in international expansion. Yet little attention is given to the learning strategy of Chinese enterprises. In Chapter 3, three authors from Tsinghua University – Fang-cheng Tang, Xu-dong Gao, and Qiang Li – develop a conceptual framework describing the learning process in Chinese international business expansion. Their chapter, written from a Chinese pragmatic perspective, studies the sources of knowledge acquisition and learning strategies to help Chinese enterprises identify knowledge sources in different stages of globalization.

Through extensive reviews of the literature, three sources of learning were identified: (1) learning by inward internationalization, (2) learning by outward internationalization, and (3) learning by doing. To understand the flexibility of learning for Chinese enterprises in globalization, the authors further identify the difference in different stages of globalization of Chinese enterprises and offer its implication for government and Chinese enterprises. The globalization process of Chinese enterprises has been supported by the Chinese government. In the early stage of globalization of Chinese enterprises, a reactive learning strategy is adopted but in the later stage of globalization, a proactive learning strategy is adopted. The reactive learning strategy is government-led. The proactive learning strategy is market-oriented. The authors urge Chinese companies to move from reactive to proactive modes of globalization to speed up the development of Chinese multinationals.

The authors suggest that the Chinese government adopt a policy that assists firms in learning from multinational enterprises (MNEs), learning from overseas direct investment, and learning by doing. For the government, such strategic moves should be used to favor firms in accumulating experiences and access to technology. Chinese companies can identify the stage of their globalization to adopt the appropriate learning strategy. However, these strategies should not be viewed in isolation; they are not mutually exclusive and can be used simultaneously to speed up the learning process to become more globally competitive.

In Chapter 4, Alon, Herbert, and Muñoz develop a conceptual and practical framework for explaining the resource gaps that exist in Chinese management for successful globalization. To achieve their full potential as global competitors, Chinese business enterprises must identify and rectify deficiencies in their resources and capabilities. These authors offer an approach to improving globalizing capabilities through the lenses of multiple response levels, including ambient factors, the individual level, the intraorganizational level, and the interorganizational level. Identifying misalignment or poor strategic fit as well as needed capabilities, plus employing analysis from a RBV, allows the firm to assess areas of investment for developing a competitive advantage. Like Chapter 2, this chapter encourages the use of RBV theory.

The authors demonstrate the utility and value of a systematic analytical approach to identifying and assessing strengths and deficiencies in the capabilities and resources applied by the globalizing Chinese firm. Specific strategic actions, pertinent to each of the three tiers in the strategic fit model, are identified, and are able to be used as beginning points for executives. The RBV formally employed, then, allows each of the strategic actions to be assessed against the criterion of its potential for contributing to competitive parity or to competitive advantage, utility in funds allocation to competing strategies and initiatives. As such, the authors identify an approach that (although not an exhaustive treatment of all possible issues of relevance) provides what they believe to be a manageable range of issues, through which actionable areas of high return for the globalizing Chinese enterprise may be specified by the executives involved.

While Chapter 2 explains the process of learning in the Chinese multinational, Chapter 4 identifies areas where learning is needed and calls for comprehensive strategies aligned throughout the organization. RBV theories are explored in Section I and attention is brought to the institutional framework within which Chinese multinational operate. Government involvement in directing the economy, although decreasing, is still high and a residue of the old economic system remains.

Section II: Institutional considerations: New pathways

Chapters 5 through 7 highlight the importance of the institutional environment. A conceptual model is given in Chapter 4 by Xiaohua Yang, Queensland University of Technology, and Clyde Stoltenberg, California

State University – Long Beach. The authors offer a preliminary framework for understanding some of the underlying forces driving the internationalization of Chinese firms. First, they articulate historical periods in which outward FDIs by Chinese firms shared certain identifiable characteristics. An important measure in this process is whether the reasons for investing are internal to the firm or driven by external factors, and how this measure changes from one period to the next. Then, the authors summarize the existing literature on institutional change and development in the context of the Chinese economic reforms. Finally, they examine the evolution of outward FDI by Chinese firms in the context of changes in relevant institutional influences to relate the investment trends to the environment in which they occur.

Chinese outward FDI has been led by state-owned or state-controlled enterprises. Therefore, the role of the state has been significant, and government policies have done much with regard to controls and incentives. However, institutions – which have emerged as reforms have shifted the economy from a planned economy to one driven more by market forces – have been increasingly important change agents affecting outward FDI practices. Capital markets and their legal (regulatory) and financial institutions have had an increasing impact on decision making by Chinese firms, as have external environmental factors, such as the impact of World Trade Organization (WTO) accession and the globalization of the world's financial markets.

Continued change in both the internal and external environments within which outward FDI decisions are made make the analysis of the phenomenon a very dynamic one. Institutional theory, and particularly the impact of institutional change, will have significant power to explain this particular component of China's internationalization. Understanding how decision making by Chinese firms is increasingly impacted by institutions associated with a market economy, but still in the context of transition in terms of property rights and management practices, will have significant implications for both policymakers and all varieties of entities dealing with Chinese firms.

In Chapter 6, Peng, Sun, and Tan consider what the strategic management and international business literature has often ignored – the "latecomers" from periphery countries. What strategies for internationalizing do these latecomers have? How do they overcome severe "resource position barriers" with limited recourses? Based on data collected form China's listed companies, the authors analyze how (1) industry dynamics, (2) resource repertoires, and (3) institutional transitions affect the scale and scope of firms' reactions to globalization pressure. The authors try to answer how the focus strategy or diversification strategy, in combination with an internationalization strategy, relates to the performance of Chinese firms.

The authors collected a sample of 2189 Chinese listed firms from 2002 to 2004, and divided them into four different categories: (1) domestic focus firms, (2) domestic diversification firms, (3) international focus firms, and (4) international diversification firms. The authors use a multivariate regression model to test the relationship between categorization and firm performance. The authors find that a focus firm will gain more competitive advantage than a diversified firm during its initial internationalization in China. The intensification of competition in domestic markets and pressures from globalization under openness policies have significantly affected the scope of all four types of firms. The authors suggest that these firms follow a "build–borrow–buy" path for their internationalization.

Chapter 7, written by Hui and Fatt from the University of Malaya, discusses the alignment of strategies with institutional influences by Chinese SOEs. The chapter examines how a Chinese SOE, Sinohydro Corporation, has aligned its business strategies with institutional influences, inherently dynamic, so as to successfully enter an international market. The setting of inquiry is the firm's taking on a large international joint venture (JV) project based in the emerging market of Malaysia. Qualitative approaches are the major data collection methods. The authors suggest that both home advantages and heterogeneous foreign markets are important to the path of internationalization; a competitively priced factor embedded with multiple valuable characteristics can be better than the ones with mere low cost; and a salient nonprice capability may fall short of competition if other capabilities are also equally demanded at the same time.

On the practical front, this research suggests that possessing distinctive knowledge assets to bundle and leverage both price and nonprice dimensions of competition, subject to organizational internal and external constraints, is crucial to sustaining a globally competitive advantage position. Though some aspects of international institutional environment have provided Chinese firms with opportunities to establish a global position, more work needs to be done before they can take up a dominant lead position in the global marketplace. Chinese multinationals are perhaps in a better position to operate in other developing countries that may experience similar economic, social, and political environments.

Section III: Regional implications: Following or leading

Section III considers the regional impacts of China's globalization. While some still debate whether China has emerged as a global leader, there is no question that regionally it has a large influence. In Chapter 8, Tom Lairson of Rollins College considers the case of Vietnam, analyzing it from a political science perspective. China's economic miracle raises concerns for many countries in Asia. This chapter examines the potential impact of China's globalization on Vietnam. One well-known approach in political science to the topic is the flying geese model (FGM), which sees industrialization transmitted from one state to another following the logic of comparative advantage. The author modifies the FGM to consider the new economic environment defined by global production networks established by transnational corporations and the importance of governments in creating complementary assets capable of making low labor costs effective as a comparative advantage. This is applied to the dynamic changes in China from globalization and the potential implications for Vietnam.

Through a conceptual reworking of existing research on Asian economic development and the FGM, Lairson defines new forms for the shifting of industrial development across Asia. This is applied to China and Vietnam, thereby defining a distinctive set of expectations for the pathways for development in these states. In this way, the author demonstrates the importance of rethinking the nature and origins of comparative advantage as a basis for understanding how economic growth in one nation can affect the prospects for others. In the case of China and Vietnam, rising costs in China present a significant opportunity for both nations. For China, Vietnam is an opportunity to maintain a position in the low end of the value chain even while moving into higher value-added products and segments. For Vietnam, China's globalization is an opportunity to gain access to the resources of enormous global and regional production as well as knowledge and financial networks centered on China. Vietnam's government has taken many of the steps toward creating the complementary assets that can attract investment from transnational firms and Chinese firms seeking to relocate labor-intensive segments of the value chain. Considerable spillover of investment from China into Vietnam is expected in the coming years.

The chapter provides a set of expectations about future developments in China and Vietnam that is of interest to governments and firms as well as scholars of the Chinese political economy. Rather than seeing China's development as a threat, governments in the region should be developing local assets capable of creating comparative advantages able to link into these global and regional networks. The chapter establishes the importance of an approach based on political economy, that is, it demonstrates the need to understand how the governments of poor states are essential to creating comparative advantage and how transnational firms create networks of global resources that are also essential to understanding the origins of comparative advantage. This approach rejects the traditional assertion that understanding autonomous markets is sufficient. Rather, global markets must be supplemented by the capacities of firms and governments. States can create advantages in a world where capital, technology, and knowledge are available in *networks*. The FGM, when updated with the perspective of political economy, can be effective in demonstrating the potential benefits to Vietnam from China's globalization.

In Chapter 9, James Johnson explores the similarities and differences between the Korean and the Chinese paths toward globalization. While Chapter 8 explains the impact of a lagging economy, namely Vietnam, Chapter 9 compares Chinese international development to a leading political economy, South Korea. In the second half of the 20 century, the People's

Republic of China and South Korea followed separate paths of economic and political development. However, they share two principal features of their economic growth: heavy dependence on exports and the preferential treatment afforded certain domestic firms. Both of these features contributed to the extraordinary progress that these nations have achieved. To understand how this advancement occurred, the author first examines the cultural similarities and differences between China and South Korea and he then traces the economic development of each country over the past 50 years. Using RBV and institutional theory, Johnson discusses the growth and development of the Korean *chaebol* and Chinese SOEs that have emerged onto the global stage.

China's political leaders face a variety of challenges to the nation's future economic development. They must maintain a high growth rate, deal effectively with the rural workforce, restructure the financial system, and continue to reform the SOEs, foster the productive private sector, promote better international cooperation, and change the role of the government in the economic system. Despite the strong similarity between Korea's growth trajectory in the 1980s and 1990s and the trajectory that China seeks to follow today, with its emphasis on a combination of SOEs in resource-dependent industries and private firms in consumer products, Johnson concludes that Chinese firms need to leapfrog the Korean model of incremental globalization through organic growth. It can do this, Johnson suggests, by acquiring external strategic resources and by relying more on inward FDI to provide the key technologies and the critical management skills that China will need in order to compete in the 21st century.

Lawton and Lin from Chung-Hua Institute and Imperial College London, respectively, in Chapter 10, describe another leading political economy in the race of globalization and in particular focus on the internationalization of Taiwanese SMEs. Their study investigates domestic interfirm network utilization in the internationalization process of Taiwanese SMEs. Given the cultural and national similarities between Taiwan and mainland China, much can be learned by examining the Taiwanese case. Taiwanese SMEs use domestic interfirm networks in their internationalization process. The authors argue that internationalizing through domestic interfirm networks is positively correlated with firms' limited nonfinancial resources, perceived uncertainties and risks associated with internationalization, and dependence on home partners. They contend that the technology level of firms and deficiencies in local knowledge and experience do not have a significant impact on decisions to utilize domestic interfirm networks in the internationalization process.

In Chapter 11 Jun Kurihara from Harvard University examines the globalization of Northeast Chinese firms as a Chinese regional case study. The purpose is to investigate the global strategies of the electronics multinational companies (MNCs) in Northeast China and to discuss policy implications for the region. The author collects data and information for the study through first-hand visits to the region and contact with key authorities, extensive interviews and document surveys in China, Japan, and the United States. The interviewees include top executives of electronics companies in the above-mentioned countries, experts in the electronics industry in the business and academic communities, and policymakers in the Chinese and Japanese governments.

Kurihara's contribution to the literature is fourfold. First, the chapter highlights regional differences: those actively expanding and those with little industrial agglomeration. The actively expanding region includes the Northern Coastal Region (Beijing, Tianjin, Hebei, and Shandong), the Yanzi Delta (Shanghai, Jiangsu, and Zhejina), and the Zujian Delta (Gangdong) while the other consists primarily of Northeast China. Second, the chapter discusses the strengths and weaknesses of the electronics MNCs located in Northeast China. Northern China has three characteristics: a rapidly growing software industry, its geographical proximity to Japan and South Korea, and the strength of traditional SOEs and local academic communities. Third, the chapter examines a prospective role played by Japan's electronics MNCs to help Northeast China's electronics MNCs become internationalized. They can help Dalian become a Chinese "multilingual" Bangalore, and they can help SOEs by an active interplay with them and through privatization. Fourth, the chapter identifies obstacles prohibiting both Japanese and other foreign MNCs from actively engaging in the interplay with Northeast China's electronics MNCs: a lack of strong leadership in the Liaoning Province and a lack of an active secondary region (either Jilin or Heilongjian).

In sum, Section III describes regional variations and shifting of economic resources both between and within countries in Asia. The rise of China has a strong economic influence on lagging countries, like Vietnam, which China is pulling into prosperity, and on developed countries, which now increasingly rely on China as a source of inexpensive production and a host of a large and growing marketplace. In addition, the globalization of China has benefited some regions that are connected to the global marketplace and neglected others, causing wide income fluctuations within China, an area of increasing emphasis for policymakers there.

Section IV: Case studies: Selected industry sectors

Section IV describes the experiences of specific industries and companies. In Chapter 12, Fetscherin and Sardy from Rollins College examine the Chinese automobile industry. Prominent Asian and Western auto manufacturers have for many years considered the competition and the marketplace to be fairly well defined. China, the newest market for automotives, has already developed into one of the largest consumer markets and the growth has just begun. Most of the automobiles consumed in China are domestically produced by local, regional, or national manufacturers. The skills and expertise that Chinese automotive firms have developed on their own or through JVs have prepared them for expansion beyond the borders of China. The authors propose a framework for identifying which Chinese auto manufacturers are most likely to export vehicles. They identify the current JVs in place with foreign partners and the sectors in which the most aggressive exporters will be found.

Through review of the literature and comparison with historic behavior of several other Asian automotive manufacturers that have become strong exporters, Fetscherin and Sardy develop a model of the current competitor's value strategy within the Chinese market. A sales-based model is then proposed to identify those firms most likely to develop a strong export strategy. When considering the direction that Chinese automobile manufactures will take over the next decade, it is fairly clear that their initial focus will be on the domestic market. It is quite probable that the economies of scale and the manufacturing insights gained from JVs in the local market will help China become an effective global competitor. The export of Chinese brands is more likely to take place among firms that manufacture their own brands rather than those producing for their JV partners. It is likely that early exports of Chinese cars will be small cars competing primarily on price. How Chinese automobile manufacturers deal with quality issues and brand perception may determine how effectively and how quickly they become global competitors.

The authors identify two groups of Chinese automobile manufacturers: state-owned national enterprises and local government or independent automobile manufacturers. Their analysis shows that the latter are more prone to internationalization in the near future, concluding that it is no longer the question of "if" Chinese manufacturers will produce cars for foreign markets but of "when" and "where." The chapter provides a window into the early development of what promises to be one of the largest automobile markets in the world and potentially one of the world's largest automobile exporters.

In Chapter 13, Simmons presents the case of Huawei as a globalizing Chinese firm. The chapter examines how a Chinese MNE, Huawei, has grown to become China's largest telecommunications equipment provider and a significant international competitor. It further looks at what issues exist for its future, particularly as they pertain to US market penetration. The chapter provides background on the company's history and approach to international expansion and examines its entry attempts into the US market. Public, secondary sources are used for data collection.

The case offers several insights. An MNE must continue to evolve and change tactics to remain competitive and grow in the international marketplace. Specifically with regard to the US market, a competitive low price structure and an attempted Western management approach are not necessarily sufficient for success, particularly when aggressive R&D tactics have created a negative perception of the enterprise in the market. Despite some weaknesses in developed countries and particularly in the American market,

Huawei is a model for other Chinese firms' internationalization. Going forward, its approach to the US market may have far-reaching implications for how Chinese and US companies interact.

In Chapter 14, Gilbert presents the Wuliangye Distillery case as a wonderful example of the new Chinese global consumer company. This MNE has captured the hearts and wallets of Chinese customers for years and now competes with the largest firms in the world for shelf space for spirit beverages. The purpose of the case is to gain insights into a world class manufacturing firm within mainland China that has embraced a multinational business strategy. The Wuliangye brand is prized in China as its Wuliangye Spirits liquor brand is used for toasts at official state functions with heads of state and dignitaries from all over the world. The firm has won 39 gold medals in worldwide competitions. The Yibin plant produces 4 types of distilled products in 25 varieties and 50 specifications of liquor with its primary brands.

The methodology for this case study is mainly secondary source materials available on the Wuliangye Group of firms and its marketing and promotion arm, the Push Group. The author finds that Wuliangye is the largest, most prestigious, and most profitable of the Chinese distillers of spirits. Its international success has spurred the firm toward other global markets, such as automobile mold design and fabrication. These new multinational manufacturing thrusts are all looking beyond the Chinese borders toward global markets. The company already competes in markets as diverse as the United States, the United Kingdom, Italy, Spain, New Zealand, Japan, Laos, and Taiwan. The authors look specifically at the Wuliangye Distillery plant in Yibin, China, but also take a peek at its many other businesses within its corporate strategy. This case gives a first insight into the international strategy of the Wuliangye Group and offers a glimpse at this major player in the distilled spirits market.

Conclusions

Collectively, the authors have developed models to enable international business as well as China scholars and business people to better understand the strategic directions that Chinese firms will take in the process of globalizing their businesses, and the impacts these decisions will have. RBV and institutional theories seem to be growing in importance in explaining the internationalization of Chinese enterprises. However, traditional Western theories of international business need to be adapted to the Chinese context or new theories altogether are necessary.

Note

1. The 11th five-year plan (2006–2010) calls for upgrading the industrial structures, developing of rural and western areas, becoming environmentally friendly,

opening markets up further, investing in science, education, and human resources, and constructing a harmonious socialist society. (China.org.cn, retrieved 2006).

References

Child, J. and Suzana B. Rodrigues (2005), "The Internationalization of Chinese Firms: A Case for Theoretical Extension?" *Management and Organizational Review* 1 (3): 381–410.

Shenkar, O. (2005), *The Chinese Century*. Wharton School Publishing, Upper Saddle River, NJ.

Yan, B. (2007), Should Government Controls Keep You From Investing in China? *Morningstar*, http://news.morningstar.com/article/printarticle.asp?id=183585 (retrieved January 28, 2007).

Part I

Resources and Outward FDI from Chinese Companies

2
Resources, Capability, and Outbound FDI from Chinese Companies

Ping Deng

Introduction

A central issue in international business studies is how firms exploit their existing assets and explore new assets in host countries through foreign direct investment (FDI) (Caves, 1996). While the conventional theories of FDI research were based on exploitation, a number of scholars have recently studied the asset-seeking motive of multinational corporations (MNCs) when they invest in developed countries (DCs) (Kuemmerle, 1999; Wesson, 1999; Frost, 2001). According to the asset-seeking perspective, FDI is viewed as a means to develop firm-specific advantages or acquire necessary strategic assets in host countries largely embedded in local firms. Such asset-seeking FDI emphasizes that a firm's subsidiaries can help to enhance its knowledge base and competitive edge through resource accumulation and capability building. While most research on asset-seeking FDI is limited to the firms from DCs, a growing number of studies have reported that emerging market firms invest in DCs to source strategic resources such as technologies, brand names, and managerial know-how typically via aggressive acquisitions of DC firms in the host countries (van Hoesel, 1999; Makino *et al.*, 2002).

As a latecomer, Chinese firms are in a more urgent position to be engaged in asset-seeking FDI in order to catch up with the incumbent global giants (Deng, 2007). Moreover, China has had the largest FDI outflows among emerging economies since the early 1990s and is expected to become one of the top sources of outward FDI in the near future (UNCTAD, 2005). However, there has been a lack of research attention on China's outbound FDI from the asset-seeking perspective (Deng, 2004; Child and Rodrigues, 2005). This chapter intends to fill this significant research issue by focusing on the rationale and the capability behind Chinese firms' FDI in DCs.

To reach the above goal, we make case studies of three leading Chinese companies (Haier, TCL, and Lenovo) by using the dynamic resource-based view (RBV) of the firm. Largely by incorporating key concepts such as organizational learning theory (OL) (March, 1991) and dynamic capability (Teece *et al.*, 1997), the RBV theory (Barney, 1991) has become one of the three most insightful theories when probing into emerging economies (Hoskisson *et al.*, 2000). Within the RBV framework, we argue that asset-seeking FDI arises when Chinese firms are in vulnerable strategic positions so that they need the resources that foreign investments bring and when Chinese firms have sufficient absorptive capacity so that they can capitalize on their existing knowledge to access or build up new resources. By arguing that Chinese outward FDI represents a means to acquire valuable resources and competencies in the logic of strategic needs and absorptive capacity, this study is of great interest not only to stimulate possible theoretical extensions but also to draw out the strategic implications for other emerging firms. Specifically, our study contends that RBV theory can shed new light into the Chinese outbound FDI.

Theoretical framework and hypotheses

RBV theory: Combining strategic needs and adsorptive capacity

The RBV theory (Barney, 1991) can be extended to combine these two themes of asset-seeking FDI by arguing that when firms are in vulnerable strategic positions they need additional resources that FDI can provide to compete effectively and when firms have sufficient absorptive capacity they can identify, acquire, and integrate the new knowledge generated with FDI. A major asset of the RBV theory is "to account for the creation, maintenance and renewal of competitive advantage in terms of the characteristics and dynamics of the internal resources of firms" (Foss, 1997: 347). In recent years, the RBV theory has been moving in a more dynamic direction particularly by incorporating key concepts from related theories such as OL theory (March, 1991) and dynamic capability (Teece *et al.*, 1997).

Dynamic capability is the capacity to extract rents from current resources as well as build new competencies; it extends the term "routines" and "resources" used in the RBV of the firm (Teece *et al.*, 1997). Of particular interest herein is that dynamic capabilities allow firms to create new resources and enable them to take advantage of new opportunities, thereby providing the basis for the firm to recognize and develop needed resources (Eisenhardt and Martin, 2000). OL is often considered a requirement for the development of a firm's resources and knowledge acquisition; successful learning is a function of the firm's absorptive capacity, which is defined as the ability to adopt knowledge, connect it with existing knowledge, and thus apply it for their purposes (Cohen and Levinthal, 1990). Direct application of the RBV approach in international business research dramatically increased in recent years. However, there has not been any application of RBV theory to the Chinese outward FDI. In this chapter, we contend that dynamic RBV theory can provide insights on how latecomers like Chinese firms overcome their initial disadvantages via FDI to seek strategic resources.

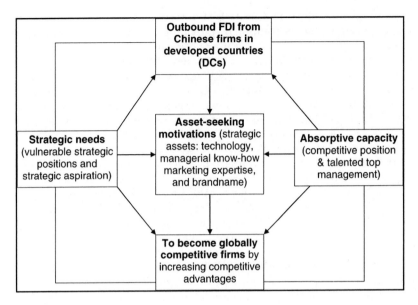

Figure 2.1 An asset-seeking model for outbound FDI from Chinese companies

Building on the RBV theory, we propose a theoretical framework of outbound FDI into DCs from Chinese firms, as shown in Figure. 2.1. The foundation of the model is that asset-seeking FDI occurs in the logics of strategic needs and absorptive capacity of firms for the purpose of enhancing a firm's competitive advantages. A strategic need for FDI refers to the reason that gives an investing firm the impetus for investing abroad. An absorptive capacity refers to an investing firm's existing abilities and skills necessary to be engaged in asset-seeking FDI. As competitive advantages of firms are based upon resources, while investing in advanced economies, Chinese MNCs are motivated primarily by accessing and acquiring strategic resources in order to address their competitive disadvantages and/or enhance their competitive advantages, thereby becoming globally competitive companies. In the following sections, we concentrate on discussing how Chinese firms' strategic needs and absorptive capacity would influence their actual asset-seeking FDI activities.

Strategic position hypothesis

Competition plays an important role in determining strategic position because when a firm faces many competitors, its strategic position is vulnerable, resources are squeezed, profits are stressed, and even survival is threatened (Dunning, 1998). In addition, because of many similar firms and products in highly competitive markets, it is difficult for firms to set themselves apart from others. China's consumer electronics and PC companies are rooted in a large and open market where their products prove themselves daily against the world's best in features, quality, and price. FDI improves a firm's strategic position by providing resources and the obtained resources give firms a cushion to weather business downturns and to ride out difficult times and learn better ways (Lecraw, 1993) and accumulate more resources to compete in highly competitive industries (Dunning, 1998). FDI also improves the strategic position of firms by enhancing corporate reputation and brand strategy and by obtaining needed skill-based resources quickly (Caves, 1996). Further, strategic asset seeking occurs among late-comers or technical laggards trying to reduce their gap by investing abroad to acquire needed resources (Wesson, 1999).

In the case of Chinese firms, research shows that the gap between top Chinese firms and their foreign counterparts is bigger than many had thought (Nolan, 2001). Most importantly, Chinese firms lack proprietary technology and innovative capability because they suffered from a weak national innovation system. In 2002, for example, China's total R&D spending was only a fraction of that of the United States, Japan, and Germany and its business R&D spending was even less than that of Korea (UNCTAD, 2005). It is increasingly recognized that lack of proprietary core technology and plenty of low-quality products have become a bottleneck for further economic growth in China (Nolan, 2001). To catch up with the established giants in the industrial nations, China needs to expand its international market, and more importantly, gain access to patents and technology information (van Hoesel, 1999; Deng, 2004).

On the other hand, a number of strong Chinese firms are aspiring to become world-class enterprises and to join the listing of *Fortune's* Global 500. They are eager to become organizations that mirror Germany's giant MNC, Siemens, or Korea's business groups (*chaebols*) largely by taking accelerated globalization strategies (Deng, 2004). As managerial and marketing resources are limited in China, Chinese companies have to go abroad to build or acquire international brand and advance product development. Such strategic need becomes even more logical for Chinese MNCs whose lack of superior technology is the biggest disadvantage in their internationalization process (Nolan, 2001). They often need managerial capabilities and know-how in order to effectively compete in their domestic markets and, even more, in international markets. According to the RBV, it is precisely because some firms may acquire resources and capabilities that others are incapable of imitating that they can obtain sustainable competitive advantage (Foss, 1997). At least partially influenced by the weakness of the national system of innovation, it is difficult for Chinese firms to access and/or develop technological capabilities and other intangible assets at home. Such inability to build the knowledge and the competencies they need forces them to search for and to acquire them overseas. Based on the above discussions, we have the following hypothesis:

H1: Chinese firms are engaged in asset-seeking FDI because they are in vulnerable strategic positions where they need strategic resources that are not available domestically so as to compensate their competitive weakness and/or enhance their competitive advantages.

Absorptive capacity hypothesis

The above hypothesis emphasizes vulnerable strategic position. Some may wonder why some aspiring Chinese firms are more active than others in asset-seeking FDI activities. One possible explanation for this question is that firms differ in their capabilities. This difference would lead to different possibilities for why the firms would engage in asset-seeking FDI. From an OL perspective, this type of capability is known as a firm's absorptive capacity, that is, the ability "to recognize the value of new information, assimilate it, and apply it to commercial ends" (Cohen and Levinthal, 1990: 128). Absorptive capacity has long been used to explain a variety of business phenomena in such fields as strategy, technology management, and international business (Zahra and George, 2002). For example, Lane *et al.* (2001) found that absorptive capacity plays a critical role in interorganizational learning and performance. Moreover, by conceptualizing absorptive capacity as an employee's capability and motivation, Minbaeva *et al.* (2003) empirically supported the notion that absorptive capacity of the subsidiary facilitates the transfer of knowledge from other parts of a MNC.

In the context of outward FDI in DCs, whether Chinese firms can actually invest abroad may depend on their absorptive capacity that supports the asset-seeking FDI. In highly competitive industries such as household appliances, consumer electronics, and PCs, a firm's absorptive capability can be well reflected in a firm's market position (Makino *et al.*, 2002). A market leadership position normally means strong absorptive capacity. Strong domestic market position, for example, indicates that the firms have a large and growing pool of talented scientists and skilled engineers as well as the financial resources to invest in DCs. Empirical study indicates that the Indonesian firms that invested abroad for resource exploration tended to be those market leaders that could leverage their domestic sources and capabilities abroad (Lecraw, 1993). In contrast, if firms lack absorptive capacity, they may be unaware of the opportunities to access strategic resources even if they do invest or may have little information with which to identify the investment projects or acquisition targets (Makino *et al.*, 2002).

In sum, whether FDI can be used as a tool to access and acquire resources is influenced by the absorptive capacity of the firm. The underlying logic is that firms need capabilities in order to build capabilities. Putting the above arguments together, we hypothesize the following:

H2: In order to be engaged in asset-seeking FDI, the Chinese firms should be those companies that possess strong absorptive capacity/capability largely in terms of domestic market leadership and a talented top management team so as to acquire, integrate, and build new sources that FDI brings.

Research method

To validate the above hypotheses, we employed a multiple-case study research method. The method is appropriate because the main question addressed is why Chinese firms invested for resources and where reliable data sets are largely unavailable (Yin, 2003). For the purpose of this chapter, we chose three well-known Chinese firms – Haier, TCL, and Lenovo – as case firms. As leading Chinese firms in their respective industries, they represent outward FDI from Chinese firms. While the companies analyzed are real, the senior managers involved in the study are disguised to ensure confidentiality. The time frame chosen for the study is the last 10 years from 1995 to 2005 when their international expansions were materialized.

To ensure validity, we collected two major sources of data. The primary data were collected during July and August 2004. The interviews were made possible due to the assistance from several trusted professionals in China. For each of the three firms, approximately 3-hour in-depth interviews were conducted with three to five senior managers who were directly involved in international expansion strategies of their firms. After the interviews, we maintained contact with the informants to help us incorporate some significant issues (e.g., Lenovo's purchasing of IBM PC units) that could not be covered during the interviews. In addition, we also collected a variety of secondary sources from corporate documents, the firms' websites, and government data releases. In the following, we will discuss how the strategic needs and absorptive capabilities of the case firms influenced their asset-seeking FDI in the context of RBV approach.

Case studies of Chinese companies

As leaders in their respective industries in China, the three companies have been engaged in a number of important foreign investments particularly in DCs, which are highlighted in Table 2.1. A complete review of their FDI activities is beyond the scope of this chapter; of particular interest to us is the rationale behind their asset-seeking FDI. According to the RBV theory, asset-seeking FDI has been increasingly used as a means for MNCs to tap into strategic resources in a foreign market, such as technological know-how, management expertise, or reputation. Moreover, we will focus on their majority-owned joint ventures (JVs) and wholly owned enterprises for the purpose of better understanding their investment rationale and strategic ability (Caves, 1996).

Table 2.1   Major outbound FDI projects by the case firms

Haier Group	TCL Group	Lenovo Group
(1) In 1999, set up manufacturing facilities in Camden, SC, for over US$40 million, the largest Chinese Greenfield investment in the United States. (2) In 2001, invested over US$15 million to purchase a building in Manhattan, NY, as Haier American headquarters. (3) Set up numerous R&D centers in DCs. (4) In 2001, acquired an Italian firm to target the EU market.	(1) In July 2004, set up US$560 million JV "TCL-Thomson Electronics" (TTE) with TCL holding a 67% stake. (2) In 2002, acquired Germany's Schneider Electronics for US$8.2 million. (3) In 2003, acquired GoVideo, a US brand of audiovisual products and DVD players. (4) In 2004, invested 55 million euro and set up 55% owned cellular phone JV – TCL & Alcatel Mobile Phones Limited (TAMP).	(1) In the 1990s, set up R&D center in Japan and marketing center in Hong Kong. (2) In April 2003, changed its brand name to Lenovo to facilitate overseas expansion. (3) In December 2004, acquired IBM's PC business for US$1.75 billion, the biggest overseas acquisition for Chinese manufacturing firms, thus becoming the world's third-largest PC maker and getting IBM's brand name and managerial teams.

Haier group

Along with other Chinese white goods manufacturers, Haier has remained highly dependent on foreign key components and technology. These include high-performance electromotors, compressors, controllers, magnetrons, and sensors. Moreover, compared to well-established multinationals, Haier is disadvantaged in brand awareness and image particularly in DCs, where consumers are familiar with brands such as GE, Electrolux, and Whirlpool, but few of them have heard of Haier or its products. In 2004, according to Euromonitor Statistics of the global white goods manufacturers, Haier was ranked fourth in revenue, but Haier is determined to gain the top position in this sector.

In 1984, soon after joining the plant, CEO Zhang Ruimin introduced technology and equipment from Liebherr, a German company, and expanded cooperation with Liebherr by manufacturing refrigerators based on its standards, and then sold them to Liebherr as a way of entering the German market. Mr Zhang later commented on this strategy, "Exporting to earn foreign exchange was necessary at that time. But, it was only one of the two purposes. We also aimed to make our brand name famous internationally." In the US home refrigeration and laundry sectors, the top five brands hold more than 80 percent of the market. "It is almost a mission impossible for us to set up a name brand particularly in the US and EU," said one of the senior managers. "But if you don't take this road, you will always work for others."

Moreover, after the mid-1990s, price wars broke out one after the other in the Chinese home appliances market. At the end of 2000, Haier's market shares of refrigerators, freezers, air conditioners, and washing machines had reached 33 percent, 42 percent, 31 percent, and 31 percent, respectively. The potential for further development in the domestic market was therefore limited. In addition, since China joined the World Trade Organization (WTO) in December 2001, almost all the international competitors have invested in China. "The best defensive strategy for Haier would be to have a presence in its competitors' home markets," commented one of the senior managers. Moreover, global giants such as Electrolux, GE Electronics, and Whirlpool tend to generate a large part of their revenue from international markets. To follow the trend, Haier believed that it had to go global. Haier's goal is to compete globally, build a globally recognizable brand, and become one of the Global 500. In reaching this goal, Haier intends to produce and sell one-third of its total output in China, make one-third of its total output in China but export it to international markets, and manufacture and sell one-third in foreign countries. As a result, Haier must develop design, manufacturing, and marketing networks internationally, particularly in the United States, to build up Haier's international brand reputation. As one senior manager put it, "We believe that the added expense of producing goods in the US will be outweighed by the ability to respond more quickly to changes in local consumer tastes. Local manufacturing helps us quickly develop a feel for the design and feature preferences of Western customers."

In China, Haier has been widely recognized as one of the most respected companies. The strong business position in China underlies Haier's sufficient absorptive capacity in terms of identifying and assimilating external knowledge, and such ability allows Haier to expand overseas for building and integrating new resources. Over the past 20 years, Haier has witnessed significant success and gained worldwide recognition. In 2005, Haier's global revenue reached RMB103.4 billion (US$12.8 billion based on the foreign exchange rate in December 2005: US$1 = 8.07RMB), with average annual growth of 56 percent between 1984 and 2005. In August 2005, the Haier brand was ranked first among China's Top 10 Global Brands by the *Financial Times*, valued at RMB61.6 billion (US$7.6 billion). In the same vein, Haier was ranked 86th among the world's 500 Most Influential Brands by World Brand Lab in 2006 – the only Chinese brand to be ranked in the top 100 for 3 consecutive years. Additional international and domestic resources at Haier's disposal include 12 technological research institutes, 48 development centers, 10 advanced laboratories, and 6 design centers.

Haier's absorptive capability also lies clearly in its consistently improving technological competence. In the period 1997–2000, Haier's investment in R&D averaged 4.7 percent of its total sales, ranking number one in the industry, and in 2000 its R&D expenditures reached RMB 1949 million (US$242 million). By April 2006, the Haier Group has obtained 6189 patented technology certificates and 589 software intellectual property rights. Technological innovation is a key to maintaining a firm's competitiveness and Haier has technological flexibility to respond to global changes in market demand globally.

TCL group

TCL's corporate objective is to "create a world-class corporation with international competitiveness." In the words of its chief financial officer (CFO), "We aspire to be the next Sony or next Sumsong." Specifically, TCL tries to transform itself from maker of conventional color TV sets into a leading electronics group focusing on high-end plasma HDTV, TFL-LCD displays, and DLP projection TVs. On the office desk of Chairman Li Dongshen lies a planning document that aims for RMB150 billion (US$18.6 billion) of sales by 2010. However, despite being a consumer electronics leader in China, TCL still lacks core proprietary technologies that are essentially held by global giants such as Sharp, Philips, and Sony. Outside China, TCL's brand is limited only to Southeast Asia and it is also unsure of its marketing skills particularly in DCs. TCL's global competitive situation is well summarized by one of its senior managers, "Compared with global giants, we obviously still lag behind, particularly in LCD and plasma HDTV technologies. The competition between global giants and us is similar to a match between lightweight and heavyweight boxers. In the new round of competition, only the best corporations will survive. Of course, we always aspire to be the best." Therefore, in order to be become a world-class enterprise, to compete in DCs is a must for TCL. After all, mergers and acquisitions (M&A) provide TCL a valuable opportunity to learn about the world market and the requisite breathing space to build its own overseas marketing capabilities.

Similar to Haier, the absorptive capacity for TCL to be engaged in asset-seeking FDI lies in its domestic market leadership. In the past 12 years, TCL achieved a record of an average rate of 42.7 percent in growth, becoming one of the fastest growing companies in China. In the year of 2002 when the domestic color TV market experienced substantial loss, TCL remained profitable. After two decades of growth, TCL has become one of China's most valuable brands. According to a national survey on most valuable brands in 2004, TCL's brand equity was RMB 30.6 billion (US$3.8 billion). In 2006, according to the Chinese Most Valuable Brands' Report, the TCL brand was ranked third with a value of RMB 36.2 billion (US$4.5 billion), just behind Haier (valued at RBM 74.9 billion) and Lenovo (at US$60.7).

TCL has already built its grand domain in the global color TV field with possession of 5 profit-making centers, 5 research and development centers, 10 manufacturing bases, and over 20,000 global marketing outlets. Since TCL started engaging in original equipment manufacturing (OEM) for some of the international brands in the mid-1990s, its overseas businesses now cover 50 countries. Before a series of acquisitions, TCL's electronics products bearing its TCL brand had been exported to many countries in the world, and it had also set up sales and representative offices and manufacturing facilities worldwide. TCL's strong absorptive capability is well illustrated in its ability to deal with post-M&A restructuring. As one of the senior managers commented during the interview, "Through reorganization, we have transferred most of the businesses to China. In Europe, we maintain R&D by focusing on new technology innovation. In so doing, we have enhanced our competitiveness." Sufficient absorptive capability also helps TCL's business after the merger. In the first half of 2005, its total sales reached RMB24.4 billion (US$3.0 billion), with overseas sales accounting for over 60 percent.

Lenovo group

The strategic needs for Lenovo to seek strategic assets via FDI are similar to Haier's and TCL's because all of them are in globally competitive industries. In the initial stage of internationalization, Lenovo had tried an approach similar to Haier's Greenfield investment, but it failed to establish its brand awareness abroad and lost tens of millions of US dollars. On the other hand, the acquisition of the IBM PC business gives Lenovo IBM's capability of R&D and notebook manufacturing and also a world-class management team. According to a Lenovo senior manager, "If Lenovo had done it itself, it would have taken several times the money and even 8 to 10 years. Most importantly, those efforts would not necessarily guarantee that we would reach that level of achievements, as IBM PC units had."

In addition, global manufacturing and marketing provides Lenovo with high-quality products. As one of the senior managers said, "Once purchasing IBM PC, we begin to acquire advantages related to 'transnationality', that is, confidence in, and knowledge of operating in a foreign market. The acquisition certainly gives us access to technology and other strategic assets such as brand names, as well as access to US markets." In the words of another manager, "Creating and sustaining brands in developed markets is complex, expensive, and uncertain. The biggest obstacle is we do not have vital marketing skills. It took years, and a great deal of money, before the giant Japanese and Korean consumer electronics companies established themselves abroad. We tried their method before, but the result was very slow." With Lenovo aiming to compete globally, it needs to move into high-technology, sophisticated products and services.

Lenovo considered its acquisition of IBM PC units as opportunistic since the acquired firm has expertise in technological innovation and managerial know-how, thereby strengthening its existing line of business and later transferring the know-how of PC businesses to other regions. Moreover, as some R&D activities were also included in the transaction, the takeover has contributed to Lenovo's R&D intensity and enhanced its innovative capabilities. Furthermore, after the acquisition, Lenovo shows a strong need for new managerial and marketing resources and that has led Lenovo to adapt to many existing business practices of the previous IBM PC units. Finally, in order to show its commitment to building the company as a truly global MNC, in May 2005, Lenovo relocated its executive headquarters to Raleigh, North Carolina, USA.

Similar to Haier's dominant position in the refrigerator industry, Lenovo dominated the Chinese PC industry with 27 percent market share in 2005. Since 1997 Lenovo has held the market share leader position in China for 8 years in a row. Its leading-edge PCs are highly acclaimed for their user-friendly, tailor-made designs and customized solutions for various customer needs, including the Tianjiao and Fengxing consumer desktops and Yangtian and Kaitian enterprise desktops. Lenovo also has a broad product line encompassing mobile handsets, servers, peripherals, and digital entertainment products. Lenovo's strong absorptive capability has certainly contributed to its business performances after the acquisition. According to IDC, a market research firm, in the third quarter of 2005, Lenovo dominated the Asian (excluding Japan) PC market with 20.4 percent of the market, higher than the second quarter's 18.5 percent, which accounted for IBM's sales' number into Lenovo's, whereas H-P and Dell were far behind Lenovo with 12.4 percent and 7.8 percent market share, respectively.

Asset-seeking FDI in the logic of strategic needs and absorptive capacity

It is clear that whether asset-seeking FDI can take place or not is influenced by a firm's strategic needs. In highly competitive markets, all the three Chinese firms need advanced technologies and marketing expertise to compete successfully, particularly in the global marketplace. As the strategic resources are not available at home and cannot be acquired easily through other channels including inward FDI and licensing, FDI provides Chinese firms with an effective means to access and acquire those resources particularly in DCs. Born into an industry that is essentially open to worldwide competition, Haier, TCL, and Lenovo have little choice but to go global and to gain competitive edge against the world's multinationals. On top of that, all the case firms are aspiring to be world-class enterprises, stimulated by the Chinese government at different levels. To reach their aspirations, they are in more urgent positions to seek strategic assets in advanced host countries and essentially embedded in foreign firms. From the dynamic RBV perspective, what the three case firms have in common is that their FDI in DCs is not based on the possession of superior assets that can be exploited abroad. Rather, their FDI has been undertaken more for the search for new resources and the acquisition of innovative capabilities for the purpose of building their competitive advantages globally.

Furthermore, although FDI provides the opportunity to access managerial and technical capabilities, it does not guarantee that firms will obtain those resources. Given the size of the Chinese market and the nature of highly competitive industries, the market leadership positions held by the three Chinese firms well indicate their sufficient absorptive capacity. Such capability enables them to leverage their domestic market power to expand internationally, a strategy that has proved to be effective among newly emerged Asian firms including Taiwan's Acer and Korea's Lucky Gold Star and Sumsang. As exploration of new resources has less certain outcomes, longer time horizons, and more diffused effects than exploitation (March, 1991), generally only the Chinese firms with sufficient absorptive capacity, as demonstrated in the three analyzed firms, tend to be able to acquire, assimilate, and exploit new resources that FDI brings.

In terms of absorptive capacity for acquiring new resources, the three companies have another common trait and that is their highly talented and top management teams, featured by their legendary leaders: Haier's CEO Zhang Ruimin, TCL's Chairman Li Dongsheng, and Lenovo's founder Liu Chuanzhi. In China, they are the most well-known entrepreneurs and they share a common strategic aspiration: building their own companies into first-class world enterprises with globally recognizable brands. Zhang's vision of Haier is of a totally internationalized company, Liu's mind-set of Lenovo is never to be the number three PC maker in the world, and Li's mission for TCL is a world-class corporation like Sony or Sumsong. One impression from the corporate interviews is that all the managers show great respect for their leaders because the three legendary leaders are keen on stimulating employee enthusiasm in independent innovation practice and cultivating the innovative mechanisms at both organizational and individual levels. As the arguments of absorptive capacity contend (e.g., Minbaeva *et al.*, 2003), an organization's compensation policies and employees' capability and motivation constitute primary elements of a firm's absorptive capacity: the ability to acquire, assimilate, transform, and exploit new knowledge. Most notably, each of the three visionary leaders along with other top managers firmly believes that their enterprises can compete successfully on the global stage and they have carefully used asset-seeking FDI as an effective means to build their competencies for their overall corporate strategies.

Discussion and conclusion

Contrary to conventional theory that views FDI as an attempt to exploit firm-specific assets abroad, the dynamic RBV approach views FDI as an attempt to access and obtain strategic resources that the investor is lacking, but available in a foreign market. According to the RBV theory, FDI is a quest for some strategic advantages in order to offset the weaknesses of the investor. By examining the asset-seeking FDI made by the three Chinese firms, we have supported the hypotheses surrounding firm-level strategic need and absorptive factors.

Specifically, we argued that increasingly global competition would put Chinese firms in vulnerable strategic positions (i.e., intense competition, lack of innovative capabilities, and weak brand name) in which they need strategic resources that are available in DCs. On the other hand, stimulated by the government, strong Chinese firms are aspiring to be global giants. Such strategic aspiration in the context of vulnerable strategic position leads Chinese firms to conduct asset-seeking FDI particularly in DCs. On top of that, consistent with the absorptive capacity hypothesis, our results emphasize the importance of a firm's capability to the formation of asset-seeking FDI. Importantly, the contribution here is to recognize a firm's absorptive capability in facilitating the rate of using FDI as resource exploration, particularly for companies from emerging economies such as China.

Taken together, these two sets of results extend the dynamic RBV theory to the asset-seeking FDI through strategic need and absorptive capacity arguments, thereby putting the RBV approach to new and potentially far-reaching applications. The rational calculus of strategic needs captured the logic underlying Chinese outward FDI in DCs. But the asset-seeking FDI was also strongly affected by absorptive capacity calculus related to the domestic competitiveness and talented top management teams. This interplay between strategic and absorptive factors becomes apparent in Chinese asset-seeking FDI. For those Chinese firms that can obtain valuable and rare resources via FDI in developed markets, they are most likely to become more competitive players in the global arena.

References

Barney, B. (1991) "Firm resources and sustained competitive advantages," *Journal of Management* 17: 99–120.

Caves, R. (1996). *Multinational Enterprise & Economic Analysis* (2nd ed.). Cambridge University Press, Cambridge, MA.

Child, J. and Rodrigues, B. (2005) "The internationalization of Chinese firms," *Management and Organization Review* 1 (3): 381–410.

Cohen, M. and Levinthal, D. (1990) "Absorptive capacity: A new perspective on learning and innovation," *Administrative Science Quarterly* 35: 128–152.

Deng, P. (2004) "Outward investment by Chinese MNCs: Motivations and implications," *Business Horizons* 47 (3): 8–16.

Deng, P. (2007). "Investing for strategic resources and its rationale," *Business Horizons* 50 (1): 71–81.

Dunning, J. (1998). "Location and the multinational enterprise: A neglected factor?" *Journal of International Business Studies* 29 (1): 45–86.

Eisenhardt, K. M. and Martin, J. A. (2000) "Dynamic capabilities: What are they?" *Strategic Management Journal* 21 (10/11): 1105–1121.

Foss, N. (ed.) (1997) *Resources, Firms, and Strategies*. Oxford University Press, New York.

Frost, T. S. (2001) "The geographic sources of foreign subsidiaries' innovations," *Strategic Management Journal* 22: 101–123.

Hoskisson, R, Eden, L., Lau, C. and Wright, M. (2000) "Strategy in emerging economies," *Academy of Management Journal* 43: 249–267.

Kuemmerle, W. (1999) "The drivers of foreign direct investment into research and development: An empirical investigation," *Journal of International Business Studies* 30 (1): 1–24.

Lane, J., Salk, E. and Lyles, A. (2001) "Absorptive capacity, learning, and performance in international joint ventures," *Strategic Management Journal* 22: 1139–1161.

Lecraw, D. (1993) "Outward direct investment by Indonesian firms: Motivation and effects," *Journal of International Business Studies* 24 (3): 589–600.

Makino, S., Lau, C. and Yeh, R. (2002) "Asset exploitation versus asset seeking," *Journal of International Business Studies* 33 (3): 403–421.

March, J. (1991) "Exploration and exploitation in organizational learning," *Organization Science* 2 (1): 71–87.

Minbaeva, D., Pedersen, T., Bjorkman, I., Fey, C. and Park, H. (2003) "MNC knowledge transfer, subsidiary absorptive capability, and HRM," *Journal of International Business Studies* 34 (6): 586–599.

Nolan, P. (2001) *China and the Global Economy*. Palgrave, Basingstoke, UK.

Teece, D., Pisano, J. and Shuen, S. (1997) "Dynamic capabilities and strategic management," *Strategic Management Journal* 18: 509–533.

UNCTAD. (2005). *World Investment Report 2005*. UNCTAD, New York and Geneva.

van Hoesel, R. (1999) *New Multinational Enterprises from Korea and Taiwan*. Routledge, New York.

Wesson, T. (1999) "A model of asset-seeking foreign direct investment driven by demand conditions," *Canadian Journal of Administrative Sciences* 16 (1): 1–10.

Yin, R. (2003). *Case study Research: Design and Methods*. London, Sage Publications.

Zahra, S. and George, G. (2002) "Absorptive capacity: A review, reconceptualization and extension," *Academy of Management Review* 27 (7): 185–204.

3
Knowledge Acquisition and Learning Strategies in Globalization of China's Enterprises

Fang-cheng Tang, Xu-dong Gao, and Qiang Li

Introduction

Since the Chinese government opened its door and launched the "going out" strategy (*zou chu qu*), we have witnessed the emergence of Chinese multinationals with a presence in both developed and developing countries (Liu and Li, 2002). Up till the end of 2005, Chinese overseas direct investment (ODI) amounted to over $50 billion, with over 10,000 overseas made in China multinationals. Having achieved an average growth rate of nearly 10 percent over the past 20 years, China already ranks as one of the world's largest economies and trading powers. This rapid economic development has strengthened China's international competitiveness. Many Chinese companies have seen the limitations of the Chinese market and are striving to become global players. Many of them have already quietly moved into international operations. Some exemplary names of Chinese multinationals include Lenovo, Haier, TCL, CNOOC, and WanXiang.

In spite of the increasing significance of Chinese multinationals in world markets, there is a dearth of literature on the activities and behavior of these made in China multinational enterprises (MNEs). Anecdotal accounts that document a few more prominent cases such as Haier suggest that the unique features found in the international expansion of Chinese firms are not comparable to these of multinationals from any other countries (Liu and Li, 2002). These unique features include the dominant types of Chinese multinationals, i.e., SOEs, which lack core technology and managerial expertise, and their international expansion is promoted and supported by the Chinese government. However, we don't know exactly how these firms acquire knowledge and accumulate experience in globalization. While there is no shortage of theories to depict the motivations for the international expansion of multinational firms from industrialized countries, there has not been a theoretical framework specifically developed to describe the learning modes these Chinese multinationals have.

This study is an attempt to develop a conceptual framework describing the learning process in Chinese international business expansion. Chinese firms have made a debut on the international markets and their internationalization occurs in two ways: inward internationalization (I-I) and outward internationalization (O-I). To secure access to intangible technology and managerial expertise and accumulate experience, Chinese firms can conduct learning via three processes: learning by I-I, learning by O-I, and learning by doing.

Two modes of reactive learning and proactive learning are further proposed to understand the learning process of these firms in internationalization. Globalization is a product of a certain stage of economic development and China follows this general rule, even if the timing and circumstances of the country's entry may differ from those applicable to other states. Chinese companies are characterized by a high level of control by the central government, strong bargaining power with the government, easy access to political and economic privileges, and soft budgets (Deng and Dart, 1999; Luo and Peng, 1999; Luo et al., 2005). China's MNEs acquire knowledge by government-led rather than by market-oriented efforts in the early stage of internationalization. But proactive learning can be a dominant mode in the later stage of internationalization.

The next section discusses the learning process of enterprises in the globalization of Chinese firms. Subsequently, a conceptual framework for international expansion in Chinese firms is presented. Finally, the last section discusses implications for government policy makers and business practitioners as well as for future research.

Learning processes in globalization of China's enterprises

In the internationalization field, new theoretical and empirical models on North American and Western European multinationals have been devised for the process by which multinational companies access locationally dispersed technological assets and strategic resources, through their own international operations and through alliances with other firms (Almeida, 1996; Cantwell and Piscitello, 2000; Dunning, 1995; Kogut and Chang, 1991). Although the internationalization of SOEs from a developing country is not a unique phenomenon and there have been extensive studies of "the third world multinational enterprises" (TWMNEs), little attention has been given to the learning process of Chinese multinationals. Theories developed in market economies are more likely to be capable of explaining the knowledge acquisition and learning process of MNEs in world markets. The explanatory power is lessened in China, where the ownership of large firms is inseparable from the government. The traditional economic analysis and the rational behavior models are likely to be insufficient in explaining the learning motivation of these Chinese firms (Yang, 2006).

In the Chinese context, the government has adopted a strategic posture in framing both their I-I and O-I policies to face new global challenges.

Learning by I-I

The Chinese government recognized the importance of using joint ventures as a means of transferring knowledge internally. Within such communities, learning is bound to take place among individuals and groups through frequent interactions (Kogut and Zander, 1992; Itami and Roehl, 1987; Maitland and Nicholas, 2002). I-FDI has been positively linked with the innovatory capacity and competitiveness of the resources of the recipient economy (Dunning, 1993). Hence, for many years, the Chinese government required foreign investors to form joint ventures with SOEs if they wished to invest in China. Such joint ventures not only allowed SOEs to obtain much needed capital and technology, but also offered the SOEs a taste of the international markets in the earlier days. Knowledge or time-based experience is a critical driving force behind multinationals' international expansion (Johanson and Vahlne, 1977; Luo, 1999).

To increase knowledge and sharpen the competitive edge, a certain amount of resources must be consumed to search for new skills and advanced technologies. For example, the Chinese government has initiated "market exchanges technology" strategy (*shi chang huan ji shu*) since the 1990s, i.e., Chinese firms have been induced to absorb the technologies by sacrificing profits for a larger market share. As a result, while penetrating of target markets in China can be facilitated, a disadvantage is the ability to access advanced technology and managerial skills, particularly as a frequent complaint against inward FDI in China has been the failure or unwillingness of European, American, and Japanese partners to introduce state-of-the-art technical expertise in their Chinese operations.

Learning by O-I

Data from studies on TWMNEs suggest there may be another component in the technological accumulation process, namely outward FDI that is designed to acquire technology from abroad. Major barriers are likely to exist to the inward transfer of the most advanced technologies through mechanisms such as licensing, and advanced country MNEs will wish to retain proprietary know-how by internalization and the formation of wholly owned subsidiaries. Under such circumstances, acquisition overseas represents a potential alternative.

Recently mergers and acquisitions have been used to penetrate host country markets (see Figure 3.1, Table 3.1).

A consistent goal of China's industrial policy has been to construct globally powerful companies that can compete on the global level playing field:

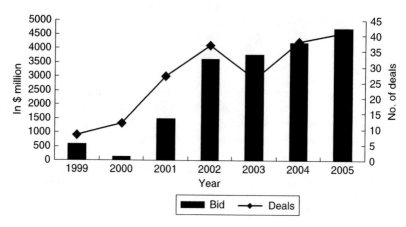

Figure 3.1   Chinese companies buying foreign companies, 1999–2005
Source: own calculations based on Chinese Statistic Yearbook 2005 and data from Ministry of Commerce of the P.R. China.

In our world today economic competition between nations is in fact between each nation's large enterprises and enterprise groups. A nation's economic might is concentrated and manifested in the economic power and international competitiveness of its large enterprises and groups...our nation's position in the international economic order will be to a large extent determined by the position of our nation's large enterprises and groups.

(Wu Bangguo, Chinese State Council, August, 1998)

The Chinese government has encouraged big SOEs to become internationally competitive corporations. "The country will develop thirty to fifty large state-owned enterprises in the next five years through public offerings, mergers and acquisitions, restructuring and co-operation" (Bai Rongchun, Director General, Industrial Planning Department, State Economic and Trade Commission, July, 2001).

For many Chinese multinationals, economic concerns and commercial interest may not be their top priorities in international expansion. Their O-FDI may have been triggered primarily by "pull" factors like the government's desire to secure supplies of key natural resources (Deng, 2003). For instance, Chinese oil companies expanded abroad because of government concerns over the energy shortage in China. What has been seen in the investment behavior in these state-owned oil companies is that they often pursue highly risky investment projects from other countries and outbid rivals by a large margin just to win contracts. It has been speculated that such behavior may derive from fear of being downsized in the continuing process of privatization and fear of being outcompeted by other oil companies in China (Wu and Han, 2005).

Table 3.1 The ten largest outbound acquisitions by Chinese companies (1999–2005)

Announcement date	Deal status	Acquired stake	Bid value US$ million	Target name	Nation	Chinese bidder
23.06.05	Aborted	100 %	18,306	Unocal	USA	CNOOC
08.12.04	Completed	100 %	1,564	IBM (personal computer business)	USA	Lenovo
11.06.2001 + 26.09.2002	Completed	100 % (80 % + 20 %)	1,385 (918 + 467)	Hyundai Display Technology Inc-Hydis	South Korea	BOE Technology
21.06.05	Aborted	100 %	1,260	Maytag	USA	Qingdao Haier
18.01.02	Completed	86 %	806	Repsol-YPF (Indonesian assets)	Indonesia	CNOOC
24.10.03	Completed	13 %	712	Oil & gas assets (Gorgon Liquefied Natural Gas Field)	Australia	CNOOC
27.07.04	Completed	49 %	503	Sangyong Motor	South Korea	Shanghai Automotive Industry
09.06.05	Completed	100 %	444	PetroChina International Ltd	Indonesia	CNPC, PetroChina
24.08.02	Completed	5 %	430	Woodside Petroleum Ltd	Australia	CNOOC
15.04.02	Completed	10 %	358	Devon Energy Corp (Indonesian oil and gas assets)	Indonesia	PetroChina

Source: own calculations based on Chinese Statistic Yearbook 2005 and data from Ministry of Commerce of the P.R. China.

Learning by doing

Regardless of I-I or O-I, Chinese firms could accumulate experience and acquire knowledge by attaining the particular task goals or doing. Although not the only source of learning, learning by doing is one of the most important sources of organizational learning (Nelson and Winter, 1982). Since knowledge incorporates implicit and tacit dimensions along with those that are explicit and codifiable (Kogut and Zander, 1992), organizations must "remember by doing" if they want to be well-versed in the tacit aspect of knowledge (Nelson and Winter, 1982). Multinational expansion can thus be regarded as an "option window" permitting MNEs to gain more tacit knowledge of a host country (Bowman and Hurry, 1993; Kogut, 1991). An initial option involves a small amount of investment in a host country that can be used to explore emerging opportunities (Chang, 1995). Once enough experience is gained and the option calls for further investment, the MNE increases its commitment to exploit more opportunities (Kogut and Kulatilaka, 1994). As a result, these real options can be called "learning options" serving as a means for organizational learning for MNEs (Peng and Wang, 2000).

Chinese firms can learn from experience and they accumulate specialized knowledge by receiving feedback from their own experiences. Even though the learning by doing process may be considered routine, these firms are still obligated to make efforts at accumulating and maintaining specialized knowledge that will allow them to work more efficiently than before. Meanwhile, acquired knowledge can accelerate the internationalization of Chinese firms.

Based on the analysis above, we can gain a conceptual framework of learning process in globalization of China's enterprises (Figure 3.2).

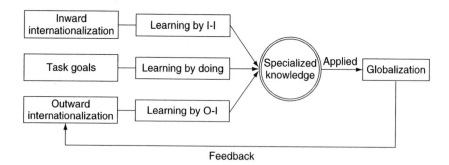

Figure 3.2 A conceptual framework learning process in globalization of China's enterprises

Learning strategies in globalization of China's enterprises

In international literature, the Uppsala stage model stipulates organizational learning (Johanson and Vahlne, 1977), consisting of small steps whereby firms gradually increase their international involvement (Johanson and Wiedersheim-Paul, 1975). In order to reduce uncertainty regarding local habits, preferences, market structure, and ways of approaching customers, the sequential steps are small.

Over the past two decades, the Chinese government persisted in a combined strategy of "coming in" (*yin jin lai*) and "going out" (*zou chu qu*). "Not only should we attract the foreign firms to actively invest in China, but also we should direct domestic firm to go out, invest abroad and exploit the local market and resources. We should not only target the markets of European Union and US, but the markets in developing countries..." (Jiang Zeming, 2002).

We have observed that Chinese multinationals initiated the establishment of overseas operations. Of particular interest in the present context is that the time order of such establishments seems to be related to the psychic distance between the home and the import/host countries (Johanson and Wiedersheim-Paul, 1975). The psychic distance is defined as the sum of factors preventing the flow of information from and to the market. Examples are differences in language, education, business practices, culture, and industrial development. Learning amounts to reducing the psychic distance between the home and the host country by expanding knowledge of local conditions (Barkema *et al.*, 1996).

However, if these firms cannot adopt appropriate learning strategies to facilitate them doing right things rather than just doing things right, they fail to increase the expected technology and management skills instead of diminishing the psychic distance in international expansion. Thus, the farther the "technological distance" of a country from the global frontier (best practice), the more difficult it is to absorb information effectively into production systems (Keller, 2002). This problem concerns the strategic flexibility of learning and little attention is given to the strategic flexibility of learning in the globalization of China's firms. The current study conceptualized the strategic flexibility of learning in terms of two dimensions. The first is reactive learning and the second is proactive learning. This framework helps in developing an understanding of the multidimensional nature of strategic flexibility of learning.

Reactive learning

In the early stage of internationalization, when many foreign enterprises entered the Chinese market, Chinese people called the phenomena as "*lang lai le*" (wolf came). Next, government pushed firms to increase their involvement in internationalization. In particular, to protect the vulnerable and developing industries, the Chinese government limited the entry of foreign firms and launched the "import • assimilate • innovate" strategy.

However, it is difficult for indigenous firms to verify the quality of the technological knowledge that they receive from MNEs. Further, technology transfer can be incomplete, since MNEs may withhold tacit knowledge from, or refuse to provide continuous technical support to, local firms (Hennart, 1989). As a result, the development of Chinese industries follows a vicious circle. On the one hand, without self-reliant innovation, Chinese firms are strongly dependent on protective industrial policies and foreign technology to develop the productions in the long term. On the other hand, as described above, many firms not only sacrificed profits for larger market share but also failed to access state-of-the-art technology.

In the Deng Xiaoping and Jiang Zeming era, the Chinese government encourages indigenous firms to utilize FDI and form joint ventures and adopts open trade policies when a "trial and error" strategy (*mo zhe shi tou guo he*) is initiated. In the early stage, therefore, Chinese firms adopted a government-led reactive learning strategy.

The government-led learning strategy seems sensible and compelling. However, the problem is that the strategy responds to any changes in the environment and has short term in focus, and generally leads to adaptive rather than generative learning (Senge, 1990). The first troublesome aspect is what Hamel and Prahalad (1994) call the "tyranny of the served market" in which managers see the world only through their current customers' eyes. As Christensen and Bower (1996) point out, existing customers can substantially constrain a firm's ability to innovate because the innovations may threaten the customers' way of doing business.

By reactive learning, however, firms are on the lookout for unexploited opportunities within the existing industry structure. Learning options that allow Chinese multinationals to "wait and see" are exploitative actions that arise from the reactive flexibility of the firm.

Proactive learning

A later stage of globalization through mergers and acquisitions (M&A) has been encouraged by the Chinese government, largely to circumvent import barriers and enter third country markets (Lei, 2000). In the Chinese context, such strategic moves were called as "*yu lang gong wu*" (dances with wolves). "*yu lang gong wu*" enables Chinese firms to form strategic alliances and cooperate projects and conduct the interactive learning with foreign firms.

In 2000, however, the "Go Global" strategy initiated by the Chinese government aimed to turn large domestic companies into global players. Since 2001, in particular, which was the year when China became a member of the World Trade Organization (WTO), the support of the overseas expansion of Chinese companies became a major concern for the government. Therefore, a number of policies were designed to help companies invest abroad. Before presenting these policies in more detail, a short look at the government's motivation to support the "going out" strategy (*zou chu qu*) is necessary.

Fischer (2002, pp.12–13) argues that the motivation of the government and the companies to pursue this strategy is not necessarily one and the same. For the government, access to overseas natural resources counts as basic motives that explain economic policy support.

When setting up production abroad, MNE subsidiaries often face operational disadvantages, a handicap called the liability of foreignness (Hymer, 1976; Zaheer, 1995). Thus, the learning strategy in the later stage of internationalization of Chinese companies is oriented by the market to be proactive learning. Proactive learning strategy represents a long-term focus on understanding local market environment and psychic characteristics and on developing innovative solutions that produce superior customer value.

Because of a dynamic and turbulent market, for generative learning, market-oriented learning strategy facilitates Chinese multinationals to conduct market experiments, learn from the results, and modify their offerings based on the new knowledge and insights (Hamel and Prahalad, 1994; Slater and Narver, 1995). Therefore, market-oriented learning can lead to radical improvements in current products and service activities.

In doing so, proactive Chinese learners have also acquired advanced foreign technology, management expertise, and personnel training. Haier Corporation, the household electronics manufacturer, for example, established a venture in Indonesia in 1996, followed later by operations in the Philippines and Malaysia. In early 1999, Haier was exporting from China to 87 countries, with 60 percent of the total destined for the United States and Europe (Taylor, 2002). By making use of designs in its global operations, Haier has been enabled to develop new technologies to better target individual markets, as indicated by its construction of a new production base in the United States, expected to produce 200,000 refrigerators per year.

According to the above analysis, the key differences between reactive learning and proactive learning are given in Table 3.2.

Implications

With closer integration into the global economy and China's accession to the WTO, the government realized that economic power and international competitiveness were the most important sources of international influence, and that globally operating companies were of crucial importance in achieving those goals.

Learning is an interacting process, and localization, especially in human resource areas, could eventually lead to a hybrid system of management, where respective partners contribute their own managerial practices, as is becoming the case with Sino-foreign ventures in China itself. As yet, however, the globalization of China's companies is still inhibited by legal, financial, fiscal, intelligence, and human resource constraints, barriers that can

Table 3.2 Key differences between reactive learning and proactive learning

	Reactive learning	Proactive learning
Strategic orientation	Government-led	Market-oriented
Adjustment style	Responsive	Proactive
Temporal focus	Short-term	Long-term
Spatial focus	Local	Global
Learning type	Adaptive	Generative
Learning approach	Deterministic	Choice
View of environment	Source of risk, uncertainty, opportunity if lucky, deterministic	Source of competitive advantage, opportunities; malleable
Learning objective	Process emphasis	Product emphasis
Learning outcome	Incremental improvement and innovation	Radical improvement and innovation

best be removed by recourse to action by government and business in partnership (Hu, 2000; Lei, 2000; Nie, 2000).

The three learning processes proposed in this study are conducive to understanding the evolution of knowledge acquisition in the globalization of China's companies. We argue that the Chinese government should adopt the policy that facilitates firms to learn from MNEs, learn from ODI, and learning by doing. For the government, such strategic moves should be used to favor firms in accumulating experiences and access to technology. For Chinese companies, the implications of this study lie in helping them with leveraging the diverse sources of learning. In the different stages of internationalization, firms have particular learning processes. But as shown in Figure 3.2, learning process follows the "learning • applications • feedback" path.

Currently, however, the globalization strategies of China's companies will only be realized through a close partnership with the government. In the reactive learning view, motivation of the companies to pursue this strategy should be in alignment with that of government.

Faced with a growing number of dumping complaints from its major trading partners, direct investment became an attractive vehicle for China. Therefore, outward investment and the support of the global expansion of large (state-owned) companies were added to the overall program of foreign economy policy. Therefore, a proactive learning strategy is proposed to analyze the motivation of China's companies in the later stage of internationalization. A proactive learning strategy allows firms to have a long-term learning focus and scan the world markets globally. Furthermore, we present the key differences between reactive learning and proactive learning. This allows us to understand the flexibility and evolution of learning strategies in internationalization.

However, there are limitations to the globalization of Chinese companies. The government has yet to establish a credible legal infrastructure. Companies, too, have a responsibility to improve the quality of management through training in areas like human resources, marketing, and foreign languages. Generally speaking about Chinese subsidiaries abroad, one of the niche specialist traders observed: "Most overseas companies are small scale, managed on a loose basis. The business depends upon the overseas subsidiary's ambitions, abilities, funds and readiness to take risks." Major challenges exist for Chinese managers and policy makers at both enterprise and national economy levels. Therefore, future research should focus on the antecedents and consequences of international expansion in Chinese enterprises from an institution-based view.

Acknowledgments

We would like to thank Professor Ilan Alon and Professor John R. McIntyre, who have provided us with an opportunity to publish our works. We would also like to thank an anonymous referee for his insightful comments on earlier versions of this chapter. Financial support in part from the National Natural Science Foundation of China (NSFC) under contract no. 70472009 and no. 70602004 and from the Key Project of the Educational Ministry of China (KPEMC) under contract no. 04JJD630001 is gratefully acknowledged.

References

Almeida, P. (1996) "Knowledge sourcing by foreign multinationals: Patent citation analysis in the US semiconductor industry," *Strategic Management Journal*, 17: 155–165.
Bai Rongchun's speech on large state-owned enterprises reform, July, 2001. http://www.xinhuanet.com.
Barkema, H. G., Bell, J. H. J. and Pennings, J. M. (1996) "Foreign entry, cultural barriers, and learning," *Strategic management Journal*, 151–166.
Bowman, E. H. and Hurry, D. (1993) "Strategy through the option lens," *Academy of Management Review*, 18: 760–82.
Cantwell, J. and Piscitello, L. (2000) "Accumulating technological competence: Its changing impact on corporate diversification and internationalization," *Industrial and Corporate Change*, 9(1): 21–51.
Chang, S. J. (1995) "International expansion strategy of Japanese firms: Capability building through sequential entry," *Academy of Management Journal*, 38: 383–407.
Christensen, C. and Bower, J. (1996) "Customer power, strategic investment, and the failure of leading firms," *Strategic Management Journal*, 17(3): 197–218.
Deng, P. (2003) "Foreign investment by multinationals from emerging countries: the case of China," *Journal of Leadership and Organization Studies*, 10(2): 113–124.
Deng, S. and Dart, J. (1999) "The market orientation of Chinese enterprises during a time of transition," *European Journal of Marketing*, 33(5/6): 6–31.

Dunning, J. H. (1993) *The globalization of business*, London: Routledge.

Dunning, J. H. (1995) "Reappraising the eclectic paradigm in an age of alliance capitalism," *Journal of International Business Studies* , 26: 461–491.

Fischer, D. (2002) Zou chu qu – Ein neuer Schwerpunkt in der chinesischen Aussenwirtschaftspolitik. in: *GVC informiert*, 1: 10–13.

Hamel, G. and Prahalad, C. K. (1994) *Competing for the Future*, Boston, MA: Harvard Business School Press.

Hennart, J.F. (1989) "Can the 'New Forms of Investment' Substitute for the 'Old Forms'? A Transaction Costs Perspective," *Journal of International Business Studies*, 20(Summer): 211–234.

Hymer, S. (1976) *The international operations of national firms: a study of direct investment*, Cambridge, MA: MIT Press.

Hu, R.D. (2000) "A discussion of possibilities, problems and policies relating to our country's outward direct investment," *Jingji Wenti Tansu*, 7: 72–74.

Itami, H. and Roehl, T. W. (1987) *Mobilizing invisible assets*, Cambridge, MA: Harvard University Press.

Jiang Zeming's speech on Socialism characterized by China. Zhongyang Wenxian Chubanshe, 2002, 190–191.

Johanson, J. and Vahlne, J. (1977) "The internationalization process of the firm: A model of knowledge development and increasing foreign commitment," *Journal of International Business Studies*, 8: 23–32.

Johanson, J. and Wiedersheim-Paul, F. (1975) "The internationalization of the firm: Four Swedish cases," *Journal of Management Studies*, 12: 305–322.

Keller, W. (2002) "Geographic localization of international technology diffusion," *American Economic Review*, 92(1): 120–142.

Kogut, B. (1991) "Joint ventures and the option to expand and acquire," *Management Science*, 37: 19–33.

Kogut, B. and Chang, S. J. (1991) "Technological capabilities and Japanese foreign direct investment in the United States," *Review of Economics and Statistics*, 73: 401–413.

Kogut, B. and Kulatilaka, N. (1994) "Operating flexibility, global manufacturing, and the option value of a multinational network," *Management Science*, 40: 123–139.

Kogut, B. and Zander, U. (1992) "Knowledge of the firm, combinative capabilities, and the replication of technology," *Organization Science*, 3(3): 383–397.

Lei, W. (2000) "New opportunities and challenges: Discussing China's multinational mergers and acquisitions," *Jingji Wenti Tansu*, 2: 15–18.

Liu, H. and Li, K. (2002) "Strategic implications of emerging Chinese multinationals: The Haier case study," *European Management Journal*, 20(6): 699–706.

Luo, Y. (1999) *Entry and cooperative strategies in international business expansion*, London: Quorum Books.

Luo, Y. and Peng, M. W. (1999) "Learning to compete in a transition economy: Experience, environment, and performance," *Journal of International Business Studies*, 30(2): 269–296.

Luo, X. L., Zhou, N. and Liu, S. S. (2005) "Entrepreneurial firms in the context of China's transition economy: An integrative framework and empirical examination," *Journal of Business Research*, 58(3): 277–301.

Maitland, E. and Nicholas, S. (2002) "Internationalization of Australian firms in Asia," *International Studies of Management and Organization*, 32(1): 79–108.

Nelson, R. and Winter, S. (1982) *An evolutionary theory of economic change*, Cambridge, MA: Harvard University Press.

Nie, M. H. (2000) "An examination of policy regarding the development of mergers and acquisitions by our country's multinationals," *Guoji Maoyi Wenti*, 3: 41–45.

Peng, M. W. and Wang, D. Y. (2000) "Innovation capability and foreign direct investment: Toward a learning option perspective," *Management International Review*, 40: 79–93.

Senge, P. M. (1990) *The Fifth Discipline*, Doubleday, New York.

Slater, S. and Narver, J. (1995) "Market orientation and the learning organization," *Journal of Marketing*, 59(3): 63–74.

Taylor, R. (2002) "Globalization strategies of Chinese companies: current developments and future prospects," *Asian Business & Management*, 1: 209–225.

The World Bank, *Policy Options for Reform of Chinese State-Owned Enterprises*, World Bank Discussion Paper No. 335, Washington, D.C. (1996).

Wu Bangguo's speech on the reform of large state-owned enterprises in China, August, 1998. http://www.xinhuanet.com.

Wu, K. and Han S. L. (2005) "State-company goals give China's investment push unique features," *Oil $ Gas*, 103(15): 20.

Yang, X. H. (2006) "Antecedents of international expansion in Chinese state-owned enterprises," IACMR.

Yin, R. K. (2003) *Case study research, design and methods* (3rd edition). Beverly Hills: CA, Sage Publications.

Zaheer, S. (1995) "Overcoming the liability of foreignness," *Academy of Management Journal*, 38: 341–363.

4

Performance Strategies for the Globalizing Chinese Enterprise: Resource and Capabilities-Based Insights from a Three-Level Strategic Fit Model

Ilan Alon, Theodore T. Herbert, and J. Mark Muñoz

Introduction

China's economy is in a lengthy transformation from a centrally planned economy (Lukas *et al.*, 2001: 409) to a socialist market economy – a market economy with uniquely Chinese characteristics, management practices, and employee behavior (Zhu and Dowling, 2000). China is "the most active internationalizing economy among the developing countries" (Child and Rodrigues, 2005: 382), surpassed in exports only by Germany and the United States (Williams, 2005). Its outward foreign direct investment is currently the fifth largest in the world (Ministry of Commerce, 2005). A successful transition has national importance, yet the means by which Chinese enterprises can achieve the capabilities needed for effective globalization are unclear.

The challenge: becoming globally competitive

Even after two decades of reform, the competitive capability of China's large firms remains weak when compared with the prosperous, highly competitive, sophisticated, experienced, and aggressive global giants (Nolan, 2001: 187; Redding, 2005: 1). Many Chinese companies have been sheltered from intensive competitive pressures and the need to improve and hone organization-wide capabilities. While fraught with difficulties, internationalizing is a means for the Chinese firm to gain flexibility and an international presence, becoming more competitive both on the world market and at home (Child and Rodrigues, 2005).

To globalize, the firm must build the skills needed to remedy performance deficiencies. A systematic analytic approach, detailed herein, can be helpful in identifying, understanding, and remedying strategic and operational deficiencies, and in maintaining and strengthening existing advantages.

Strategic fit and alignment of organizational initiatives

To become successful in an intensely competitive global marketplace requires attending to the full but prioritized set of elements central to the firm's competitive and operational conditions. Focusing on improving the performance of a specific function such as production efficiency, while neglecting how that function interacts with other elements in the business system, inevitably leads to overall suboptimal performance or outright dysfunction. Yet paying attention simultaneously to all relevant facets of organizational performance is a skill normally acquired only through extensive experience. To achieve this important skill requires being able to articulate what the important strategic elements are and how they must "fit" together in concert with overall performance requirements.

Strategic fit

The concept of strategic fit (Miller and Friesen, 1983) is useful for systematically identifying the business's elements that affect organizational performance; one can make decisions designed to ensure all the parts fit, yielding higher coordination and overall performance. For fit to exist, the components of a system must be mutually consistent, toward the end of optimizing their respective coalignments with each other, and then ensuring still another fit between the coaligned system and its environment. When fit is attained, the organization can achieve higher levels of performance (Peng, 2003). Implicitly, using strategic fit criteria also includes identifying deficiencies that need to be remedied.

The validity of the concept has been extensively investigated in Western organizations, with consistent positive results (Venkatraman and Prescott, 1990). The few studies in transitioning economies have generally yielded positive results, including fit between generic strategy and national culture in China (Ross, 1999), and fit between Chinese electronics firms' strategies and their environments (Lukas *et al.*, 2001).

The strategic fit approach thus offers a means by which to investigate and identify Chinese firms' opportunities or deficiencies in becoming effective as competitors against more globally experienced companies. It then may be applied to identify appropriate strategic responses to rectify any imbalances or lack of alignment, or to maintain required coalignment of company resources and capabilities.

Identifying the firm's levels for analysis

An important question pertains to the proper scope of any initiative for improving global performance capabilities. The answer may be approached by relating the initiatives to the level at which their primary sources and effects lie, at one of three related conditions or levels of analysis: the individual level, the intraorganizational level, and the interorganizational level. Each level has separate implications for performance in globalizing competences and for fit.

The "individual level" consists of those elements that operate through the capabilities, resources, and processes of individual members, important for overall performance through effective and efficient human resources.

The "intraorganizational level" focuses on those capabilities, resources, and processes relevant to the effectiveness and efficiency of operations within the organization. These factors may include deficiencies in needed capabilities and resources, structural adjustments, technological innovations, and process improvements to the various business functions.

The "interorganizational level" focuses on the interactions between firms. These are external to their boundaries, either *local* or *global*. The local sublevel pertains to in-country relationships with the government and other domestic stakeholders. The global sublevel consists of, for example, cross-border business strategies or strategic alliances/partnerships, and competitive strategies needed for success in the global marketplace.

Alignment across levels

Companies run a significant risk of pursuing conflicting or malaligned strategies across these three levels. For instance, interorganizational actions may prove to be incompatible with the requirements of the individual level, resulting in organizational conflicts or failure. Performance is optimized when the requirements of each of the three levels are identified, the levels aligned (investigated for inconsistencies or conflicts, and those found are rectified) with each other, and all levels also be found to be consistent with (fit) the relevant external environmental conditions. If conflicts across two or more levels are identified, conscious trade-offs can be made.

In the next section, we review the resource-based view (RBV) of the firm for assessing initiatives' opportunities to generate competitive advantage to the globalizing firm.

The resource-based view of the firm

The RBV of the firm focuses on the performance-relevant assets of the firm and their derived skills (Barney, 1991). Any firm's assets can be categorized as tangible or intangible resources, which are "all assets, organizational processes, firm attributes, information, knowledge, etc., controlled by a firm that enable the firm to conceive of and implement strategies that improve its efficiency and effectiveness" (Barney, 1991, 101). Tangible resources include financial, physical, technological, and organizational assets; intangible resources include human, innovation and creativity, and reputation assets. Capabilities are the skills or competencies used by the firm to create and deliver its goods or services.

To assess its ability to confer competitive advantage, each resource is evaluated for its value, rarity, ability to be imitated, and substitutability.

For example, a given resource may be evaluated as having no value (i.e., does not contribute uniquely to a firm's efficiency or effectiveness), is not rare (is available easily to others), is readily imitated or duplicated (is not unique), and is easily substituted (has equivalent but different alternatives). No competitive advantage is then attained through acquiring or enhancing that resource. Alternatively, when a resource is valuable, rare, inimitable, and nonsubstitutable, competitive advantage may be attainable through its acquisition or enhancement. Varying combinations of the assessments of these four attributes yield no sustainable competitive advantage; yet oftentimes resources are necessary simply for staying in the game, for attaining competitive parity with adversaries. The RBV approach allows prioritizing actions or investments by their value either for attaining competitive parity or for gaining competitive advantage in the global marketplace.

Levels of strategic response and their interactions

Having dealt with several means for evaluating strategic initiatives, we now consider the "backdrop" of organizational functioning, then review the natures of the separate levels and their potentials for mutual interactions. We discuss also the critical importance of ensuring that the actions taken at each separate level are consistent with (fit) those at the other levels, followed by steps that address deficiencies.

Ambient factors

Backdrop or "ambient" factors are those cultural or institutional elements that permeate the organization through common culture and history. These affect almost all organizational members, specific intraorganizational factors, and some aspects of the firm's interorganizational elements. These cultural and institutional forces are many, but discussion is limited to those that have immediate implications for globalizing Chinese firms.

One such factor is Confucianism's continuing influence over individuals and their beliefs and behaviors in the Chinese culture (Lu, 2003), particularly through personal relationships. Philosophically aligned with the Confucian values of maintaining relationships, *guanxi* is associated with helping those in need and fully reciprocating favors; it works to maintain network harmony, sets the rules of cooperation, secures knowledge and resources, and lowers the transaction costs of doing business (Davies *et al.*, 2003). Without appropriate *guanxi*, even the most highly endowed and technologically sophisticated organization may not achieve its objectives without enormous extra effort and resources (McInnes, 1993). An important *caveat* is that *guanxi*'s critical requirement in emerging economies' early phases becomes "necessary but insufficient for good performance" in later phases, requiring the addition of conventional strategic elements of market and competition-based capabilities (Peng, 2003).

Culture-based differences between two organizations and their separate business practices, such as culture-specific work goals, must also be identified and factored into strategies. Joint ventures or strategic alliances with foreign personnel offer opportunities for conflicts from differing work goals, which should be anticipated and preempted.

The ambient factors identified above illustrate the potential of this category of factors to influence organizational functioning. They also should point the thoughtful executive to examine critically those cultural or institutional factors relevant to the specific Chinese firm's needs and situation, rather than being overlooked due to overfamiliarity.

Nested within the ambient factors are the three levels directly relevant to the globalizing Chinese firm, the first of which is the individual level.

The individual level

As China evolves, employees increasingly face the need to upgrade their competences, since they are likely to possess uneven skill sets, interests, and predispositions toward foreign cultures and organizations. Yet simply acquiring skills or technical capabilities is insufficient for ensuring that the individual meshes seamlessly with organizational needs and strategic elements. The organization's and its members' attributes must be consistent with each other. Such fit is a significant factor in organizations endeavoring to conduct business globally. Organizations in China must examine and assess their employees' suitability to the organization and its strategies in order to optimize its individual level challenges.

Specific managerial responses to those challenges resident at the individual level include the following:

1A: Identify the relevant skill sets for members and executives for the business strategy, assess current skills, and remedy any deficiencies.
1B: Ensure that members' beliefs, work values, motivational levels, and personal goals are consistent with those of the organization.
1C: Investigate culturally derived processes such as *guanxi* for their possessors within the firm, as a firm asset available for exploitation.
1D: Review work histories and work orientations of members to uncover and retrain inappropriate habits from planned-economy organizations.
1E: Review and improve members' language skills and foreign-culture knowledge.

RBV perspective: Each of these actions is important for the firm to ascertain the value of its resources and capabilities. But remedying deficiencies does not make it difficult for competitors to imitate or substitute them; attaining satisfactory levels and matches of individual resources and capabilities is certainly not rare among global competitors. At best, raising firm resources and capabilities to a level dictated by the firm's aspirations and strategies can but yield competitive parity. Sustainable competitive advantage must be sought elsewhere.

The intraorganizational level

The globalizing corporation's business skills evolve to become better associated with economic performance (Peng, 2003), with necessary transitions in mode, scale, and business functions (Geng, 1998), all of which must also fit each other.

A critical constraint in transforming or operating a firm is the managerial resource. China's current scarcity of management talent is traceable to the practices of the Cultural Revolution, decades of subsistence-level living, and the historic large-organizational managerial roles of compliance and implementation rather than initiative (Redding, 2005). While entrepreneurial talent in small and medium-sized organizations has quickly emerged, a cadre of professional managers best-suited to building and strengthening large-scale world competitors remains underdeveloped.

Ongoing challenges are the traditional Chinese management practices developed under the former centrally planned economy. Those include the following:

(1) *Top-down decision making*: Workers wait for and follow the orders from superiors, and do not think creatively because the traditional reward system depended on age and time in service, not performance.
(2) *Vertical communication*: Ineffective communication processes exist between different management levels, and getting information from lower levels is slowed by the organization's multiple levels.
(3) *Focus on production*: In order to meet the production targets assigned by the central planning body, managers were trained to focus on production.

As a result, traditionally experienced Chinese managers tend to be risk-aversive, do not understand the need for linking pay and performance, have little or no financial management skills, are unfamiliar with marketing activities, are unaware of the need to create competitive advantage, are unfamiliar with leadership and governance skills, and are specialized in a single function rather than having cross-functional or integrative skill sets (Bai and Enderwick, 2005: 26–27). Developing appropriately entrepreneurial, risk- and marketing-oriented members of the firm, then, can be a critical challenge.

Some Chinese industrial sectors have low-cost competitive advantages. But the typical Chinese firm faces important disadvantages in its global strategy, since nation-specific endowments like low labor costs cannot be exported (Sinha, 2005). Similarly, failure to develop branding identities or opting to specialize in commodity-like products can limit the potential for global success. Such deficiencies are apparent only upon evaluating the success of the strategy, unless the thoughtful executive remedies them beforehand.

The ability to manage its human resources and the followers' perception of the leader are important contributors to the Chinese firm's performance

(Law *et al.*, 2003). Particularly for larger firms, developing effective human resource management systems and ensuring they are carefully aligned with its selected developmental strategy are important elements in a successful global strategy.

The implications for managerial actions to identify and remedy the challenges posed at the intraorganizational level may include the following:

2A: Review management practices to ensure they are consistent with goals and resources; if not, undertake developmental activities.

2B: Consider the form of organization and ownership, changing it for greater appropriateness in a global context.

2C: Assess and modify leadership roles and functions for consistency with the needs dictated by the firm's globalization strategy.

2D: Review and modify the firm's administrative practices for human resources and refine a skills inventory for appropriate skill sets.

2E: Conduct an internal audit of resources (technological, *guanxi*, physical, capital, competences) and capabilities.

2F: Review and modify, if appropriate, governance and managerial processes, including decision-making practices.

RBV perspective: Many of the suggested actions are oriented toward attaining consistency among internal levels of resources and capabilities, the requirements for reaching parity with the new global strategy, and the resources and capabilities of more experienced global competitors; these include assessment of current management practices (2A), form of organization and ownership (2B), human resources practices (2D), auditing resources (2E). While important, none seem to offer unique advantage by being valuable, rare, inimitable, or nonsubstitutable.

Depending on the unique circumstances of the firm and its global industry and competitors, developing leadership (2C) and decision-making skills (2F) could be assessed as being valuable, rare, inimitable, and nonsubstitutable, and hence could be investments that rise above gaining parity.

The interorganizational level

The interorganizational level refers to the conditions within both local and global environments that separately affect or influence the organization's dynamics. A *local* response pertains to actions regarding relationships with the government and other domestic stakeholders, while the *global* response refers to actions regarding strategic alliances and partnerships developed across borders and the integrated web of activities pursued within an overall global framework.

The local environment and the firm: Social institutions play an important role in a transitioning economy, and the regional economy also has the ability to affect firm performance (Law *et al.*, 2003). The globalizing Chinese firm may wish to achieve economies of scale through intra-China operations to help finance its international operations. This strategy may be difficult, especially since China consists of 23 provinces and 5 autonomous regions. Each region has its own cultural and economic characteristics, and its separate legal system that may differ substantially by region, each of which operates to increase local protectionism. Thus, for the firm with pan-Chinese aspirations, each region must be dealt with and organized for separately, generating cost inefficiencies rather than economies of scale for funding the globalization effort. Working with local, regional, and national governments, then, is vital. In fact, most Chinese companies have a government relations officer who is responsible for both monitoring and managing relations with government agencies and individuals.

Maintaining good *guanxi* has been identified as the single most important business activity (Leung *et al.*, 1996); we consider it here because, as an ambient factor, it can affect an entire organization. It becomes available because it begins with and resides within a specific individual (Davies *et al.*, 2003), so it can be an ephemeral asset. Over time, though, the personal basis of *guanxi* can benefit or accrue more broadly to an employing department or organization (Grainger, 2003). It directly affects the Chinese legal system, employment nepotism, promotions, occupational advantages and disadvantages, corporate relations, international political structures, recruitment, transfers, apartment allocations, and banquets (Grainger, 2003). Western joint venture partners typically remain unfamiliar with the nuances of *guanxi*, treating important outsiders collectively rather than individually. For Chinese and Western partners, differing interpretations of *guanxi* can create difficulties, with implications for both management dynamics and the formulation of strategy.

Infrastructure is another important factor to consider in transitioning environments. While there are emerging opportunities in media expansion, challenges exist in governmental censorship and intellectual property, calling for the need to carefully assess the landscape.

Managerial actions suitable for identifying and accommodating the local sublevel's implications include the following:

3A: Consider how the expansion strategy is appropriate for the domestic market needs across China's regions.
3B: Assess the impact of governmental relations processes at home, in other Chinese regions, and in foreign markets on operations.
3C: Investigate the effects of ambient cultural factors on foreign partners' negotiating or establishing working relationships.
3D: Understand and optimize local market factors and dynamics for performance, especially for transferring skills to broader marketplaces.
3E: Consciously audit ongoing organizational *guanxi* and maintain proper relationships with those involved.
3F: Monitor the emerging nature of the local and global mass media and develop a strategy for them.

RBV perspective: Competitors would likely have varying but minor capabilities in ambient cultural factors (3C), leveraging local-market-based skills (3D), and consciously managing *guanxi* (3E). These would seem to be, for now, relatively rare but valuable, inimitable, and nonsubstitutable. Such abilities to mount local resources and apply local competences are then an opportunity for achieving competitive advantage, at least in the short to intermediate term. In contrast, evaluating the impact of the expansion/global strategy (3A), managing governmental relations (3B), and developing mass media strategies (3F) are likely to be commonly valued actions, with currently widespread applications, and hence would be parity-oriented.

The global environment and the firm: Organizations in China should implement strategic approaches alongside individual and organizational factors. For perspective, the scope and influence of China's outward foreign direct investment reaches 139 nation states and territories, heavily concentrated in Australia, the United States, Hong Kong, Thailand, Russia, New Zealand, South Africa, and Macao (Taylor, 2002). Chinese overseas ventures are typically small-scale, with an average capitalization of US$3 million, are predominantly in service and processing, are increasingly directed toward high technology, and are likely to further expand (Taylor, 2002).

Internationalizing organizations' objectives and strategic actions vary with their experience, and most Chinese businesses are in the initial stages of internationalization (Geng, 1998). According to Lall, firms in newly industrializing economies achieve success through specialized efficiencies, while developing a strong outward orientation and pursuing strategies that are consistent with changing costs and technologies. They tend to restructure, manufacture labor-intensive goods, transfer low-technology activities to lower-wage areas, and locate final manufacturing operations near new markets. This suggests that organizations must adapt, and respond well to a global environment.

For international expansion, business success is also based on partnership selection. A potential partner's strategic, organizational, and financial characteristics must be carefully examined when considering international joint ventures (Luo, 1998). Another factor is that of cultural and values compatibility in alliances; for example, important differences were found between Chinese and French managers in an automobile joint venture. Cultural disparity affected managerial perceptions and business activities that led to serious and mutual misunderstandings (Tian and Cone, 2003). Even within Greater China (Hong Kong, Taiwan, and the People's Republic of China (PRC)) managerial values have been found to differ and thus need to be understood and reconciled. PRC managers have been found to display higher power distance and less concern for deadlines and plans than do managers in Hong Kong and Taiwan, with higher levels of materialism among managers in the PRC and Hong Kong than in Taiwan (Cheung and Chow, 1999). This suggests that compatibility between cross-border partners can affect the dynamics of international alliances and so should be given careful consideration before any agreement is finalized.

When marketing products globally, companies in transitioning environments should not neglect pricing and branding issues. Customer performance satisfaction decreased when Chinese exporters pursued price-leadership product strategies, but increased when Chinese exporters used a branding product strategy (Brouthers and Xu, 2002).

Managerial actions suitable for identifying and accommodating the global sublevel's implications include the following:

4A: Learn the issues important for global production and consumption, and set training goals as appropriate.
4B: Formulate a global vision and develop strategies for market expansion.
4C: Analyze value chains for efficiencies and effectiveness.
4D: Evaluate potential partners for strategic, organizational, and financial attributes, as well as for values and cultural consistency.
4E: Evaluate e-commerce opportunities and the skills they require for execution.

RBV perspective: Developing entry-level competences (4A) action is parity-oriented. The other action elements provide a means for achieving competitive advantage through formulating a global vision and developing explicit strategies based on that vision (4B), performing thoughtful analyses of the firm's value chains (4C), going beyond superficial reviews of potential partners (4C), and becoming versed in the emerging advantages provided through e-commerce (4E). Each of the latter action elements is more or less rare, certainly valuable, not able to be imitated, and cannot be substituted; hence these four action elements contribute directly to attaining the resources and capabilities needed for sustainable competitive advantage.

Cross-level effects

The opportunities for conflict between the conditions at two or more levels should be apparent. Compatibility between the actions taken at several different levels, alternatively, is necessary but not necessarily sufficient to yield higher levels of performance. For example, hiring new managerial employees with high entrepreneurial potential (individual level) would be inappropriate within a tightly regulated, high-security industrial sector (interorganizational level), since poor alignment or poor fit would result.

Key factors for Chinese firms are effective management of external relations, resource and skill building, and utilization of resources (Li *et al.*, 1998), so fit among these components would be conducive to higher performance. Thus, the external and intraorganizational levels in the Chinese business environment play significant roles. The individual level, too, must be explicitly considered, and strategic action across all three levels must be closely aligned and integrated.

The following managerial implications from considering cross-level fit should be considered:

5A: Create an optimal set of global capabilities that are mutually consistent across relevant levels.
5B: Develop a strategic/global mind-set among members to allow the firm to remain true to important cultural values, while improving other capabilities.

RBV perspective: These final managerial actions are directed at achieving sustainable competitive advantages for the globalizing Chinese firm. They are certainly valuable, rare in that they are not commonly possessed by competitors, inimitable, and nonsubstitutable, and hence are actions that will develop competences and resources that yield sustainable competitive advantages.

Discussion and conclusions

Especially for the previously globally isolated emerging firm, evaluating traditional or current business practices against the requirements imposed by experienced global competitors is a necessary first step. Yet, at this step many firms stumble.

It is tempting to focus on a single key or obvious skill or resource, such as increasing production efficiency or partnering with a foreign firm with complementary skills. The reality, though, is that for any firm there are many distinct areas for skill development, perhaps interwoven, which must be identified and assessed for improvement. One must also question whether any specific skill set contributes to developing a sustainable competitive advantage, or whether acquiring or enhancing those skills create no advantage at all, perhaps not even leading to competitive parity with important competitors.

The systematic analysis of the firm's skills and resources, coupled with an explicit assessment of their potential for yielding competitive advantage, is essential for the globalizing firm's success in global business endeavors. A holistic model is useful for identifying and assessing the firm's skills and resources, allowing the deconstruction of firm activities into three distinct elements (levels) for focus and evaluation, those being the individual, intraorganizational, and interorganizational levels. These play separate but interrelated and important roles in the organizational dynamics of companies in a transitioning environment such as China. Each of the three levels is likely to be interconnected with at least one of the other two; strategic measures pursued at one level could affect the other levels. Critical to the strategic success of the entire system is the necessity that they all fit, both with each other and for the entire organizational system with its environment.

Consequently, we have proposed an integrated approach. An organizational assessment is necessary for each level, so that companies can understand their current strategic position. Additionally, planned strategies have to be implemented with a clear view of how each of the levels fit together. The final stage of this analytic process is assessing the resulting managerial action elements against their yielding competitive advantage against, or (at best) competitive parity with, the firm's competitors. Investing scarce resources, such as executive attention or finances, should be allocated on a priority basis to those programs that build skills or resources that lead to attaining competitive advantage. The criteria for assessing such potential include the extent to which each investment would build a skill or resource that is valuable, rare, inimitable, and nonsubstitutable. Simply investing in building or remedying skills or resources without considering their impacts on long-term performance through competitive advantage runs the risk of approving poor uses of scarce resources and squandering significant opportunities to build a sustainable high-performance position in the global economy.

Consider this hypothetical case. A successful Chinese toy manufacturer has experienced moderate business success in Yunnan, China, for the past 5 years. As the company endeavors to build its consumer base, it launches and operates a website and runs a national advertising campaign. Due to its exceptional product quality, orders pour in and sales expand rapidly. After 3 months, the company also receives a partnership offer from a US firm, and requests for agency agreements in Thailand, Brazil, and Germany.

Based on the approach we have suggested, the Chinese enterprise should assess its individual, intraorganizational, and interorganizational dimensions. With expanding sales in the domestic environment, the resulting effects on its employees and organizational structure need to be considered. Additionally, an assessment of the external environment has to be made in the context of local, international, and global pressures.

If the firm's head decides to appoint the three interested international distributors, he or she must consider individual- and intraorganizational-level implications. At the individual level, some employees will need to be trained in international cultures, and language skills may need to be improved to facilitate international communication. At the intraorganizational level, a new department may need to be created to support international sales. At the interorganizational level, new means may be needed to foster better relationships with the new distributors, and market expansion may be given priority in markets close to the distributors' locations. The approach suggests that the selected strategic actions of the Chinese company must tie in at all the levels, or risk failure to achieve the desired objectives.

In addition, each recommendation must be evaluated for creating resources that are scarce, rare, unable to be imitated, and unable to be substituted. The individual-level recommendations would certainly be valuable and nonsubstitutable, but are not rare or inimitable, suggesting that these actions would lead to competitive parity at best. Similar analysis for the intraorganizational recommendation for a new international sales department shows this would be useful, but is neither rare nor inimitable. The interorganizational recommendations, for fostering better relationships and expanding in specific geographic areas, similarly allow the conclusion of being nonrare initiatives that are able to be imitated, however valuable and nonsubstitutable they are.

This analysis suggests that the firm must remedy its existing deficiencies to be able to enter the global business it intends, and also that it must focus significant attention on building additional strengths through capabilities and resources that will allow developing competitive advantages. Some initiatives that might yield results beyond simple parity to achieving an advantage might include negotiating exclusive rights to manufacture popular toys, formulating an innovative product-development program with distributors, implementing a new electronic real-time inventory-management system with distributors linked to production and logistics, and so on.

Although the example and the approach we have discussed specifically focus on China, a similar approach may be used in other transitioning economies experiencing the rapid and broad forces brought about by a global environment. The strategic fit approach highlights the need for tighter and more thorough integration of organizational actions by the globalizing firm in a transitioning economy, and provides a framework for an effective strategic response to the challenges posed by globalization. And, an emphasis on evaluating any program of actions against its potential for developing a competitive advantage, can help to ensure that the long-term sustainability of the emerging global firm is enhanced.

References

Bai, X. and Enderwick, P. (2005) "Economic transition and management skills: The case of China," in I. Alon and J.R. McIntyre (eds) *Business and management education in China*, Singapore: World Scientific Publishing, pp. 21–45.

Barney, J. (1991) "Firm resources and sustained competitive advantage," *Journal of Management* 17(1): 99–120.

Brouthers, E. and Xu, K. (2002) "Product stereotypes, strategy and performance satisfaction: The case of Chinese exporters," *Journal of International Business Studies*, 33(4): 657–677.

Cheung, G.W. and Chow, I.H. (1999) "Subcultures in Greater China: A comparison of managerial values in the People's Republic of China, Hong Kong, and Taiwan," *Asia Pacific Journal of Management*, 16(3): 369–387.

Child, J. and Rodrigues, S.B. (2005) "The internationalization of Chinese firms: A case for theoretical extension?" *Management and Organization Review*, 1(3): 381–410.

Davies, H., Leung, T.K.P., Luk, S.T., and Wong, Y.H. (2003) "*Guanxi* and business practices in the People's Republic of China," in I. Alon (ed.), *Chinese Culture, Organizational Behavior, and International Business Management*, Westport, CT: Praeger, pp. 41–55.

Geng, C. (1998) "The evolutionary process of global market expansion: Experiences of MNCs in China," *Journal of World Business*, 33(1): 87–110.

Grainger, S. (2003) "Organizational *guanxi* in China's hotel sector," in I. Alon (ed.), *Chinese Culture, Organizational Behavior, and International Business Management*, Westport, CT: Praeger, pp. 57–71.

Law, K. S., Tse, D. K., and Zhou, N. (2003) "Does human resource management matter in a transitional economy? China as an example," *Journal of International Business Studies*, 34(3): 255.

Leung, T., Wong, Y., and Wong, S. (1996) "A study of Hong Kong businessmen's perceptions of the role of '*guanxi*' in the People's Republic of China," *Journal of Business Ethics*, 15: 749–758.

Li, S., Li, M., and Tan, J. J. (1998) "Understanding diversification in a transition economy: A theoretical exploration," *Journal of Applied Management Studies*, 7(1): 77–94.

Lu, L. (2003) "Influences of Confucianism on the market economy of China," in I. Alon (ed.), *Chinese Culture, Organizational Behavior, and International Business Management*, Westport, CT: Praeger, pp. 27–39.

Lukas, B. A., Tan, J. J., and Hult, G. T. M. (2001) "Strategic fit in transitional economies: The case of China's electronics industry," *Journal of Management*, 27: 409–429

Luo, Y. (1998) "Joint venture success in China: How should we select a good partner?" *Journal of World Business*, 33(2): 145–166.

McInnes, P. (1993) "*Guanxi* or contract: A way to understand and predict conflict between Chinese and western senior managers in China-based joint ventures," in D. McCarty and S.J. Hille (eds), *Research on Multinational Business, Management and Internationalisation of Chinese Enterprises*, Nanjing: Nanjing University, 345–351.

Miller, D. and Friesen, P. H. (1983) "Strategy-making and environment: The third link," *Strategic Management Journal*, 4: 221–235.

Ministry of Commerce (2005) *China Outbound Investments Statistics Report for 2004*, Beijing: Ministry of Commerce and State Statistical Bureau.

Nolan, P. (2001) *China and the Global Economy*, Basingstoke, UK: Palgrave.

Peng, M.W. (2003) "Institutional transitions and strategic choices," *Academy of Management Review*, 28(2): 275–296.

Redding, G. (2005) "Feeling the stones on the river bed: Prospects and implications for China's entry into the world of global competition," *Ivey Business Journal*, May–June: 1–9.

Ross, D.N. (1999) "Culture as a context for multinational business: A framework for assessing the strategy-culture 'fit'," *Multinational Business Review*, Spring: 13–19.

Sinha, J. (2005) "Global champions from emerging markets," *McKinsey Quarterly* No. 2. [www document] http://www.mckinseyquarterly.com/article (accessed 28 December 2005).

Taylor, R. (2002) "Globalization strategies of Chinese companies: Current developments and future prospects," *Asian Business and Management*, 1(2): 209–225.

Tian, Z. and Cone, M. (2003) "Cultural conflicts between Chinese managers and foreign managers in joint ventures," in I. Alon (ed.), *Chinese culture, Organizational Behavior, and International Business Management*, Westport, CT: Praeger, pp. 137–149.

Venkatraman, N. and Prescott, J.E. (1990) "Environment-strategy coalignment: An empirical test of its performance implications," *Strategic Management Journal*, 11: 1–23.

Williams, F. (2005) "China overtakes Japan as third largest exporter," *Financial Times*, April 15: 9.

Zhu, C. J. and Dowling, P. J. (2000) "Managing human resources in state-owned enterprises in transitional economies: A case study in the People's Republic of China," *Research and Practice in Human Resource Management*, 8(1), 63–92.

Part II

Institutional Considerations: New Pathways

5
Growth of Made-in-China Multinationals: An Institutional and Historical Perspective

Xiaohua Yang and Clyde Stoltenberg

Introduction

By the mid-1990s, China became the largest outward investor among emerging countries and the eighth largest supplier of outward investment among all countries (The World Bank, 1997). However, the momentum did not really become apparent until the late 1990s, when the Chinese government launched the "Go Global" strategy in 1999, followed by a series of international expansion activities by companies such as Haier Electronics Group and Shanghai International Securities Co. Recently, the world has witnessed a number of high-profile cases of Chinese firms acquiring, or attempting to acquire, well-known firms in North America and Europe. Examples include Lenovo, the leading Chinese PC maker, acquiring the IBM PC division and TCL, the leading Chinese electronics company, acquiring a majority interest in the television division of France's Thomson SA and the handset division of France's Alcatel SA. Commentators have suggested that even recent unsuccessful high-profile bids (Haier for Maytag and CNOOC for Unocal) "reflect China's global ambitions" (Hemerling, 2006).

The most recent data further reinforce the fact that multinationals from China have been expanding abroad rapidly. Since 1986, there have been 223 acquisitions of foreign operations by Chinese companies, with a total value of some US$18 billion (Hemerling, 2006). Over the last 5 years, the total outward foreign direct investment (O-FDI) from China has averaged more than US$3 billion annually, with a total market capitalization of US$104 billion in the US market. While these figures only comprise less than 1 percent of the world's total O-FDI, they represent a significant increase over the 1980s and 1990s (Quan, 2005; Steinbock, 2005). Today, Chinese multinationals have foreign direct investment (FDI) in virtually every country in the world. In fact, the 12 largest Chinese multinationals now control over US$30 billion in foreign assets across the whole spectrum of business activities, with over 20,000 foreign employees and over US$30 billion in foreign sales. Thus, what do we know about the firms? Their strategies? Their interface with their environment?

Li and Tsui (2002) suggest that the key challenge for management and organization scholars is to understand the complexities and continuing changes in the institutional environment in China and implications for different organizational patterns embedded in this complex environment, given economic reforms, enterprise reforms, and growth in China over the past two decades. In particular, what are the implications for institutions of Chinese firms going abroad to compete with Western multinationals for both resources and customers? There has been relatively little research completed on the internationalization of firms from emerging markets, as noted by Wright *et al.* (2005) in their special issue on "Strategy Research in Emerging Economies" and Peng and Dellios (2006) in their editorial for the special issue on "Asian Business Groups and Conglomerates." Ramamurti (2004) also clearly recognized the need for research in this area in the July issue of *JIBS* when he suggested that international business (IB) scholars must pay more attention to the behavior and performance of a new generation of home-grown multinational enterprises (MNEs) in countries like China and India. Hong and Sun (2006) concur, noting the need to put the Chinese phenomenon of outward investment "into the context of the rise of East Asian capital outflows and to examine the shifts in economic motives and strategic orientations of Chinese multinationals at the firm level." Given the volume and significance of increasing O-FDI from emerging economics such as China, as noted above, the need for research on the firms and the questions raised is likely to increase. This chapter seeks to contribute to the discourse on the influence of institutional factors on the international expansion of Chinese firms.

Scholars have come to terms with the notion that institutions matter, but how they matter remains contentious. Furthermore, how they matter for growth of Chinese MNEs remains largely unanswered. We agree with Peng and Dellios' (2006) argument that what determines the international expansion of firms from emerging Asian economies lies in institutions, given Asian governments' continued intervention in resource allocation and distribution systems; this is especially salient in the case of the Chinese government (Li and Tsui, 2002). We will use the case of international expansion of state-controlled enterprises (SCEs) in China to explore the relationship between this phenomenon and institutional change in China. The justification for using the term state-controlled enterprise (SCE) interchangeably with state-owned enterprise (SOE) is that the ownership and governance form of traditional SOEs have been undergoing tremendous change as part of the central government's effort to privatize them. Thus, the boundary between purely state-owned and partially privatized firms has blurred. Scholars, however, tend to agree that most of these SOEs are still controlled by the central government.

We will begin by discussing the stages of growth in made-in-China MNEs from a historical perspective. The second section will focus on the growth of Chinese MNEs and the role of the government from an institutional perspective; it will discuss how the Chinese government shapes international expansion strategies of these firms both as an enabler and controller. The third section will provide implications and conclusions.

Growth of made-in-China MNEs: a historical perspective

Although the phenomenon of Chinese firms' international expansion has attracted attention only recently (Deng, 2003; Luo *et al.*, 2005; Peng and Dellios, 2006), we argue that the roots of their international expansion go back some five decades. The growth of Chinese enterprises and their transition into MNEs has gone through two major historical periods: Period One was from 1949 (establishment of Chinese Communist Regime) to 1978 (beginning of economic reforms) and Period Two was from 1978 to the present. Each period can in turn be broken down into three stages.

Stage one: 1949 to mid-1950s: After the establishment of the communist regime, the Chinese government established a few overseas enterprises in Hong Kong to support necessary import–export business, including a subsidiary of the Bank of China, a foreign investment bureau, the Huarun Company, and the China Tourism Company. However, these overseas enterprises did not attract any attention due to their limited number, small size, and narrow business scope.

Stage two: Mid-1950s through mid-1970s: This stage, characterized by preinternationalization activities, consisted of providing economic and technical aid in the form of development project support, technical aid, material supply aid, and financial aid to third-world countries struggling for independence. Although these activities were not strictly FDI and multinational activities, such involvement paved the way for multinational management and developed a talent pool for later expansion.

Stage three: Mid- to late 1970s: The main international activities involved construction project contracts and labor export. In 1978, China set up the first project contract company, China Construction and Engineering Corporation. The number of such companies increased to 27 by 1982, and contractual agreements for construction projects and labor export reached 755 in 45 countries in Asia, Africa, Latin America, and Europe. The contracted amount reached US$1.2 billion. This type of business activity was the main form of China's international economic involvement at the time. While relatively preliminary and simplistic, these activities helped lay the foundation for further internationalization of Chinese firms.

Stage four: 1979–1995: The major demarcation for internationalization of Chinese firms came when the Chinese government clearly established

"Go Abroad" economic policies on August 13, 1979. This is the first time that China included O-FDI in the national economic development program, thereby paving the way for large-scale overseas expansion activities. The first FDI project was the joint venture between Beijing Friendship Commercial Service Corporation and Japan Commercial Conglomerate, named "Jin He Sharing Holding Limited Company" in Tokyo, Japan.

The unique feature about this stage is transformational development. During this phase, the Chinese government initially promoted O-FDI by granting permits to large state and provincial trading houses to set up overseas operations. As a result, many of the FDI projects were set up in Southeast Asian and developing countries to facilitate Chinese petrochemical and machinery exports. Thus, the government's diplomatic agenda became the impetus for the growth of the first group of Chinese multinationals (Wu and Chen, 2001). These firms attempted to operate like Japan's *keiretsu* through networks of subcontractors. However, they were unlike their counterparts in the West, Japan, and South Korea in terms of their motivations, behavior, and strategies; their approach tended to leapfrog and take short cuts in internationalizing operations. While the Chinese government played a pivotal role in promoting O-FDI as part of its economic and foreign policy, the market behavior and motives were minimal in these Chinese MNEs, and many of the FDI projects were poorly managed and underperformed. As Hong and Sun (2006) observe, the key decisions on overseas investments during this period, including choices of location and sector "were mainly determined by the consideration of enhancing China's political and economic influence and expanding its international trade relationships rather than that of maximizing market profit."

Government policies resulting in decentralization of economic decision making were also reflected in liberalization of O-FDI. The "Provisional Regulations Governing the Control and the Approval Procedure for Opening Non-Trade Enterprises Overseas" issued by MOFERT in July 1985 set forth principles pursuant to which "all enterprises, if they [had] sufficient capital, technical and operating know-how, and suitable foreign partners, [could] apply for permission to establish subsidiaries in foreign countries." This provided local governments with an opportunity to "push and help local foreign trade corporations and foreign business oriented companies to establish overseas operations, [the objectives of which] were the capital and technology as well as trade expansion gains" (Hong and Sun, 2006).

Later in this stage (after 1991), the Chinese government began to grant permits to large SCEs to allow these firms to directly access international markets, thus bypassing large state-owned trading companies to further economic liberalization. This move contributed to competitive growth of these SCEs in the international markets (Luo *et al.*, 2005). During this phase, the government's motivation to promote O-FDI was characterized by the recognition of natural resource constraints to further development (Hong and

Sun, 2006) as well as the desire to shift mature technologies and industries to other developing countries to maximize profits by using some comparative advantages. The total investment reached US$1.591 billion, with 355 firms approved for O-FDI (Wu and Chen, 2001). However, at the beginning of 1993, the government undertook rigorous screening of O-FDI projects due to the overheating of the economy, and the level of investment and number of projects fell over the previous years.

Stage five: 1996–2003: Normal development and adoption characterizes this stage. Starting in 1996, a large group of enterprises established after the 1978 economic reforms sought to internationalize their business. As Table 5.1 illustrates, many of these firms concentrated on home appliances and vehicles as the domestic markets in these sectors began to become saturated around that time. All seven of these cases involved greenfield investment.

A significant development during this period affecting the form in which Chinese companies could pursue outward investment lay in the increasing number of firms listed on developed country stock exchanges "as an important way to raise equity capital directly in hard currency and to establish international image and reputation" (Hong and Sun, 2006). Capital raised in this manner by highly publicized initial public offerings (IPOs) has gradually allowed transnational M&A to become the main form of China's direct investment abroad and, in the process, led to further privatization of SCEs. "The major explanations for this increased M&A by Chinese companies include[d] the need for direct access to natural resources, overcoming the low brand value of Chinese products, and obtaining as quickly as possible advanced marketing and distribution networks and R&D operations" (Hong and Sun, 2006).

Table 5.1 Chinese Firms' initial foreign ventures

Company name	Year, FDI destination, FDI Project
Little Swan	1995, Malaysia – built a home appliances plant
Haier Group	1996, Indonesia – built a home appliances plant
Haixin Co.	1996, South Africa – built a home appliances plant
Huawei Co.	1996, Hong Kong – engaged in a telecommunication project
Jicheng Group	1996, Columbia – built a motorcycle plant
Wanxiang Group	1997, UK – acquired AS Co.
HuaYuan Group	1997, Nigeria – acquired a textile plant

Source: Kang, Ke, and Xu, 2006.

Stage six: 2004 to the present: This stage is characterized by acceleration of overseas expansion activities in the form of mergers and acquisitions, such as Lenovo acquiring IBM's PC business in December 2004. Such an acceleration can be partially explained by the perceived onslaught of foreign competition after China's 2001 accession to the WTO (Kwan, 2006).

Further facilitating this trend, China's State Administration of Foreign Exchange issued new regulations in October 2005 in its "Notice on Issues Relating to the Administration of Foreign Exchange in Fundraising and Reversed Investment Activities of Domestic Residents Conducted via Offshore Special Purpose Vehicles [Notice 75]." Where prior regulation had created hurdles for Chinese firms seeking to restructure their domestic businesses under an offshore holding company as a prelude to overseas fundraising, Notice 75 established a consistent foreign exchange registration system to facilitate offshore restructurings (Foo, 2006).

At the same time, regulation of M&A within China has also continued to evolve, with the 2003 M&A Rules replaced by the 2006 M&A Rules. The 2006 M&A Rules expressly allow (for the first time) the use of a foreign publicly listed company's shares as consideration for the exchange of Chinese equity securities in connection with an M&A transaction (Hsia *et al.*, 2006). Concurrently, the Ministry of Finance has issued a series of new and revised Accounting Standards for Business Enterprises (effective beginning in 2007), which largely reflect the approaches and principles of the International Financial Reporting Standards, and the China Securities Regulatory Commission has been promoting since April 2005 a share liquidity reform program under which listed companies are being restructured to convert almost all nontradable legal person shares into freely tradable A shares within 2 years (Hsia *et al.*, 2006). Along with promulgation of the new Company Law effective January 1, 2006, all of these developments reflect continued Chinese government policy moving business enterprise decision making toward economically motivated goals and policies rather than the pursuit of state-imposed mandates.

To summarize the above, the internationalization process in Chinese firms cannot be viewed in isolation from the institutional environment in which it has taken place. In the first three stages, internationalization was not market-oriented; rather it was orchestrated by the government, and only SOEs participated. Even in the latter three stages, though, internationalization still was not totally market-oriented, government involvement remained prevalent, and the SOEs continued to dominate the whole scene. Table 5.2 summarizes these six stages:

Table 5.2 Growth stages of Chinese MNEs

Stages	Government goals and actions	Main features
Stage One 1949-mid-1950s	To support Chinese import–export business	Limited number of overseas enterprises, small sizes, and narrow business scope
Stage Two Mid-1950s to mid-1970s	Provide economic and technical aid to the third-world countries	Focused on development project support, technical aids, material supply aids, and financial aids
Stage three Mid- to late 1970s	To be involved in global economy	Involved in construction project contract and labor export
Stage Four 1979–1995	To develop large global firms Reorganized trading houses Urged SOEs to go abroad Rigorously screened IFDI projects	Rise of overseas subsidiaries of large trading houses Establishment of 113 outward FDI projects valued at $US14m 355 SOEs set up FDI ventures valued at US$1.591b Drop in the number of OFDI projects
Stage Five 1996–2003	Mix of encouragement and control	Normal development and adoption Home appliances and automobile manufacturers led the pack
Stage Six 2003–present	To deliver WTO promises To seek natural resources abroad to maintain economic growth at home	Acceleration of overseas expansion

Growth of Chinese MNEs and institutional change

Institutions, institutional reform, and evolution

North (1990) defines institutions as "the humanly devised constraints that shape human interaction." Institutions "structure incentives in human exchange, whether political, social, or economic...[and] institutional change shapes the way societies evolve through time." While North's influential work is predicated almost entirely on Western economic history, his observation that "the agent of change is the individual entrepreneur responding to the incentives embodied in the institutional framework" strikes a responsive chord when one considers the last 25 years of economic reforms in China.

As Lin *et al.* (1998) has pointed out, "although, by definition, the state owns the SOEs, the state cannot operate them by itself and needs to delegate their control to the enterprises' managers." While traditional SOEs in the Chinese economy lacked autonomy, the success of China's gradualist reforms in its own unique context has depended on a "process of institutional changes from those of a planned economy to those of a market economy." Lin points out that this approach has achieved dynamic growth because it "continues to provide protection and subsidies to the nonviable enterprises while allowing for entry of enterprises which are consistent with China's comparative advantage." China's approach to both inward FDI (I-FDI) and O-FDI and its gradualist approach to piecemeal privatization of SOEs has, in fact, allowed existing enterprises to evolve toward forms consistent with China's comparative advantage, with a feedback effect driving continued change of the institutional environment. The completion of China's transition to a market economy, according to Lin, will eventually require "elimination of institutional distortions in the planned economy."

Consistent with institutional reform and evolution, Fan (1994) has pointed out how China's reform "has been characterized by gradual changing of its reform objectives." The changes in objectives reflect "first, the increasing knowledge in China about the merits of different resource allocation mechanisms" and "second, and more fundamentally, the changes in the social balance between various interest groups and the changes of economic structure resulting from the process of reform and development itself." As a result, "people become more convinced about the superior efficiency of the market system and hence offer less resistance to more profound changes." Thus, there is a continuous two-way feedback effect between firms' evolution and the institutional environment in which they function. Or, as Liu (1997) has described it, the reforms have inserted "one by one new institutional elements into the existing framework, thus changing the dynamic of the institutional matrix."

With an ultimate goal of productivity growth, the reforms through the mid-1990s redefined the role of the state with its enterprise by dismantling central planning and creating markets. The objectives were "to separate management from bureaucratic state control, to ensure enterprise accountability, and to increase efficiency." Ultimately, to achieve efficiency in capital allocation and management, institutions must emerge to "dilute state ownership by injecting non-state property into it. This highlights the risk of property use in market competition" (You, 1998). With this backdrop of institutional change growing out of China's economic reforms, we can proceed to explore the relationship between developments in China's O-FDI and relevant institutional factors.

Institution-based view of Chinese MNEs

Given the influence of the institutional environment on a firm's behavior, any strategic choices that firms make are inherently affected by their "rules of the game" (North, 1990). This is particularly salient in the context of Chinese MNEs due to the transition from a planned economic system to a market economic system (Zheng, 2004). Accounts that have documented a few more prominent cases, such as Haier (Liu and Li, 2002), suggest that the unique features found in the international expansion of Chinese firms are not comparable to multinationals from any other countries. These unique features include that the dominant type of Chinese multinationals are SOEs, and their international expansion is promoted and supported by the Chinese government.

These Chinese SOEs have operated in different ownership structures and in different institutional environments than multinationals in developed countries and other emerging economies. They have been characterized by a high level of control by the central government, strong bargaining power with the government, easy access to political and economic privileges, and soft budgets (Deng and Dart, 1999; Luo and Peng, 1999; Luo *et al.*, 2005). It is widely recognized that the Chinese government has played a crucial role in shaping the country's O-FDI (Deng, 2003; Zhan, 1995).

The Chinese government has adopted a strategic posture in framing both their I-FDI and O-FDI policies to meet the demands of new global challenges and their own domestic economic interests. The government's attitudes and actions in relation to multinational activity and growth have been integral parts of allocation and upgrading of national resources. The Chinese government has placed the creation of an internationally competitive industrial base on the national agenda of economic liberalization. Early on, this led to lack of efficiency due to ownership structure and corporate government structure, low level of market behavior, and relatively liberal access to state bank loans (Luo *et al.*, 2005). In addition, traditionally, SOEs have not been mandated to utilize an incentive structure that aligns with the financial bottom line (Luo and Peng, 1999). Thus, what can explain the "public good" characteristics of these SOEs becomes an interesting question.

What has prompted these Chinese SOEs to expand internationally may not appear to be a logical decision that a Western firm may pursue. Aharoni (1966) classified antecedents of international expansion into two groups: internal forces and external forces. He suggested that the international expansion process is not a simple and logical decision process due to human beings' bounded rationality. A firm's motivation to expand abroad is influenced by interaction between and among internal and external forces, such as government and competition.

The Chinese government has taken a radically different path to reform its economy and transform its SOEs than its counterparts from other emerging economies, which have begun to abandon industrial policies. China has chosen to follow the industrial policy models developed in Britain during the Industrial Revolution and in the United States and continental Europe in the 19th century, and more recently the models developed in Japan, South Korea, Taiwan, and Singapore (Nolan, 1995; Nolan and Zhang, 2002). These authors have noted that a consistently stated goal of China's industrial policy is to construct global powerhouses that can compete on a global scale.

In the pre-reform period, Chinese firms' international activities were mainly guided by the government's needs for diplomatic policies and its desire to promote allegiance from third-world countries. During this period, Chinese firms exhibited minimal market behavior and motives, and many of those early O-FDI projects were poorly conceived and managed (Zhou, 2004). However, in the post-reform period, influences of the institutional environment on firms have become far more complex and dynamic. During the fourth stage, the main motivations informing government policy were twofold: to grow globally powerful companies and to engage in diplomatic policy by developing closer ties with other Asian and developing countries through O-FDI in these countries. Large state and provincial trading houses had to undertake FDI projects to further the diplomatic agenda of developing closer ties with Southeast Asian and developing countries. During 1984–1985, the government carried out the reorganization of these MNEs based on the lessons learned from the first phase. As a result, 113 O-FDI projects were approved involving US$14 million, across a wide range of industry sectors. Compared to the first phase, there was a much greater outward expansion.

The more substantial growth of Chinese MNEs occurred when, in the latter part of Stage Four, the Chinese government used Chinese MNEs as a vehicle to obtain natural resources in an attempt to sustain domestic economic engine of growth. Thus, many large Chinese resource firms were granted permit to directly invest in foreign countries. This move contributed to the competitive growth of these SOEs in the international markets (Luo *et al.*, 2005). The Chinese government was also in a bid to shift Chinese firms' mature technologies and industries to other developing countries to maximize profits by using some comparative advantages (Wu and Chen, 2001).

During stages five and six, particularly from the year 2001 onward, Chinese MNEs' international expansion was characterized by an acceleration of overseas expansion activities in the form of mergers and acquisitions. Such an acceleration can be explained by two main forces:

(1) the perceived onslaught of global competition after China's accession to the WTO in 2001 (many Chinese SOEs believe that to survive means global expansion); and
(2) the Chinese government's pressure on SOEs to seek natural resources abroad in order to maintain economic growth and deal with a shortage

of natural resources at home, as seen in the case of Huaneng Energy Group setting up a joint venture in Australia.

In each of these stages, Chinese MNEs behaved somewhat like incubators, both enabled and controlled by their institutional environment. Chinese institutions have evolved toward a more systematic and holistic approach to the internationalization of large SOEs in a configuration that aims to promote the country's long-term international competitive advantages. Consistent with the nation's industrial policy and economic welfare goals, the Chinese government's push for and regulation of O-FDI framed the motivations and strategies of Chinese multinational firms' international expansion. In turn, the firms' survival and growth hinged significantly on their ability to legitimize their existence and their fit with the government's national agenda.

In two and half decades, China's large SOEs have undergone tremendous transformation and have grown rapidly in many areas: increased sales volume, absorption of a great deal of modern Western technology, learning to compete in the marketplace, upgrading much human capital; upgrading managerial systems, and gaining understanding of global markets (Nolan and Zhang, 2002). These SOEs still account for the major portion of the national GDP. Thus, they are vital to the overall economic and social welfare of the country. Their performance can directly impact on the nation's economic growth. It is not surprising that they have been the targeted audience of major economic and industrial policies.

Impact of I-FDI on O-FDI

In particular, it must be noted that the growth of Chinese firms has been intricately linked to the inflow of FDI in China throughout the reform period. Unlike their counterparts from other countries during the same period, Chinese firms started mustering their capabilities and knowledge from a humble background by wooing foreign investors to bring their capital into China. In 1979, I-FDI was legally permitted in China. In just 25 years from an initial FDI inflow of US$2.427 billion per year in the early1980s to an FDI inflow of US$153.47 billion with 43,664 FDI projects in 2004, from initial investment projects as small as US$2 million on average in the early 1980s to Motorola's pledge of US$10 billion investment in China by 2006, China has been the world's largest FDI recipient in recent years (The US China Business Council, 2005.). Table 5.3, noted earlier, demonstrates the growth of I-FDI in China over the last two decades.

This large injection of foreign capital has played a crucial role not only in China's economic liberalization, but also in the rise of Chinese multinationals (Steinbock, 2005). In the 1980s and part of the 1990s, the Chinese government devised foreign investment laws purposely favoring SOEs. Thus, the firms that received foreign capital and technology and management systems through joint ventures, licensing agreements and other forms of

Table 5.3 China's FDI by five periods (in $US Billion)

Period	Project numbers	Contracted investment	Utilized investment
1979–1986	8, 295	19.413	8.304
Annual average	1, 037	2.427	1.038
1987–1991	34, 208	33.179	16.754
Annual average	6, 842	6.636	3.351
1992–1996	241, 317	416.799	151.537
Annual average	48, 263	83.36	30.307
1997–1999	57, 718	144.328	131.118
Annual average	19, 239	48.109	43.706
2000–2004	167, 402	482.88	254.45
Annual average	33, 480	96.58	50.89

Source: Wang, Johnson, and Yang, 2003; The US China Business Council.

strategic alliances were state-owned firms. These large SOEs became sought-after partners for MNEs from developed countries. Some of these SOEs have since shed their archaic planned-economy style management systems, outdated technology, and the old brick-and-mortar approach; instead, they have equipped themselves with many modern technologies, loaded with localized "foreign" capital and some Western management skills as well as international contacts and networks through various partnership arrangements.

This process helped Chinese SOEs gain knowledge and experience of foreign markets. Chinese SOEs took such a path as part of the central government's foreign policy, which encouraged O-FDI by large SOEs in neighboring Southeast Asian and other developing countries. The policy benefited Chinese SOEs as the culture in Southeast Asian countries is similar and easy for Chinese managers to assimilate, and markets in developing countries are less complex for Chinese multinationals to deal with. They gradually gained experience and confidence from these operations. In particular, Southeast Asian countries provide a training base for the new players in O-FDI as they can learn the complexities of international expansion at a lower cost.

This is evidenced in the case of the Haier Group, the leading home appliance company in China and the world's sixth largest home appliance maker (Fonda, 2002). After a number of years' experience as an exporter, Haier started Greenfield investments in Indonesia and the Philippines in 1996. This was followed by a few more FDI projects in other developing countries before launching its the first operation in the United States in 1999. Starting in 2001, Haier embarked on the process of acquiring other companies overseas (Liu and Li, 2002). Today, Haier trains its international managers in the Philippines before they are sent to the North American market.

The advantage of internal transfer of knowledge lies in its ability to overcome the failure of an external market and is thus critical to the growth of firms (Buckley and Carson, 1976; Hennart, 1982; Kogut and Zander, 1993; Rugman, 1982). The Chinese government recognized the importance of using joint ventures as a means of transferring knowledge internally as such joint ventures with Western firms would create communities in which critical tacit knowledge and modern Western technology would be shared and communicated. Within such communities, learning is bound to take place among individuals and groups through frequent interactions (Itami and Roehl, 1987; Kogut and Zander, 1993; Maitland and Nicholas, 2002). I-FDI has been positively linked with the innovatory capacity and competitiveness of the resources of the recipient economy (Dunning, 1993). Hence, for many years, the Chinese government required foreign investors to form joint ventures with SOEs if they wished to invest in China. In addition to that requirement, joint ventures were required to export a certain percentage of products to foreign markets. Such joint ventures not only allowed SOEs to obtain much needed capital and technology, but also offered the SOEs a taste of the international markets in the earlier days.

Many of the sectors and firms that the Chinese government promoted for international collaboration in the earlier phase of economic reforms have become more competitive and, thus, have become the very sectors that the government has been promoting for overseas expansion. These joint venture operations provided an organizational way to transfer tacit knowledge and technology for the SOEs. Such accumulated knowledge or time-based experience about market and institutional environments has been a critical driving force behind Chinese MNEs' international expansion (Johanson and Vahlne, 1977; Luo, 1999). Thus, Hong and Sun (2006) argue that Chinese enterprises' establishment of joint ventures within China before making overseas investments represents a key distinction between China's O-FDI and that of third-world peers.

Conclusions and implications

We hope that this chapter has introduced some useful observations about Chinese firms' outward investment in the context of the country's evolving institutions. Stopford (2002) has urged IB researchers not to treat government as a "black box" but rather to explore the complex phenomena of the role of governments and public policies as they impact a firm's behavior. This is especially important in a transition economy as unique as China's. While some recent outward investment may be explained in economic terms of profit motive or simply as part of the regular problem of capital flight, many SOE managers are interested in noneconomic objectives when deciding where and how to go abroad, and that particular motivation in a number of instances has been driven by the strong political and diplomatic motivation of the central government behind many O-FDI projects. The unique institutional environment in China has not only shaped the motivation of these made-in-China MNEs, but also affected how they behave.

The institutional mix at any given time, as it impacts SOE ownership structure and corporate governance, may explain why Chinese firms do not behave like their counterparts from Western economies or even other emerging economies when it comes to international expansion. A Chinese energy company may expand abroad because of the government's concerns over future oil demand in China, but, beyond that, the institutional environment in which the Chinese firm exists may enable it to pursue a more risky project that would typically be shunned by multinationals from other countries and outbid rivals by a large margin just to win contracts. Institutional factors may explain such behavior as deriving from fear of being downsized in the continuing evolutionary privatization process for Chinese SOEs (Wu and Han, 2005).

As the reforms have continued and deepened, both internally and as driven by external factors such as WTO accession, the relationship between governmental institutions and SOE behavior has shifted significantly, with market forces playing an ever-increasing role. This may make Chinese firms appear to be more like those in historically market-driven environments than they are in fact. This has implications for the Chinese state and the Chinese firms and entities dealing with them. To maximize chances for success in such endeavors, one must study not only the current institutional milieu in which the particular Chinese firm is functioning, but how it has gotten to where it is, with careful attention to those forces that are stable versus those that are still in flux. The phenomenon is complex, not unlike that of a kaleidoscope in which all the pieces are shifting, and the movement of one affects that of others, but not uniformly. In any event, the process is a dynamic one, and Chinese firms, as they themselves change, have feedback effect on the institutions in which they are functioning, changing them as well.

References

Buckley, P.J. and Carson, M. (1976) *The Future of the Multicultural Enterprise*, London: Macmillan.

Deng, P. (2003) "Foreign Investment by Multinationals from Emerging Countries: The Case of China," *Journal of Leadership and Organization Studies* 10(2):113–124.

Deng, S. and Dart, J. (1999) "The Market Orientation of Chinese Enterprises during a Time of transition," *European Journal of Marketing* 33(5/6):631–652.

Dunning, J.H. (1993) *The Globalization of Business*, London: Routeledge.

Fan, G. (1994) "Dual-track transition in China," *Economic Policy* ____: 100–122.

Fonda, D. (2002) "Look out, Whirlpool: Appliance Maker Haier Quietly Went Global, and Now its White Goods are Everywhere," *Time* 159(5).

Foo, T. (2006) "Investors cheer reversal of Chinese offshore controls," *International Financial Law Review* (2) [www.document] http://www.iflr.com (accessed September 5, 2006).

Hemerling, J. (2006) "For China, It's Mergers and Ambition," *Business Week* 09/19 [www.document] http://www.businessweek.com/print/globalbiz/content/sep2006/gb20060919_357419.htm (accessed September 27, 2006).

Hennart, J. (1982) *A Theory of Multinational Enterprise*, Ann Arbor: The University of Michigan Press.

Hong, E. and Sun, L. (2006) "Dynamics of Internationalization and Outward Investment: Chinese Corporations' Strategies," *The China Quarterly* 187: 610–634.

Hsia, T., Li, C. and Eich, P. (2006) "Chinese M&A: Moving Target," *International Financial Law Review* (10) [www.document] http://www.iflr.com (accessed October 10, 2006).

Itami, H. and Roehl, T. (1987) *Mobilizing Invisible Assets*, Cambridge MA: Harvard University Press.

Johanson, J. and Vahlne, J. (1977) "The Internationalization Process of The Firm: A Model of Knowledge Development and Increasing Foreign Commitment," *Journal of International Business Studies*, 8:23–32.

Knag, R., Ke, Y. and Xu, H. (2006) *Champion's Path: Strategic Formulation and Implementation*. China Translation and Public Corporation, Beijing.

Kogut, B. and Zander, U. (1993) "Knowledge of the Firm and the Evolutionary Theory of the Multinational Corporation," *Journal of International Business Studies*, 4: 625–645.

Kwan, C. (2006) "Cross-Border Mergers & Acquisitions in Post-WTO China," *The China Business Review* 33(5): 76–77.

Li, J. and Tsui, A.S. (2002) "A citation analysis of management and organisation research in the Chinese context: 1984–1999," *Asia Pacific Journal of Management*, 19 (1):87–107.

Lin, Y., Cai, F. and Li, Z. (1998) "Competition, policy burdens, and state-owned enterprise reform," *American Economic Review*, 88(2): 422–427.

Liu, L. (1997) *China's Gradual Approach to Reforming Its State-Owned Enterprises*, in Lieberthal, K., Lin, S., and Young, E. (eds) *Constructing China: The Interaction of Culture and Economics*, Ann Arbor: University of Michigan.

Liu, H. and Li, K. (2002) "Strategic Implications of Emerging Chinese Multinationals: The Haier Case Study," *European Management Journal*, 20(6):699–706.

Luo, Y. (1999) "Time-based Experience and International Expansion: The case of an Emerging Economy," *The Journal of Management Studies*, 36(4): 505–534.

Luo, Y. and Peng, M.W. (1999) "Learning to Compete in a Transition Economy: Experience, Environment, and Performance," *Journal of International Business Studies*, 30(2):269–296.

Luo, X., Zhou, L. and Liu, S. (2005) "Entrepreneurial Firms in the Context of China's Transition Economy: An Integrative Framework and Empirical Examination," *Journal of Business Research*, 58(3): 277–284.

Maitland, E. and Nicholas, S. (2002) "Internationalization of Australian Firms in Asia," *International Studies of Management and Organization*, 32(1):79–108.

Nolan, P. (1995) *China's Rise and Russia's Fall*, London: MacMillan Press.

Nolan, P. and Zhang, J. (2002) "The Challenge of Globalization for Large Chinese Firms," *World Development*, 30(12): 2089–2107.

North, D. (1990) *Institutions, Institutional Change and Economic Performance*, Cambridge: Cambridge University Press.

Peng, M. and Dellios, A. (2006) "What determines the scope of the firm over time and around the world? An Asia Pacific Perspective." *Asia Pacific Journal of Management*, 23 (4), forthcoming.

Quan, S. (2005) "Overseas Investment, A Risk Worth Taking," *China Daily*, New York: April 23, 2.

Ramamurti, R. (2004) "Developing Countries and MNEs: Extending and Enriching the Research Agenda," *Journal of International Business Studies*, 35(4):277–283.

Rugman, A. (1982) "Internalization as a General Theory of Foreign Direct Investment: A Re-Appraisal of the Literature," *Weltwirt-Schoftliches Archives*, 116:365–379.

Steinbock, D. (2005) "China's lessons for India," *Businessline*, Chennai, September 26, 1.

Stopford, J. (2002) "The Oxford Handbook of International Business: A Review," *Journal of International Business Studies*, 33(4): 839–342.

The US China Business Council (2005) "FDI in China (Total and US) 179-2004," www.uschina.org (Accessed 31/10/05).

The World Bank. (1997) "FDI Statistics," http://www.worldbank.org/ (Accessed 31/10/05).

Wang, G., Johnson, M.V. and Yang, X. (2003) "China's revised FDI laws and WTO entry create changing patterns of FDI in China: Implications for investors and policy makers," *Journal of Emerging Markets*, 8(3): 5–15.

Wright, M, Filatotchev, I, Hoskisson, R.E. and Peng, M. (2005) "Guest Editors' Introduction: Strategy Research in Emerging Economies: Challenging the conventional wisdom." *Journal of management studies*, 42:1: 1–33.

Wu, H.L. and Chen, C.H. (2001) "An Assessment of Outward Foreign Direct Investment from China's Transitional Economy," *Europe – Asia Studies*, 53(8):1235–1254.

Wu, K. and Han, S.L. (2005) "State-Company Goals Give China's Investment Push Unique Features," *Oil $ Gas*, 103(15): 20.

You, J. (1998) *China's Enterprise Reform: Changing State/Society Relations After Mao,* London: Routledge.

Zhan, L. (1995) "$210 Million Deals Signed Guangzhou Attracting Investors," *China Daily*, May 1, 5.05.

Zheng, Y. (2004) *Globalization and State Transformation in China,* Cambridge: Cambridge University Press.

Zhou, W. (2004) *Internationalization of Chinese Enterprises: Government Policies and Case Studies*, Economics and Sciences Publisher: Beijing.

6
Competing on Scale or Scope? Lessons from Chinese Firms' Internationalization

Li Sun, Mike Peng, and Weiqiang Tan

Introduction

"What determines the international success and failure of the firm?" is the fundamental issue in strategy (Rumelt, 1974; Peng, 2006). In emerging economies, most scholars have paid attention to how multinational enterprises (MNEs) successfully enter and compete effectively in these countries. However, relatively little is known on how firms in emerging economies develop their strategies to survive and thrive in this new world order (Arnold and Quelch, 1998; Li *et al.*, 2006). There has been a debate on whether latercoming international players from emerging economies have varying catch-up strategies different from the traditional strategies of MNEs (Dunning, 2006; Mathews, 2006; Narula, 2006).

In the strategic behavior of large MNEs, both internationalization and product diversification play a key role. Building on the seminal work of Vernon (1966) and Rumelt (1974), international management scholars have explored the potential explanations for performance difference among MNEs (Stopford and Dunning, 1983; Hitt *et al.*, 1997), and found that MNEs that employ dominant-constrained or related-constrained diversification strategies gain the highest levels of performance. They also found that the degree of internationalization of a MNE is positively correlated to the performance (Geringer *et al.*, 1989). However, strategy management and international business literatures have often ignored the "latecomers" from periphery countries (Mathews, 2006). What are their strategies on internationalization? How can they overcome severe "resource position barriers" (Wernerfelt, 1984) with limited recourses? Based on data collected form China's listed companies, we analyze how (1) industry dynamics, (2) resource repertoires, and (3) institutional transitions affect the scale and scope of firms to react to the pressure of globalization. We try to answer how the focus strategy or diversification strategy, combined with the degree of internationalization, relates to Chinese firms' performance.

Competing on scale or scope?

Describing the epic rise of the modern industrial enterprise, Chandler (1990) concentrated on two patterns of growth and competitiveness in the United States, Germany, and Great Britain. One pattern is competing on *scale*. "Economies of scale may be defined initially as those that result when the increased size of a single operating unit producing or distributing a single product reduces the unit cost of production or distribution" (Chandler, 1990, p. 17). We call this approach *focus strategy*, which is aimed at appealing to single target customer needs and to target a single market segment rather than the whole market. Firms with low market share were successful because they used market segmentation to focus on a small but profitable niche market. Focus strategies aim at cost advantage (cost focus) or differentiation (differentiation focus) "in a narrow segment" (Porter, 1985, p. 11).

Another pattern is competing on *scope*. Economies of scope refer to "economies of joint production or distribution," which, "are those resulting from the use of processes within a single operating unit to produce or distribute more than one product" (Chandler, 1990, p.17). We call this approach *diversification strategy*. Chandler's model suggests that firms adopt different strategies at different stages in their life cycle in order to meet growth and profit objectives, and that the dominant growth path for the majority of US enterprises is from specification to vertical integration to diversification (Chandler, 1977).

In the global arena, MNEs that have grown and are extended in a broad geographic scope of operations yield competitive advantage by permitting them to exploit the benefits of performing more activities internally (Rugman, 1981). A diversification strategy also allows a firm to exploit the interrelationships between segments, geographic areas, or related industries (Porter, 1985).[1] However, since Rumelt's (1974) pioneering study, relatively little consensus has emerged as to the impact of corporate diversification on performance.

Recent research around the world and especially in Asia (Peng and Delios, 2006) has started to sketch the contours of an institution-based view of diversification strategies. To answer the question of what drives internationalization strategy, this view complements the existing industry- and resource-based views on diversification (Figure 6.1 and Peng, 2006, for details on these two views), and provides a leading perspective.

A core proposition of the institution-based view is that variation in national institutional environments enables and constrains different strategic choices such as specialization or diversification (Khanna and Palepu, 1997, 2000; Peng, 2002, 2003; Peng and Heath, 1996; Peng et al., 2005; Wright et al., 2005; Meyer, 2006). Under this framework, focus strategy and diversification strategy have different implications for a firm, depending on its institutional environment, industrial competition, and resource situation. Specifically, we argue that firms embracing a focus strategy compete primarily on scale, and that firms adopting a diversification strategy compete primarily on scope.

Figure 6.1   What drives internationalization strategies?
Source: Inspired form Peng M. W 2006, Global Strategy (p. 368) Thomson South-Western.

Conceptual framework

Focus firm and diversified firm

Industry-based considerations

Two key features of the current process of globalization are increased trade in intermediate inputs and increased flows of foreign direct investment (FDI). For the last several decades, growth of overall world trade has been driven in large part by the rapid growth of trade in intermediate inputs (Hanson *et al.*, 2002). This input trade results in part from MNEs choosing to outsource input processing to their foreign affiliates or strategic partners, thereby creating global production networks in which each actor is vertically specialized. Hummels *et al.* (2001) identify *vertical specialization* – production arrangements in which goods are made via multiple stages located in multiple countries – as an important aspect of intermediate-input trade. They calculate that from 1970 to 1990, the increase in exports associated with vertical specialization accounted for one-third of world export growth.

What is the driving force of the spread of vertical specialization in global production networks? Explanations include falling trade barriers and low host-country wages (Hummels *et al.*, 2001). Low wages are China's main competitive advantage, and give China great opportunities to join the global competition amphitheater.[2]

After market reforms began in 1978, China's industries have recorded an impressive growth in output, labor productivity, and exports as well as a dramatic upgrading of the quality and variety of output. However, in the initial stages of internationalization, China did not have leading conglomerate MNEs (such as South Korea's *chaebol*, for example Samsung or Daewoo), but many small or middle-size manufactories joining the vertical specialization in the global value chain. Such focus firms rely on networks of exchange relationships among firms as a major coordinating mechanism within market economies, and as a major source of collaborative advantage for entering foreign markets. The team of Center of China Economic Research at Peking University finds that the vertical specialization ratio in China's whole export has risen from 14 percent in 1992 to 21.8 percent in 2003, and that the ratio is higher in China's exports to the United States. The market-orientation reforms that facilitate interfirm transactions and benefit the focus firm is the most significant driving force behind the vertical specialization process that occurred in China's manufacturing firms (Zhang, 2004).

The vertical specialization in the global value chain benefits focus firms by finding an appropriate position in the division of labor in global market. For example, major changes in how the world's biggest automakers operate – outsourcing everything from design to component manufacturing – are making it easier for Chinese auto firms to join the ranks of globally competitive car producers in far less time than it took Japan and South Korea. An appropriate example is Geely, an aggressive Chinese auto firm that has exported more than 20,000 cars to 42 countries and buys fuel-injection systems from Robert Bosch GmbH of Germany. Interior parts come from a Chinese company that also supplies Volkswagen AG and General Motors Corp. Its steel plate comes from the same mill that sells to Ford, GM, and Volkswagen. Dies and other manufacturing equipment come from a Taiwanese company (Fairclough, 2006). Under such vertical specialization, car manufacturing in China has a significantly different cost structure from what is in place today in the United States or other developed economies.

The rising vertical specialization within multinational firms is fueled by widening factor-price differences between countries. Average wages in China, at the official exchange rate, were 2 percent of those in the United States in 2002. The price of labor relative to the price of capital is 6 percent of that in the United States. In other words, Chinese labor, compared to labor in the United States, is cheap in absolute terms as well as relative to capital (Holz, 2006). China's accession to the World Trade Organization (WTO) and subsequent external trade liberalization allow these advantages to come into full play. According to Porter, "if a focuser's target segment is not different from other segments, then the focus strategy will not succeed" (1985, p. 16). The advantage of low cost of wages makes China's firms focus more on adopting established production processes rather than on investing new products, while a firm's resources do not permit it to go after a wide segment of the total market. Therefore, firms employing a focus strategy can increase production capacity in the global division of labor and be more equipped to enjoy the economies of scale than diversified firms.

Resource-based considerations

The resource-based view emphasizes the advantages of organization-based capabilities (Barney, 1991), and "the existence, boundaries, nature and development of the firm is the capacity of such an organization to protect and develop the competences of the groups and individuals contained within it, in a changing environment" (Hodgson, 1998, p. 189). Thus, the potential for organizational growth is always limited on the firm's scale and scope. Different market and exchange relationships may stimulate the firm to develop different capabilities (Nelson and Winter, 1982). These new capabilities have to be managed and organized in an evolutionary process under the resource-based view.

Across all patterns of economic development, China is at the early stages that other countries, including Japan, Korea, Hong Kong, and Taiwan, experienced before. The past 20 years is the first phase of China's internationalization process. Looking back on how Japanese and Korean firms became global leaders, a common trajectory emerges with three distinct phases: they first built local manufacturing (often in order to provide low-cost sourcing to MNEs), then they borrowed capabilities through technology licensing and joint ventures (to improve quality and processes and begin exporting), and finally, they bought asset and brands abroad to secure their global positions (Ellis and Godiesh, 2006). This "build–borrow–buy" path is similar to the latecomer's catch-up strategy centered on "linkage, leverage, and learning" as identified by Mathews (2006). Learning or absorptive capacity plays an important role in the gradual acquisition, integration, and use of market and operational knowledge for firms in institutional transitional economies.

Organizations use two major mechanisms to facilitate learning from experience. The first is simplification where a firm seeks to simplify experience, to minimize interactions, and to restrict effects to the spatial and temporal neighborhood of actions in order to learn. The second mechanism is specialization where firms tend to focus attention on narrow areas of competence (Levinthal and March, 1993). The essence of the focus strategy is to specialize in a limited market segment, which allows a company to learn the needs and preferences of a limited group of clients, gain a competitive edge in winning the patronage of these clients, and carve out its own market niche. For firms at the initial stage of internationalization, completion of scale results in learning on the capability of magnification and processes employing low-cost labor, which will make Chinese firms earn the first entry ticket to join the global competition (Sun and Cao, 2005).

Some scholars at Uppsala University present their observations in a process or stage model and argue that internationalization is a logical sequence of an increasing international commitment through the gradual acquisition of foreign market knowledge (Johanson and Vahlne, 1977). The path of "build–borrow–buy" fits the stage model in an evolutionary and learning process, and also provides a prediction about the Chinese firm's strategic choice in the next phase. Chinese firms will extend their capability on marketing, brand building, and strategic alliances. They will encourage customer, supplier, and even competition collaboration on R&D, look outside – even beyond their own industry – for innovation. At this phase, competitions on scale will be alternated by competition on scope, and diversified firms will likely gain more competitive advantage on innovation, brand, and complex multidivisional management, especially on the knowledge-intensive industries.

Institution-based considerations

Similar to conglomerates in other emerging economies, Chinese business groups always leverage their connections with governments by obtaining licenses, arranging financial packages, hiring and training the elite, and establishing supply and distribution channels. Most business groups are state-owned enterprises (SOEs), and can easily access the financial resource from state-owned or -controlled banks, and get capital from a government quota on the initial public offering (IPO) or refinancing market. However, learning from the crash of Asia's conglomeration in the East Asia financial crisis in 1997, the Chinese government dramatically changed the policy and encouraged the development of small and private-owned enterprises.

The Chinese government found that most of the nonperforming loans within the banking system were linked to the bad performance of an overdiversified business group. This led to a restructuring of the banks and the big business groups, which was largely completed by 2005. Business groups have been seriously regulated by different government departments. Some had gone bankrupt or had been restructured by spinning off unrelated businesses, such as the famous 999 Group or Delong Group. Others had transferred debt into equity, or gotten refinance in securities markets by governments, such as the Shoudu Steel Group. Diversified firms lost favor with the Chinese government, but focus firms that were open to the overseas market had gotten strong support from the government's endorsed guarantee (the Lenovo Group acquired International Business Machines Corp.'s personal computer division for $1.25 billion and China's CNOOC Ltd made a $18.5 billion bid for Unocal Corp.).

At the same time, China joined the WTO in 2001 after ambitiously accepting concessions more extensive than those agreed to by other developing countries. Being a WTO member and thus a global player has a heavy impact on key aspects of many of China's industries including in the matter of regulation and competition. For example, in the telecom industry, the Ministry of Information Industry (MII) provided more comprehensive telecom regulations for both domestic players and foreign investors. Regulators broke up China Telecom, the dominant fixed-line operator, and spun off China Mobile, China Unicom, China Netcom, China Railcom, ChinaSat, and Jitong (which focus on different target markets). Regulators hoped competition would strengthen Chinese carriers as the country joins the WTO and prepares to open its closed market. When the WTO drove initiatives to redefine the legal framework and speed up the deregulation procedure, the diversification business group lost most benefits in the "political rent" (McChesney, 1987).

Thus, the logic presented above suggests the follow hypothesis:

Hypothesis 1: Under the pressure of globalization and deregulation, a focus firm will outperform a diversified firm.

According to Rumelt (1974), the relationship between diversification and a firm's performance has attracted serious attention in the strategic management research area. Varadarajan and Ramanujam (1987) suggested that related diversification may be a necessary but not sufficient condition for superior performance, and that unrelated diversification serves a number of firms as well, if not better than, as more related or focused strategies.

In emerging economies, the institutional contexts may more substantially affect strategic choice than those in the developed economies (Peng, 2003). Khanna and Palepu (1997) argued that firms in emerging economies may need to engage in unrelated diversification to cope with the challenges in the environment. Through internal processes or internalization of key external institutes, firms may effectively undertake tasks that would otherwise be performed by external entities. However, firms filled in those institutional voids also have a poor governance structures to solve the principal–agent conflicts. In China's enterprise reforms from the mid-1980s, the shareholding system was introduced to deal with property rights relations. Although it seems to have contributed to some improvement in enterprise performance, there still remains the problem of expropriation of state assets by agents seeking irregular private gains (Lee, 1993; Xu *et al.*, 2005). The controlling shareholder, especially in a diversified firm, may engage in expropriation of minority shareholder through illegal tunneling or legal related transactions. Overinvestment and internal corruption also destroys the advantages of the internal capital market in the diversified firms. Through internal processes or internalization of key external institutes, diversified firms may not effectively undertake tasks that would otherwise be performed by external entities, and cannot react to the MNEs' competition pressure in a sophisticated manner, even in a familiar domestic market that is more open and deregulated.

Hypothesis 2: Under the pressure of globalization and deregulation, a product diversification strategy, whatever domestic diversification or international diversification, is negatively related to a firm's performance.

International focus and domestic focus

As firms start international expansion, there are some positive or negative direct impacts on performance. On the one hand, internationalization provides new market opportunities in which a firm can sell its production innovations or improve production efficiencies and provide learning processes through leveraging a firm's skills and products over a broader array of markets (Hitt *et al.*, 1997). Internationalization also provides economies of scale in a geographical market (Caves, 1982), thereby boosting growth and profitability (Geringer *et al.*, 1989; Hennart, 1991), and increases the chances of survival (Hill *et al.*, 1994). An international strategy also makes firms open up new overseas businesses in-house, including the sharing of markets, products, and related technologies, as well as foreign business experience. Such internalization of operations in the cross-border markets results in synergy benefits and reduced transaction costs (Dunning and Rugman, 1985). Both the Uppsala model and the eclectic paradigm, concentrating on the autonomy of the firm in developing its international marketing activity, support that all modes of entry, if implemented effectively, should have positive effects on a firm's performance. It is consistent with evidence that new ventures with international operations usually outperform those that are without them (Oviatt and McDougall, 1994).

On the other hand, internationalization also has some disadvantages for firms from emerging economies, especially when MNEs of developed economies maintain their hegemony power in global markets. International firms face more uncertain environments, such as trade barriers, cultural diversity, exchange rate fluctuations, as well as political risks. Palich *et al.* (2000) argued that management coordination in the same country is much easier than cross-market activities such as advertising and distribution. Meanwhile, the internal organization involved complicates cross-country transactions and coordination and increases the administration cost. Myerson (1982) argued that the information asymmetry between the company's headquarters and department managers also increases the costs, and generates agency problems when the manager wants to control the assets in their hands as much as possible (Rajan, 2000). Therefore, what decides the successful strategy of internationalization is the trade-off between the value created by internationalization and the cost of international operation.

For most Chinese focus firms, their strategy and pattern of internationalization is different from that of their Western counterparts. At the initial phase of internationalization, they always use direct exports, not direct investment or active organizational presence abroad, as the main channel for overseas sales. Chinese firms also imitated the strategy that the firms from the four tigers of East Asia implicated through original equipment manufacturing (OEM) or subcontracting to avert risk and decrease administration costs on overseas business. As Child and Rodrigues (2006) suggested, Chinese firms are engaging in "inward" internationalization by means of OEM and joint venture partnerships and will benefit from the initial knowledge of internationalization and avoid most risks. Although they have been heavily exploited by MNEs and kept a low margin of profit, they quickly acquired a more invaluable experience through stable orders from MNEs than did their counterparts that only operated in the domestic market. Also, they accumulated more capital from MNEs' stable cash flow than did domestic competitors, which slumped in delayed receivables and bad debts.

Thus,

Hypothesis 3a: Under the pressure of globalization and deregulation, an international focus firm outperforms a domestic focus firm.

Driving force of Chinese firms' internationalization

If internationalization is defined as "the crossing of national boundaries in the process of growth" (Buckley and Ghauri, 1999, p. ix), then at present

China may be the most active internationalizing economy among developing countries (Child and Rodrigues, 2006). Mainland Chinese firms had established 7470 companies in over 160 countries or regions by 2004 (Chung, 2004). For most Chinese firms, the impetus for the first overseas venture was furious domestic competition after they consolidated their businesses at home.

After China entered the WTO in 2001, the increasing openness of China's economic policy sped up the focus firms' learning and competitive capability (Sun and Zhu, 2003; Sun and Cao, 2005). The rapid increase in foreign-owned production capacity in China further expanded foreign competition in the domestic market, and the pervasiveness of foreign competition is forcing domestic firms to update their operations or face serious competitive difficulties. Some local firms fall, but survivors improve their product lines and marketing skill, and change to faster responses and become more competitive. In a large survey conducted by *Fortune* (China) in 2002, 83 percent of the responding foreign firms considered increasing competition as a major challenge facing their firms, even more significant than such institutional factors as government relations, labor management, and policy uncertainty (Jiang, 2002).

As said by Zhang Ruimin, CEO of Haier Group, "If we cannot win in our domestic market, we will not succeed internationally." After successes from furious competition in the domestic market, most focus firms start an aggressive international extension plan. For example, the privately owned Lifan Group, Geely Automobile, Greatwall Motor, and the state-owned Shanghai Automobile, Chery Automobile, all set aggressive export plans in 2006. So the motive for most Chinese focus firms to internationalize is to extend their successful experience and knowledge in the domestic market into the global market (Sun, 2006). Thus,

Hypothesis 3b: When domestic market turns more competitive under the openness policy, the better performing focus firm will start to internationalize to increase their scale.

In summary, all hypotheses can be expressed in Figure 6.2.

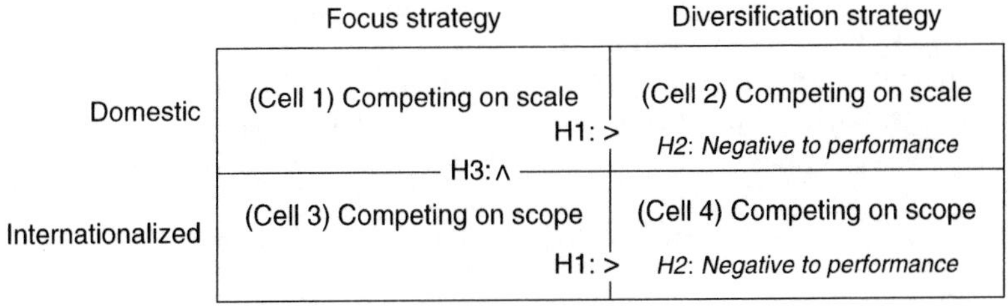

	Focus strategy	Diversification strategy
Domestic	(Cell 1) Competing on scale H1: >	(Cell 2) Competing on scale *H2: Negative to performance*
	H3: ∧	
Internationalized	(Cell 3) Competing on scope H1: >	(Cell 4) Competing on scope *H2: Negative to performance*

Figure 6.2 Hypotheses

Methods

Sample

Our sample was drawn from the listed companies in the A shares stock market of China from 2002 to 2004. We excluded all the financial and insurance companies because of the peculiarity of their balance sheet. We also excluded Special Treatment (ST) firms[3] and firms with no positive sales revenue. Firms that do not disclose revenue data by industry and by region in annual reports were also excluded. When handling multiindustry data, we loosened the criteria set by Berger and Ofek (1995) and other product diversification references in sample selection, and only excluded the companies that have balances larger than 10 percent between the total sales revenue in industry segments and the real sales revenue. We also excluded the multiindustry firms that have revenues from the financial industry. According to method implemented by Denis *et al.* (2002), we do not require firms survive from 2002 to 2004. The final sample comprised 2189 firm year observations from 2002 to 2004.

China Securities Regulatory Commission (hereafter CSRC) issued the *Industry Classification Guide of Listed Companies* (hereafter *Guide*) in April 2001, which categorized sales revenue by industries. We collected the segment sales revenue from the annual reports of the listed firms. All other data are drawn from the WIND database.[4]

Primary measures

Performance: There are two accounting-based measures that are considered as possible indicators of a firm's performance: return on assets (ROA) and return on sales (ROS). To analyze the relationship between ROA and ROS, we are also using the assets turnover (TURNOVER), which is a measure of the total sales divided by the total assets, to test the turnover rate of the asset.

Product diversification: We use three indexes to measure product diversification strategy. First, the industries number *(M)* that is involved in operations is measured. Second, the Herfindahl index, which is defined as

$$HI = \sum_{i=1}^{M} P_i^2,$$

where P_i is the sales attributed to segment *I*, is measured.

The entropy measure of product diversification has become increasingly popular in strategic management research (Hitt *et al.*, 1997; Palepu, 1985). So we are also using the entropy measure of product diversification (EI), which is defined as

$$EI = \sum_{i=1}^{M} [P_i \times \ln(1/p_i)],$$

where P_i is the sales attributed to segment *i*. The measure considers both the segment number and the proportion of total sales of each segment.

Internationalization: Several measures of internationalization have been used in previous research. The most common form has been a unidimensional measure of international sales as a percentage of total sales. Although this measurement cannot tell the whole story of internationalization, compared with other measurements, it still has great advantages, hence it is being used broadly (Geringer *et al.*, 2000; Hitt *et al.*, 1997). In this study, we use the ratio of a firm's nondomestic sales to its total sales (hereafter FSALES) to measure internationalization. Due to the institutional differences between Hong Kong/Macau/Taiwan and the mainland of China, sales in those regions will be counted in nondomestic sales revenue.

Control variables

We included several control variables, similar to those used in previous studies. Firm size (SIZE), measured by the natural logarithm of the book value of total assets that is deflated using the CPI into 2002 RMB, was employed to control for economies and diseconomies of scale at the corporate level. Leverage has been argued to affect a firm's performance (Hitt *et al.*, 1997). We measure leverage as a firm's total debt to total assets (LEVERAGE). Profitability is measured as earnings before interest and taxes divided by total sales (EBITR). Sales growth is measured as growth rate between current year and the year before (GROWTH).

We employ dummy variables to control for industry effects and year effects. The industry dummy variables represent each firm's primary industry classification following CSRC's *Guides* as a measure of industry effects in the regression equation. Also, the year dummy variables measure the year effect as the dependent variable.

Results

Table 6.1 reports the summary description of the sample in the study. The full sample is divided into four different categories: domestic focus firm (DF: 27.59 percent of total sample), domestic diversified firm (DD: 41.98 percent of total sample), international focus firm (IF: 11.88 percent of total sample), and international diversified firm (ID: 18.55 percent of total sample). The proportion of product-diversified firms in the total sample is 60.52 percent, and the proportion of internationalized firms in the total sample is 30.42 percent.

Table 6.1 provides the means and median for all variables used in the study. Focus firms' performance is better than diversified firms', both ROA and ROS. Also, the turnover of total assets is highest for IF firms than for any other firms.

Table 6.2 show univariate test statistics of a firm's performance ROA in the four different groups testing the hypotheses. The difference in mean tests (*t*-statistics) and Wilcoxon sign rank median difference tests are presented. The last column in Table 6.2 provides the mean and median ROA for

Table 6.1   Descriptive statistics

		DF	DD	IF	ID	Full sample
N		604	919	260	406	2189
N%		27.59%	41.98%	11.88%	18.55%	100%
M	Mean	1.000	2.576	1.000	2.599	1.958
	Median	1.000	2.000	1.000	2.000	2.000
HI	Mean	1.000	0.557	1.000	0.537	0.728
	Median	1.000	0.544	1.000	0.526	0.733
EI	Mean	0.000	0.733	0.000	0.759	0.448
	Median	0.000	0.674	0.000	0.688	0.438
FSALES	Mean	0.000	0.000	0.275	0.265	0.082
	Median	0.000	0.000	0.162	0.174	0.000
ROA	Mean	0.026	0.016	0.034	0.016	0.021
	Median	0.028	0.022	0.034	0.022	0.025
ROS	Mean	0.057	0.043	0.051	0.020	0.043
	Median	0.051	0.049	0.052	0.034	0.046
TURNOVER	Mean	0.661	0.469	0.789	0.697	0.602
	Median	0.494	0.377	0.593	0.575	0.470
TOTAL ASSET	Mean	3180.0	1950.0	2970.0	2270.0	2470.0
(RMB millions)	Median	1460.0	1310.0	1510.0	1510.0	1390.0
SALES	Mean	1890.0	938.0	2560.0	1760.0	1550.0
(RMB millions)	Median	801.0	504.0	921.0	906.0	679.0
LEVERAGE	Mean	0.494	0.493	0.474	0.519	0.496
	Median	0.475	0.493	0.449	0.512	0.489
GROWTH	Mean	0.527	0.321	0.350	0.231	0.365
	Median	0.168	0.172	0.182	0.191	0.178
EBITR	Mean	0.118	0.089	0.077	0.042	0.088
	Median	0.087	0.101	0.079	0.067	0.086

domestic and international firms while the last row provides the mean and median ROA for specification and diversified firms. Consistent with earlier findings and our Hypothesis 1, Table 6.2 shows that product diversification reduces firms' performance statistically significantly. ROA of product-diversified firms is 2.83 percent, which is lower by 1.24 percent when compared to the focus firms. From Table 6.2, a diversified firm, be it domestic diversification or international diversification, underperforms a focus firm significantly. This finding is consistent with the findings of Denis *et al.* in a US sample (2002). The statistically significant *t*-statistics and the *Z*-score provide support for Hypothesis 1 and Hypothesis 2. More interestingly, an international focus firm significantly outperforms a domestic focus firm, which implies that focus firms benefit from internationalization.

Table 6.2 Univariate test on ROA[a]

	Focus	Diversification	t-test Z-score	GeographicAll
Domestic	0.02572 [0.0278] (N = 604)	0.0160 [0.0218] (N = 919)	2.8149*** 3.666***	0.0198 [0.0245] (N = 1523)
International	0.0343 [0.0339] (N = 260)	0.0158 [0.0223] (N = 406)	3.9826*** 4.450***	0.0230 [0.0277] (N = 666)
t-test	−1.7852*	0.0580		−1.0545
Z-score	−1.711*	0.358		−0.780
Industrial All	0.0283 [0.028] (N = 864)	0.01591 [0.022] (N = 1325)	4.4320*** 5.501***	

[a] Difference in mean tests and nonparametric Wilcoxon sign rank median difference tests are provided. [ ] median, ( ) number of firms are in the parentheses.
* p<0.10.
** p<0.05.
*** p<0.01.

Table 6.3 Univariate test on TURNOVER[a]

	Focus	Diversification	t-test Z-score	Geographic
Domestic	0.6605 [0.4943] (N = 604)	0.4694 [0.3769] (N = 919)	8.1616*** 6.865***	0.5452 [0.4160] (N = 1523)
International	0.7888 [0.5928] (N = 260)	0.6974 [0.5754] (N = 406)	1.8976* 1.068	0.7331 [0.5873] (N = 666)
t-test	−2.7362***	−9.7433***		−7.9717***
Z-score	−3.997***	−10.594***		−10.718***
Industrial All	0.6991 [0.5262] (N = 864)	0.5393 [0.4265]	7.1880*** 6.256*** (N = 1325)	

[a] Difference in mean tests and nonparametric Wilcoxon sign rank median difference tests are provided. [ ] Median, ( ) number of firms are in the parentheses.
* p<0.10.
** p<0.05.
*** p<0.01.

Table 6.3 presents the difference in mean tests (t-statistics) and Wilcoxon sign rank median difference tests. We find that the asset turnover of focus firms is significantly faster, and that of international firms does as well. Linking with the findings on Table 6.1, though ROS of international focus firms is lower than that of domestic focus firms, the firm will still go to internationalization because the higher asset turnover brings more profit and gets a higher return-to-assets rate than that of domestic focus firms. Thus, the results given in Table 6.3 support Hypothesis 3a.

Overall, the results given in Table 6.3 are consistent with Hypothesis 1 and Hypothesis 2, while Hypothesis 3 needs further analyses. We use the domestic focus firms as benchmarks to examine the effects of product diversification and internationalization. And we construct three dummy variables: DD Dummy is defined by dummy variable equal to 1 if the firm is a domestic diversified firm and zero otherwise, IF Dummy is defined by dummy variable equal to 1 if the firm is an international focus firm and zero otherwise, ID Dummy is defined by dummy variable equal to 1 if the firm is an international diversified firm and zero otherwise. Also, we define DDUM as dummy variable equal to 1 if the firm is a diversified firm and zero otherwise, and IDUM as dummy variable equal to 1 if the firm is an international firm and zero otherwise.

The correlation matrix in Table 6.4 presents more details on the relation between product diversification and internationalization. Table 6.4 shows that the relation between HI and a firm's performance such as ROA and ROS is significantly positive, which implies that the relationship between product diversification degree and a firm's performance is negative, while the internationalization dummy variable is insignificantly positive related to ROA and is significantly negative related to ROS. This finding may come from interactions between internationalization and product diversification. Further, Table 6.3 shows that DD dummy and ID dummy are negatively related to a firm's performance, and IF dummy is positively related to a firm's performance.

Table 6.5 shows the effects of both product diversification and internationalization on a firm's performance after controlling for size, leverage, profitability, and sales growth. In the multivariate regression model, the independent variable includes ROA and ROS. Model 2 and Model 5 control the year effects and Model 3 and Model 6 control the year and industry effects at the same time.

These results lead to the similar conclusions that are based on the univariate tests performed in Table 6.2 .The relationship between international specification and ROA is largely positive while there is a negative relationship between international specification and ROS. The regression coefficient of international diversification is significantly negative whatever be the independent variables ROA or ROS. The multiple regression model provides support for Hypothesis 2.

The control variables are generally consistent with previous studies of product diversification and internationalization. A firm's size and performance have a significantly positive relationship, which indicates that after controlling the strategies for a firm's product diversification and internationalization, firms that have a larger size will perform better. This could

Table 6.4 Correlation matrix

	ROA	ROS	TURNOVER	DD Dummy	IF Dummy	ID Dummy	IDUM	DDUM	FSALES	HI
ROA	1.000									
ROS	0.831*** (0.000)	1.000								
TURNOVER	0.168*** (0.000)	−0.024 (0.263)	1.000							
DD Dummy	−0.064*** (0.003)	−0.004 (0.869)	−0.220*** (0.000)	1.000						
IF Dummy	0.077*** (0.000)	0.019 (0.380)	0.133*** (0.000)	−00.312*** (0.000)	1.000					
ID Dummy	−0.038* (0.080)	−0.071*** (0.001)	0.088*** (0.000)	−0.406*** (0.000)	−0.175*** (0.000)	1.000				
IDUM	0.023 (0.292)	−0.047** (0.029)	0.168*** (0.000)	−0.563*** (0.000)	0.555*** (0.000)	0.722*** (0.000)	1.000			
DDUM	−0.094*** (0.000)	−0.060*** (0.005)	−0.152*** (0.000)	0.687*** (0.000)	−0.455*** (0.000)	0.385*** (0.000)	0.006 (0.785)	1.000		
FSALES	0.013 (0.533)	−0.028 (0.189)	0.114*** (0.000)	−0.370*** (0.000)	0.377*** (0.000)	0.464*** (0.000)	0.657*** (0.000)	−0.004 (0.841)	1.000	
HI	0.091*** (0.000)	0.054** (0.011)	0.179*** (0.000)	−0.581*** (0.000)	0.398*** (0.000)	−0.363*** (0.000)	−0.027 (0.210)	−0.875*** (0.000)	0.003 (0.872)	1.000

* $p<0.10$.
** $p<0.05$.
*** $p<0.0$.

Table 6.5 Multiple regression models[a]

Independent variable	ROA			ROS		
	Model 1	Model 2	Model 3	Model 4	Model 5	Model 6
Constant	−21.422***	−21.059***	−21.067***	−65.029***	−65.541***	−55.786***
	(−7.160)	(−6.980)	(−5.250)	(−8.770)	(−8.760)	(−5.700)
DD Dummy	−0.668**	−0.662**	−0.568*	−0.540	−0.531	−0.958
	(−2.160)	(−2.140)	(−1.780)	(−0.700)	(−0.690)	(−1.230)
IF Dummy	0.701	0.689	0.895**	−0.935	−0.933	0.487
	(1.610)	(1.580)	(1.980)	(−0.860)	(−0.860)	(0.440)
ID Dummy	−0.720*	−0.714*	−0.438	−3.071***	−3.055***	−1.816*
	(−1.900)	(−1.890)	(−1.110)	(−3.270)	(−3.260)	(−1.880)
SIZE	1.304***	1.290***	1.155***	3.751***	3.755***	2.876***
	(9.320)	(9.180)	(7.930)	(10.820)	(10.790)	(8.100)
LEVERAGE	−7.727***	−7.760***	−7.927***	−18.570***	−18.509***	−18.120***
	(−16.520)	(−16.530)	(−16.550)	(−16.030)	(−15.920)	(−15.510)
EBITR	0.024***	0.025***	0.022**	0.104***	0.105***	0.098***
	(2.800)	(2.840)	(2.510)	(4.890)	(4.930)	(4.650)
GROWTH	0.302***	0.299***	0.291***	0.643***	0.640***	0.585***
	(4.890)	(4.840)	(4.730)	(4.200)	(4.180)	(3.890)
Year Dummies	Yes	Yes	Yes	Yes	Yes	Yes
Industry Dummies	Yes	Yes	Yes			Yes
F	59.70***	46.78***	16.91***	62.62***	48.90***	20.55***
R²	0.16	0.16	0.17	0.16	0.16	0.21

[a] Year and Industry dummy variables are included in the models, but regression coefficients are not shown for them. *t-statistics* values are in the parentheses.
For all models, n=2189.

* *p*<0.10

** *p*<0.05

*** *p*<0.01

possibly be due to better management skills and more resources than in the past and so they could grasp market changes accurately, and then perform better. There is a significantly negative relationship between financial leverage and a firm's performance while there is a positive relationship between a firm's profit margin and performance. The regression coefficient of sales growth is significantly positive.

To discuss Hypothesis 3b, we can compare the growth opportunities between international focus firms and domestic focus firms in detail. Table 6.1 shows that the domestic focus firms have a better growth rate and a better gross margin rate than international focus firms; however, the former firms cannot outperform the latter firms in terms of ROA. Therefore, a reasonable explanation for focus firms to exploit international markets is that these firms face more intense rivalry in the domestic market (Sun and Zhu, 2003) and keep a lower gross margin rate than domestic players that do not exploit international markets. The international focus firms improve their performance usually through elevating the economies of scale. These indirectly support Hypothesis 3b.

Discussion

Can the internationalization of Chinese firms be explained in terms of mainstream theory derived largely from Western MNEs, or in terms of the analyses that have so far been offered for developing country multinationals (Child and Rodrigues, 2006)? International business theory (Rugman, 1981) argued that firms can only be successful abroad if they possess some type of intangible knowledge that makes them competitive in foreign markets. International business theory thus focuses on the creation of isolation mechanisms, which means that MNEs use the process of "internalization" to replace an external market by an internal market, through setting up foreign subsidiaries. However, in China's case in initial internationalization, compared to their Western counterparts, relatively few Chinese firms invested in building extensive networks of subsidiaries with sales, manufacturing, and service operations, as well as support functions around the world. Most Chinese firms use the process of "externalization" – direct export, OEM, joint venture with MNEs, etc., all heavily relying on the MNEs' supremacy on the global vertical specialization pattern.

"Externalization" governance mechanism embedded into MNEs' value chain can avoid so-called "liability of foreignness," although no isolation mechanism to protect Chinese firms has been exploited by MNEs. In our analysis, the margin of profit in international focus firms is not higher than in domestic focus firms in our data analysis. But why did international focus firms have the best performance among the four types of firms? The reason is that international focus firms are more focused on the *scale* - by improving processes and increasing turnover. Using a comprehensive firm-level data set in China's manufacturing sector, Zhang (2004) also finds that vertical specialization increases the total factor productivity of firms.

What will happen in China's next phase of internationalization? The inevitable result of vertical specialization in the MNEs' value chain is a low margin of profit. "Build–borrow–buy" is perhaps a long path for future growth. For example, Geely crudely built hatchbacks, powered by Toyota-designed engines in 1999, and annual production was less than 5000. However, 6 years later, Geely makes 180,000 cars a year, with models including sedans and a sports car. It has engineered its own six-cylinder engines and is selling cars not just in China, but in Latin America, the Middle East, and Russia as well (Fairclough, 2006). A coevolutionary perspective would provide an appropriate analytical framework regarding whether China will shift the "externalization" strategy and adapt to the internalization strategy in the future.

Future research

Our study indicates a number of opportunities for future research. We will note four such possibilities. First, the strategy literature suggests that firms adapt different strategies at different growth stages (Chandler, 1962, 1977) under the presence or absence of increasing returns and attendant path dependencies (Teece, 1977). The strategic choice of Chinese firms under institutional transitions provides a goldmine to test and extend these theories (Peng, 2005). If we can collect and analyze 10–15 years' longitudinal data, we may be able to explain Chinese firms' dynamic growth mechanism in greater detail and contribute to strategic management theory.

Second, a research possibility is to develop our knowledge of Chinese firms' "externalization" in the global vertical specialization trend to enrich the "catch-up" perspective (Mathews, 2006), and explain how new globalization alters ecologies and zoologies in international business.

Third, a research opportunity is to examine how the related diversification and unrelated diversification affect Chinese firms' performance. Rumelt (1974) found that the related diversified firms outperform the nondiversified and unrelated diversified firms. The unrelated diversification strategy was found to be one of the lowest performing on average. We can analyze the data more carefully and find whether China's related diversified firms outperform unrelated diversified firms, and if not, why?

Fourth, an interesting question emerging in our analysis is how the degrees of internationalization affect Chinese firm's performance. In our regression model, we have not found direct linear cause-effect relationship. What mechanisms are behind these? What will happen when China's current labor cost advantage is diminished?

Since Chandler, scholars have developed many theories to explain the scale and scope of firms. We developed a model to argue that focus firm will gain more competitive advantage than diversified firm during their initial internationalization in China. It is our conjecture that the intensifying competitions in domestic market and pressures from globalization under openness policy have, and will continue to, affect the scope of the firm.

Notes

1. There are two types of diversification: product diversification and geographic diversification (Peng and Delios, 2006). Because of limited data on China, the "diversification" discussed in this chapter refers to product diversification.
2. There is considerable debate about whether the Chinese yuan has been severely and "artificially" undervalued.
3. Since 1998, Shanghai and Shenzhen Stock Exchanges have classified some listed firms as Special Treatment (ST) firms. A firm will be labeled as an ST firm if there is certain abnormality in its financial status and other aspects, resulting in investors having difficulty in judging the company's prospects, which consequently harms investors' benefits or interests.
4. The WIND database is widely regarded as one of most comprehensive and authoritative data sources of the publicly listed firms in China.

References

Arnold, D.J. and Quelch, J.A. (1998) "New strategies in emerging markets," *Sloan Management Review* **40**(1): 7–20.

Barney, J. (1991) "Firm resources and sustained competitive advantage," *Journal of Management* **17**(1): 99–120.

Berger, P. and Ofek, E. (1995) "Diversification's effect on firm value," *Journal of Financial Economics*, **37**: 39–65.

Buckley, P.J. and Ghauri, P.N. (eds.) (1999) *The Internationalization of the Firm*, London: Thomson Business Press.

Caves, R.E. (1982) *Multinational Enterprises and Economic Analysis*, New York: Cambridge University Press.

Chandler, A.D. (1962) *Strategy and Structure*, Cambridge: MIT Press.

Chandler, A.D. (1977) *The Visible Hand: The Managerial Revolution in American Business*, Cambridge: Harvard University Press.

Chandler, A.D. (1990) *Scale and Scope: The Dynamics of Industrial Capitalism*, Cambridge: Harvard University Press.

Child, J. and Rodrigues, S.B. (2006) "The internationalization of Chinese firms: A case for theoretical extension?" *Management and Organization Review*, 1(3):381–410.

Chung, O. (2004) "Outward FDI tops US$33bn," *The Standard*, October 7, www. thestandard.com.hk.

Denis, D.J., Denis, D.K., and Kevin, Y. (2002) "Global diversification, industrial diversification, and firm value," *The Journal of Finance*, **57**(5): 1951–1979.

Dunning, J.H. (2006) "Comment on Dragon multinationals: New players in 21st century globalization," *Asia Pacific Journal of Management*, **23**(2): 139–141.

Dunning, J.H. and Rugman, A.M. (1985) "The influence of Hymer's dissertation on the theory of foreign direct investment," *American Economic Review*, **75**(2): 228–232.

Ellis, S. and Godiesh, O. (2006) "Outsmarting China's start-arounds," *Far Eastern Economic Review*, **169**(6): 5–9.

Fairclough, G. (2006) "In auto business, China jumps in," *The Wall Street Journal*, November 7.

Geringer, J.M.,Beamish, P.W., and daCosta, R.C. (1989) "Diversification Strategy and Internationalization: Implications for MNE Performance," *Strategic Management Journal*, **10**: 109–119.

Hanson, G.H., Matalont, R.J., and Slaughter, M.J. (2002) "Vertical production networks in multinational firms," NBER Working Paper No. W9723.

Hennart, J.F. (1991) "The transaction cost theory of joint ventures: An empirical study of Japanese subsidiaries in the United States," *Management Science*, 37(4): 483–497.

Hitt, M., Hoskisson, R., and Kim, H. (1997) "International Diversification: Effects on Innovation and Firm Performance in Product Diversified Firms," *Academy of Management Journal*, 40: 767–798.

Hodgson, G. (1998) "Competence and contract in the theory of the firm," *Journal of Economic Behavior & Organization*, 35: 179–201.

Holz, C. (2006) "Why China's rise is sustainable?" *Far Eastern Economic Review*, 169(3): 41–46.

Hummels, D., Ishii, J., and K. Yi, (2001) "The Nature and Growth of Vertical Specialization in World Trade," *Journal of International Economics* , 54(1): 75–96.

Johanson, J. and Vahlne, J.(1977) "The internationalization process of the firm: A model of knowledge development and increasing foreign market commitments," *Journal of International Business Studies*, 8(1): 23–32.

Jiang, W. (2002) "Impression of China-2002 foreign investments survey," *Fortune (China)*, 41(May): 10–17.

Khanna, T. and Palepu, K. (1997) "Why focused strategies may be wrong for emerging markets," *Harvard Business Review*, 75 (July-August): 41–51.

Khanna, T. and Palepu, K. (2000) "Is group membership profitable in emerging markets: An analysis of diversified Indian business groups," *Journal of Finance*, 55: 867–891.

Lee, K. (1993) "Property rights and the agency problem in China's enterprise reform," *Cambridge Journal of Economics*, 17(2): 179–194.

Levinthal, D. and March, J. (1993) "The Myopia of Learning," *Strategic Management Journal*, 14: 95–112.

Li, M., Gao, X., and Wu, Y. (2006) "External environments, strategy, and high tech new ventures in China," in H. Li (ed.) *Growth strategies of new technology ventures in China*. Northampton: Edward Elgar, 112–142.

Mathews, J. (2006) "Dragon multinationals: New players in 21st century globalization," *Asia Pacific Journal of Management*, 23(1), 139–141.

Meyer, K.E. (2006) "Globalfocusing: From Domestic Conglomerate to Global Specialist," *Journal of Management Studies*, 43: 1109–1144.

McChesney, F.S. (1987) "Rent extraction and rent creation in the economic theory of regulation," *The Journal of Legal Studies*, 16(1): 101–118.

Myerson, R. (1982) "Regulating a monopolist with unknown costs," *Econometrica*, 50: 911–930.

Narula, R. (2006) "Globalization, new ecologies, new zoologies, and the purported death of the eclectic paradigm," *Asia Pacific Journal of Management*, 23(2): 143–151.

Nelson, R. and Winter, S. (1982) *An Evolutionary Theory of Economic Change*. Cambridge: Harvard University Press.

Oviatt, B.M. and McDougall, P.P. (1994) "Toward a theory of international new ventures," *Journal of International Business Studies*, 25(1): 45–64.

Palepu, K. (1985) "Diversification strategy, profit performance, and the entropy measure," *Strategic Management Journal*, 6(2): 239–55.

Palich, L., Carini, G., and Seaman, S. (2000) "The impact of internalization on the diversification-performance relationship: a replication and extension of prior research," *Journal of Business Research*, 48: 43–54.

Peng, M.W. (2002) "Towards an institution-based view of business strategy," *Asia Pacific Journal of Management*, 19: 251–267.

Peng, M.W. (2003) "Institutional transitions and strategic choices," *Academy of Management Review*, 28: 275–296.

Peng, M.W. (2005) "From China strategy to global strategy," *Asia Pacific Journal of Management*, 22(2): 123–141.

Peng, M.W. (2006) *Global Strategy*, Cincinnati: Thomson South-Western.

Peng, M.W. and Delios, A. (2006) "What determines the scope of the firm over time and around the globe? An Asia Pacific perspective," *Asia Pacific Journal of Management*, 23(4): 385–405.

Peng, M. W. and Heath, P. (1996) "The Growth of the Firm in Planned Economies in Transition: Institutions, Organizations, and Strategic Choice," *Academy of Management Review*, 21(2): 492–528.

Porter, M. (1985) *Competitive Advantage*, New York: Free Press.

Rajan, R., Servaes, H., and Zingales, L. (2000) "The cost of diversity: the diversification discount and inefficient investment," *Journal of Finance*, 55: 35–80.

Rugman. A. (1981) *Inside the Multinational: The Economics of Internal Markets*, New York: Columbia University Press.

Rumult, R.P. (1974) *Strategy, Structure, and Economic Performance*, Cambridge: Harvard Business School Press.

Stopford, J. and Dunning, J. (1983) *The World Directory of Multinational Enterprises, 1982-1983 Company Performance and Global Trends*, Gale Research Company, Detroit, MI.

Sun, L. (2006) "China's opportunities in global auto industry," *CEO & CIO China*, 196(18): 56–67.

Sun, L. and Cao, S. (2005) *Running on Fit Shoes: Benchmark Management for High Growth Companies*, Beijing: China Social Science Press.

Sun, L. and Zhu, W. (2003) "The value drivers of corporate performances," *Peking University Business Review*, 4 (3): 48–61.

Teece, D.J. (1977) "Technology transfer by multinational firms: the resource cost of transferring technological know-how," *The Economic Journal*, 87(346): 242–261.

Varadarajan, P.R. and Ramanujam, V. (1987) "Diversification and performance: a reexamination using a new two-dimensional conceptualization of diversity in firms," *Academy of Management Journal*, 30(2): 380–393.

Vernon., R. (1966) "International investment and international trade in the product cycle," *Quarterly Journal of Economics*, 81:190–270.

Wernerfelt, B. (1984) "A resource-based view of the firm," *Strategic Management Journal*, 5(2): 171–180.

Wright, M., Filatotchev, I., Hoskisson, R., and Peng, M.W. (2005) "Strategy research in emerging economies: Challenging the conventional wisdom," *Journal of Management Studies*, 42: 1–33.

Xua, D., Pan, Y., Wu, C., and Yim, B. (2006) "Performance of domestic and foreign-invested enterprises in China," *Journal of World Business*, 41(3): 261–274.

Zhang, Y.(2004) "Vertical Specialization of Firms: Evidence from China's Manufacturing Sector," Unpublished working paper.

7
Aligning Strategies with Institutional Influences for Internationalization: Evidences from a Chinese SOE

Loi Teck Hui and Quek Kia Fatt

Introduction

Accelerated internationalization has been one of the most significant developments in the business world over the past few decades. Multinational corporations (MNCs) have used different entry modes to enter overseas markets. McDonald and Coca-Cola, for instance, have established a pretty consistent global image as a corporate strength. IKEA's furniture operations in China have sought to be more flexible, adapting to each local area. Despite these attempts, the MNCs are often facing enormous tasks of coordinating activities of a heterogeneous group of home entities and overseas subsidiaries operating with a diverse range of cultures, institutional factors, and behavior patterns.

This chapter focuses on the business activities of Sinohydro Corporation (SHC) at the subsidiary level in Malaysia. The perspective of the firm's internationalization processes is taken mainly in the Malaysian Bakun Hydroelectric Project (BHP) context. We aim to examine SHC's organizational competences and how do they organize and leverage the competences in response to the institutional pressures presented in carrying out the project for international expansion. This chapter fills a gap in the literature as it may contribute to the sparse literature on successful internationalization of firms from nontriad countries. It has the following organization. The "Theoretical Framework" section develops the theoretical viewpoints of the institutional influences. "Methods and Data" section then discusses research setting and data collection approaches. We present in the subsequent two sections the strategic opportunities and challenges that the institutional-level factors present and the ways the SHC employs for aligning its resource capabilities with the factors before we make some concluding remarks.

Theoretical framework

Institutional influences

One of institutional theory's central concepts has been to explain the existence of institutional norms such as the rules set down by regulatory agencies and the isomorphism of organizational fields. Firms that exist in a highly isomorphic field will have a relatively small range of variation in organizational performance, although in reality no two organizations are identical (DiMaggio, 1988; DiMaggio and Powell, 1991; Scott, 1987). Institutional environments are characterized by the collection of rules and regulations that constrain a firm's behavior by defining moral, legal, and cultural boundaries (Hinings and Greenwood, 1988; Meyer and Rowan, 1977; Scott and Meyer, 1983). Individual firms need to conform to institutional requirements in order to establish their own social credibility and acceptability if they are to receive legitimacy and more active support from stakeholders. The firms could do so by adopting appropriate organizational structures, procedures, and practices that conform to social norms (Ashforth and Gibbs, 1990; Suchman, 1995), which are inherently subjective and subject to different interpretations.

Consequently, institutional-based influences are becoming a powerful driving force in formulating firms' strategies and plans. Governments and regulatory agencies enforce varying degrees of policies across industries. This has created more diversified business contexts in which it is hard to reach a general consensus on what really constitutes legitimacy. Highly institutionalized organizations divert managerial attention significantly from a crucial internal focus toward conformity with external requirements (Scott and Meyer, 1983). The firms' congruence with the institutional constraints in which they are embedded gains legitimacy. They will be judged illegitimate if not (Meyer and Scott, 1983; Suchman, 1995). Conforming organizations could increase their legitimacy and thus survival capabilities (Meyer and Rowan, 1977; North, 1990; Scott, 2001). Hence, competence in aligning firms' specific characteristics with industry forces is central to manage institutional influences and sustain competitive advantage.

Reconciliation strategies

Achieving above-the-average performance is a central topic in strategic management. A firm practising legitimacy would enjoy better returns when an exchange partner is more willing to concede in contract negotiations with the firm as such tie could enhance the former's perceived legitimacy. The firm could also use legitimacy as a competitive weapon to source better supplies and charge a premium on outputs (Galaskiewicz, 1985; Wood, 1991). On the other hand, for less legitimate firms, external stakeholder groups may demand higher prices in exchanges from the firms for their hazard risk (Cornell and Shapiro, 1987; Miller and Bromiley, 1990). Internal stakeholders may depart the firms, thus reducing the quality of organizational decision making and earnings (Hambrick and D'Aveni, 1992). Institutional theory could therefore integrate with strategy discipline if it could increase the firm's financial performance. Effective strategy is the mediating force between the firm and the environment and appears as a series of compounded assets or practices (Henderson and Mitchell, 1997; Hitt *et al.*, 2001; Hui, 2004). Institutional arrangements have always existed to influence firms' foreign market servicing policies. Oliver (1997) finds that firms' economic performance is closely linked to their ability to manage institutional context decisions. The institutional contexts include organizational internal cultures and broader influences from the external institutions that collectively define the firms' socially acceptable economic behaviors. The success of the going-global plan, thus, lies in the firms' abilities to effectively bundle and leverage both organizational internal and external institutional influences as an integrated capability in alliance with their business strategies.

Methods and data

Analysis unit

SHC is the largest contractor for the construction of water and hydropower projects in China. It is currently working on a number of projects at home and overseas including the Three Gorges Dam project, the largest hydropower dam in the world that perhaps costs more than virtually any other single construction project in human history. "Organizational corporatization, management modernization, business internationalization" is the firm's strategic growth motto. SHC set up its international business division only in 2000, driven by growing businesses in overseas markets and corporate missions. In 2002, the growing overseas businesses accounted for about 8 percent of the total corporate revenues for the year. Through the Sime Darby Berhad-led consortium, the Malaysia–China Hydro Joint Venture (MCH JV) in which the Sime Joint Venture (led by Sime Engineering Services Bhd) holds 70 percent stakes and SHC 30 percent, SHC partakes in the construction of, amongst others, the CW2 package, the main civil works for the BHP located on the Balui River, Bintulu, the State of Sarawak, Malaysia. The construction of BHP started in 2003 and the Bakun Hydroelectric Dam will have an ultimate installed capacity of 2400 MW. In addition to the BHP, SHC has also been engaged in a portfolio of projects in Malaysia, including construction and commissioning of the SG Kelalong Dam at Bintulu in 2001, and dredging, reclamation, and sand filling by Beaver of several industrial parks.

Setting selection

We selected SHC as the analysis unit in the context of the BHP for this research as there are growing influences of China in the world's political and socioeconomic arenas. SHC is the main contractor of the controversial Three Gorges Dam project, as well as one of the largest of its kind, the BHP. While there is rich literature written on the operations of developed economies' MNCs, little is known about the mysteries behind the emerging nations' MNCs. Our setting selection is particularly useful in providing a suitable platform for us to investigate the central idea of this chapter – aligning strategies with institutional influences is crucial for an emerging firm's success in entering an international market.

The BHP was first proposed in 1981, and then postponed in 1985 as a result of the economic recession. There was renewal of the project in the early 1990s following intense lobbying by its proponents. In 1994, Ekran Berhad-Swedish ABB Corporation received the project's contract, and started the construction in 1996. The project was shelved in September 1997, the second postponement, due to the Asian Economic Crisis. Ekran Berhad-Swedish ABB Corporation ended their involvement in the project. Nonetheless, the project, scaled down to RM 9 billion from the original RM 13 billion, was resumed in 1999 under the control of the Malaysian government. The MCH JV received a letter of acceptance from the Malaysian government for the project in 2002, and the execution of the civil work began in late 2003.

Data collection

Interviews

SHC's main office in Malaysia is located in Kuching, the capital of Sarawak. Its BHP operational office is based in Bintulu. Guided by participation observations in the company since January 2004, as further elaborated later, an author of this paper (author X) has spent about 9 months between January 2004 and August 2004 to carry out a mixture of semistructured and open-style interviews with four members of the firm's BHP senior management team and a member of its Malaysia Board of Directors seconded from the headquarters, international business division, in Beijing. The former, at deputy general manager level of seniority in different functional areas such as quality control, accounting, and engineering, are based in the Bintulu site office, whereas the latter is in Kuching, the regional headquarters. Both teams work closely on the BHP and are involved in SHC's internationalization initiatives. They are all China-based personnel working in Malaysia with considerable experiences in projects based both in China and overseas. In addition, author X had also worked closely with many employees at middle and operational levels. Author X took notes on the related issues aligning with this research during the interviews.

Participation and observation

Author X began his full-time in-company participative observation in January 2004. Engaged in SHC at a senior executive role, he was able to phase in relatively quickly and directly to the mainstream and daily operations of SHC, in particular its BHP undertaking. The participative observations allowed him to learn more personally the key issues and variables we attempted to find out for this research. We also used nonparticipative observations to make some generalizations of the key issues under study and to complement the data collection methods used. For instance, author X learns the progress of power tunnel construction, an area that he is not directly involved, through a series of informal discussions with the firm's personnel responsible in the area and external related parties. He can then evaluate the facts learned against the true pictures presented on the construction, internal documentations, and other related official correspondences about the actual progress of the power tunnel works. The local relevancies of our work have further benefited from author X's attachment with the University of Putra, Malaysia, Bintulu Campus, as a visiting lecturer when this research was conducted.

Archival records analysis

One of the pertaining features of collecting data from SHC is that there are large sources of internal records information written mainly in Mandarin Chinese. Fluency in the language could be an added advantage if one would like to conduct research in this setting, where Mandarin Chinese is the major medium of communication. Some typical in-company archival documents available that we read and referred to are as follows:

(1) Speeches and correspondences from the senior management, especially those based in Beijing headquarters and the BHP senior management team.
(2) Corporate policy handbooks, SHC's monthly internal BHP newsletters, internal rules and regulations, functional business and technical reports, agreements, operating principles, etc.
(3) Project annual reviews and SHC's official website. In addition, we also assembled a rich external secondary source of information such as newspapers, press releases, magazines, etc., written mainly in English, as one of the multiple sources to complement our understanding of SHC and to reduce retrospective bias.

Institutional pressures and implications

The Association of South East Asian Nations (ASEAN) operates in a constantly changing context. It is transitioning to a multipolar power landscape from the Cold War (Pushpanathan, 2003; Yong, 2003). Malaysia is balancing its energy supplies and demands by emphasizing a more balanced mix of the energy policy and reforming its power sector to make it more competitive (Allison, 2000). In what follows, we will look into how the institutional environments that embed SHC and the BHP provide both challenges and opportunities to SHC for discharging its BHP-related obligations.

Multidimensional pressure

The BHP is opposed by many indigenous communities, political opposition parties, a coalition of local and international nongovernmental organizations, individuals, etc. (Friends of the Earth, 1996). The commencement of the project requires timber extraction from a forest of 69,000 ha, an area as large as Singapore, which will be submerged. More than 800 species of rare plants and animals are in danger of destruction (Friends of the Earth, 1996; Matthias, 2001; Then, 2002). In addition, by changing the water quality and river flow patterns, it will potentially affect thousands of people living downstream of the Bakun Dam, on the Rajang River (Friends of the Earth, 1996). Despite these concerns, the main dam will create a water catchments reservoir 700 feet deep and can withstand an earthquake measuring up to 7.3 on the Richter scale (Then, 2003). Local youths will be trained at the project site in collaboration with the MCH JV consortium. These workers would be more employable in a market economy after the project is completed (New Straits Times, 2003).

Regulative monitoring

The Malaysian government shelved the BHP during the 1997–1998 Asian Economic Crisis but resumed it in mid-1999 (Matthias, 2001). Beyond the economic viability, the BHP has been justified in terms of meeting the overall economic development of Malaysia to become a fully industrialized nation by year 2020. Consequently, the government has established formal mechanisms to assist the implementation of the project so that the project will bring about the expected benefits. These mechanisms are in the form of specialized committees and task forces, for instance, a cabinet committee overseeing the successful implementation of the project, and an independent board of reviewer. This board is composed of local and foreign experts on hydroelectric projects. It aims at reviewing, on a regular basis, the BHP's design, construction, and performance during its operation with respect to its safety and adequacy (Then, 2003).

Compliance and cultural concerns

Bidding firms for the BHP will be post-qualified prior to consideration for the contract award. Amongst others, the firms shall be technically competent and financially stable. They shall allocate no less than 30 percent of the contract awarded to local companies and also have to commit the work, supply, and services to be allocated to the said local firms. In addition, the contractors for the BHP have to obtain various approvals from the relevant government authorities on several matters under the existing laws and regulations such as land matters, industrial health and safety standards, Environmental Impact Assessment reports, and quality control (Allison, 2000). At the micro level, two combined engineering and construction bureaus of SHC basically spearhead the firm's undertaking in the BHP. Though such a combination is not new for the firm's major home and international projects, there might be a concern for the bureaus to adapt strategically to the Malaysian local culture, standards, governances, and work practices largely influenced by capitalist ideologies, as the BHP is also closely monitored by various appointed task forces. This concern would have knock-on effects on the firm's internal organization and external obligations.

Industry structures and competences

The Malaysian construction industry has long been known for its cyclicality being dictated by various predictable and unpredictable forces. The industry is very disparate whereby large and small construction firms exist side by side. Although large projects may be awarded to multinational giants or joint ventures (JVs), in the end, smaller contractors will carry out a large part of the work. The larger contractors would generally act as the project planners and financiers. Nonetheless, large MNCs continue to dominate higher value-added projects, for instance, the Kuala Lumpur International Airport (Dynaquest, 2000). SHC's competence in handling major hydroelectric projects, especially the Three Gorges Dam, could have earned SHC its reputation as a highly sought reliable contractor for the BHP. This competence to assist the firm to meet its obligations and attain above-the-average returns will depend on the interplay of various variables, subject to the combining of the firm's internal and external effects that exist within a particular industry.

Relationship networks and learning

The Malaysian construction industry has depicted seesawing trends whereby the total number of firms rises during an upswing and shrinks when the industry recedes. The intensified competition among rivalries could further result in a great variation in the number of contracts secured from year to year. The earnings of the contractors seesaw even during a boom time. Despite difficulties in quantifying, the institutional environment plays a major part in servicing lucrative contracts in the local construction industry. It is generally perceived that a significant portion of the major local privatized infrastructural contracts have been secured by groups with strong political linkages (Dynaquest, 2000). In terms of managing the dynamic aspects of local business, SHC would have benefited from the presence of overseas Chinese business groups in Malaysia that control a considerable portion of the private sector businesses in the ASEAN. Before embarking on the BHP, SHC had already formed alliances with local Chinese firms such as Soon Hup Construction Co. to construct and commission the Bintulu SG Kelalong Dam project and other civil engineering undertakings. The incremental learning effects from previous contracts would have prepared SHC better than its competitors to operate in the Malaysian hydropower industry.

Leveraging competences for performance

The type of strategies pursued will affect resources allocation required to support the success of those strategies. SHC bundles and leverages a number of competences as discussed below in view of both institutional challenges and opportunities encountered.

Competitive costs

A strategy of competitive cost will require emphasis on cost-efficient value chains and systems. The MCH JV received the Bakun main dam contract at a tender price of RM 1.788 billion. The consortium's tender submission is said to have been the lowest bid among four competing short-listed Malaysian-led consortia for the work. Competitive cost is one of the strategic imperatives for the MCH JV competing in a price-sensitive market and also its success in securing the BHP. There are a number of factors that would challenge the viability of the BHP. The reliability of the project's anticipated electricity outputs is subject to the accuracy of a number of assumptions made on the project itself regarding, for example, the efficiency of the dam, the speed of construction, and downstream effects. A wrong judgment of any one thereon would throw the viability of the project into doubt. As a result, the projected costs and time to complete the project are likely to be overrun and therefore will destroy its economic justifications.

A factor is competitive when it is embedded with multiple valuable characteristics than merely a predominant feature such as cheap in price. The price of such a factor might still be low but it is a lot more competitive as it embraces different useful dimensions. As such, it is competitive at an acceptable price than by merely being low cost. The competitive cost orientation has provided SHC with a number of strategic flexibilities. The tender's bid price submitted, which was then accepted, would practically rule out the consideration on the next most efficient bidder as a substitute for SHC. Within SHC's organization, there is a large reservoir of competitively priced skillful hydraulic engineering workers in different areas, nurtured partly through the booming large hydraulic power industry at home. There is also the wide availability of specialized tools, consumables, and equipment that have been developed to cope with hydroelectric projects of different sizes carried out in different geographical parts of China and elsewhere. Consequently, SHC is able to maintain competitive factor costs to cope with any potential price increases imposed by powerful factors' suppliers.

Technological capabilities

The global dimensions of environmental forces are powerful and dynamic. Firms could respond to market competition and gain strategic advantages through some nonprice factors such as technological capabilities. For example, IBM's strategy is to offer high-performance servers at premium prices. The Bakun Dam is a 205-m-high concrete face rockfill dam (CFRD), with a length of crest of 740 m. It is higher than the Foz de Areia rockfill dam in Brazil and the Aguamilpa in Mexico and is the second highest in the world after the Shuibuya Dam in China. According to the original BHP plan, the transmission of the dam's electricity to Peninsular Malaysia would have necessitated some 1500 km of overland wires and four 650-km-long undersea cables, under the South China Sea. The submarine cables are far longer than the longest existing undersea power cables, between Denmark and Sweden. The BHP contract was awarded to the MCH JV's predecessors on the confidence that they are recognized as the global leader in advanced power generation and transmission technology.

Competing on nonprice dimensions does have its downside. The customers' perception of exclusivity is not always compatible with high market share, that is, they might not be willing to pay prices significantly higher than the industrial average. The scaled-down BHP was restarted in 1999 but without the original undersea cables across the South China Sea to Peninsular Malaysia, and the work on the proposed CFRD remained. The geological assessments have concluded that the Bakun site would suitably allow the building of a more cost-effective rockfill dam about 200 m high. Meanwhile, there has been an upsurge of dam construction in China. Being the largest player in China, SHC has developed and will pay more attention to the technologies of high dam construction under complicated conditions including reconnaissance, design, construction, and management especially the complete technologies to build dams 200–300 m high. Notably, the firm is carrying on with this by meeting the current BHP challenges with the experiences and competences in building and completing the world's tallest Shuibuya Dam and a number of other dams at home and overseas.

Global experiences

International operations are far more complex than those confined to the domestic scale. While domestic competition is vital as a spur to innovation and also as an enhancement to global competitiveness, there are many clear differences for a firm operating internationally in a global industry compared to a national company competing in the same industry. China has been a sizeable international market in the aspects of specific equipment of dam construction and large hydropower station facilities. In terms of the total number of dams, it currently holds the first place in the world, and the installed capacity ranks the third. International firms in the field of design, consultation, and construction have entered China's hydropower industry. On the other hand, China-based firms are also gradually moving toward the international markets and competition. The relevant Chinese authorities have given the green light to the controversial Three Gorges Dam project after receiving the feasibility study reports completed in 1988, which were prepared by a Canada-based engineering consulting consortium, Canadian International Project Managers Yangtze Joint Venture. Also, instead of relying on foreign financiers, domestic contractors to the project such as SHC would receive financial sources from China's State Development Bank, one of the most important sources of funds for China's power industry, in carrying out the project.

Likewise in the BHP context, the Malaysian government has engaged international consultants drawn from Germany and the United States to conduct the feasibility studies for the project. Past responses from home and abroad on the Three Gorges Dam project based in China, for instance, would have provided SHC invaluable experiences and hindsight in managing institutional pressures on the BHP. Combining experiences and learning from a number of international dam projects in emerging markets, and more importantly, with the successful completion of the SG Kelalong Dam project, SHC is better positioned in terms of aligning both home and hands-on local experiences to carry out the BHP.

Relationship management

The BHP tender's overseas bidders are expected to allocate no less than 30 percent of the work secured to local companies, to go into joint production of parts and components with local manufacturers, to commit to providing technical support on the work and services allocated to the local companies, and to include as one of its members a registered Class A local contractor. At the firm level, SHC subcontracts as required about 30 percent civil work of its BHP contract secured to an incorporated JV entity, Intraxis Engineering, controlled by Malaysian Chinese-based businesspeople. The JV consists of two members of the MCH JV, WCT Engineering and MTC Capital. The JV will be responsible for the supply of materials and to an extent the construction of the main dam and related electrical and mechanical installations, while SHC is in charge of the more specialized areas of dam construction and design. Engaging local partners provides SHC with some potential advantages. Firstly, it speeds up the firm's learning and therefore averts unnecessary costly miscalculations on the local regulative environments, work practices, and other related compliance concerns. For instance, the local laws, industrial health and safety standards, quality controls, and engineering protocols are to an extent influenced by Western methodologies. They are somewhat different from those experienced in China. Mediating through the differences, at times, could be time-consuming and costly. Leveraging local partners' competences suitably in different areas of the contract secured would therefore enable SHC to expand business networks, refine knowledge assets to fulfill its contractual obligations, and promote its reputation as an emerging international player.

Strategic uncertainties

Change is ever present and occurring at an ever increasing rate in this globalized world marketplace. The impelling forces for change could be attributed to organizational internal and external stimuli. Concerns from economic, ecological, technical, and social perspectives have been raised on the viability of the BHP. The implementation of the project has been fuelled with uncertainties as a result. Prior to the engagement of the MCH JV, there are significant uncertainties expressed on the security and technical worries related to the cables that will deliver power to the Peninsular Malaysia from the Bakun Dam, in the Sarawak State. Taking into consideration a number of assumptions made on the BHP regarding, for example, rainfall, sedimentation rates, speed of construction, and experience of other large dams around the world, the projection of the costs and time completion for the project are likely to be overrun. On the other side of the coin, there were some major external shocks such as the 1997–1998 Asian Economic Crisis and the global war against terrorism taking place in the past decade that would have prompted the local authorities concerned responsible for promoting the BHP to relook on the overall viability of the project. Because of the prevailing micro and macro scenarios coupled with the Chinese government's encouragement to its business firms to go global, SHC could have capitalized on the uncertainties surrounding the BHP and international relationship as a valuable opportunity to fulfill its corporate missions.

Discussions and conclusions

Strategic management is sometimes opportunistic rather than systematic when we attempt to exploit, for example, the fall and rise of an international JV initiative in a dynamic institutional environment. Conventional wisdom suggests that the uncertainty of strategy makings and institutional influences could be greatly reduced if the developments in an industry are closely watched and a firm is in direct touch with people who actually frame policies. We envisage some knowledge assets or propositions from this case research:

- Demand at MNCs' home markets could pressurize the firms to innovate and therefore prepare them better for establishing a global position. Foreign markets, though possibly being smaller, could also provide unique opportunities for firms based in a transitional economy to gain valuable global experiences that could be transferred to the entire global network of the firms.
- Some foreign markets could be better developed in terms of legal systems and professional practices in relation to the home market under transition. The institutional influences often vary from one nation to the other. While the growing complexity of the legal environment in the foreign markets could reduce operational uncertainties, the MNCs must be ready to consider overseas affiliates as part of their global unitary enterprise, and develop a strategic relationship with the host country.
- Low prices of factors need not always provide a good defense against competitive forces. To be valuable, the factors, for instance, human capital, must be embedded with characteristics such as special engineering

skills that are highly and continuously in demand and must be trainable. This human resource, if strategically priced at a relatively attractive level, will become competitive than merely low cost. The firms that possess such factors would compete more effectively than those based on price dimensions.

- The competitive advantages on price dimensions could be eroded by other nonprice dimensions of competition, such as the firms' technological capabilities, cultures, and long-term relationship-building potential with the host country. Nonprice dimensions of competition could also defend against external forces. The bidders for a particular contract could be evaluated against these dimensions. Weaker competence in one area at times could be offset by a stronger performance on other areas. One competence could become irrelevant to competition when other areas of competences are somehow equally insisted.

Therefore, the firms must be proficient in bundling and leveraging their price and nonprice capabilities, subject to organizational internal and external effects, in managing institutional influences for internationalization. This proficiency would constitute a hard-to-emulate tacit knowledge asset that can contribute to a continuous stream of rent generation. We believe this assertion is capable of analytical generalization to other major firms.

As at the end of year 2004, the progress of the power tunnels construction, a major component of SHC's contract on the BHP, is ahead of schedule. The CEO of the firm in his recent visit to the BHP site mentioned:

The BHP is the 'Three Gorges Dam' in Malaysia. Malaysian government, opposition parties and people pay high attention to it. We must accept the fact that the project is progressing satisfactory. We have faced many challenges. . . . We are committed to the project's completion. [1]

The managing director of Sime Engineering Services Bhd also commented:

The construction of the Bakun hydroelectric dam is progressing well and is on schedule. . . . [W]e take a very prudent stance on the provisions. At this moment, we do not foresee having to make any more provisions.
(The Star, 2005)

The complexity of the BHP cannot be overlooked. SHC may have gained greater autonomy and representation within the organizational structures of the MCH JV.

On the other side of the coin, there have been exciting conversations that characterize Chinese firms' global competitiveness. Lenovo, for instance, recognizes that by handing over the management of the recently acquired IBM PC unit to a group of senior IBM executives they could be better off as the firm may not have the required expertise to run the new company (Barboza,

2004). In reflecting on the rich opportunities for advancing the understanding on the vibrant Chinese economy, several strategic research questions for future research could therefore be asked: What really is the state of Chinese firms' corporate governance? How do the firms sustain and leverage their knowledge management systems? Will they be more ready to compete on nonprice dimensions? What are the major differences between operations of emerging nations' MNCs and the global strategies by the MNCs in developed economies? While some puzzles surrounding the Chinese firms are yet to be fully understood, the growing calls for adherence to the "multipolar world" in managing global affairs might have provided the firms valuable opportunities to align strategies with institutional influences inherently dynamic in entering and consolidating foreign markets somehow "neglected" by others.

Acknowledgments

This research has benefited from the Sarawak Foundation's financial supports (Ref. No: YS/LP/007228). We are grateful to the comments of the business faculty, our learned Chinese colleague Dr Haiguang Zhong, the anonymous reviewers, and conference chairs on an earlier version. Jill Gable's administration work is excellent.

Note

1. This is a direct translation from Mandarin Chinese. See Qiang (2006). The CEO, SHC Malaysia's managing director, and several other key corporate personnel of the firm visited the site of BHP in April 2006.

References

Allison, T. (2000) "Malaysia's Bakun Project: Build and be Damned," *Asia Times Online*, 28 October.
Ashforth, B.E. and Gibbs, B.W. (1990) "The Double-edge of Organizational Legitimation," *Organization Science*, 1(2): 177–194.
"Bakun Dam Project on Schedule," *The Star*, October 21, 2005.
Barboza, D. (2004) "Chinese Buyer of PC Unit is Moving to IBM's Hometown," *The New York Times*, 25 December.
Cornell, B. and Shapiro, A.C. (1987) "Corporate Stakeholders and Corporate Finance," *Financial Management*, 16(1): 5–14.
DiMaggio, P.J. (1988) "Interest and Agency in Institutional Theory," in L.G. Zucker (ed.) *Institutional Patterns and Organizations: Culture and Environment*, MA: Ballinger.
DiMaggio, P.J. and Powell, W.W. (eds) (1991) "Introduction," *The New Institutionalism in Organizational Analysis*, Chicago: University of Chicago Press.
Dynaquest. (2000) *Industry Sector Analysis (Apparel – Chemicals)*, Vol. I., Kuala Lumpur: Dynaquest.
Friends of the Earth. (1996) *Briefing Sheet: The Bakun Hydroelectric Project – Malaysia*, London: Friends of the Earth.
Galaskiewicz, J. (1985) "Interorganizational Relations," *Annual Review of Sociology*, 11: 281–304.

Hambrick, D.C. and D'Aveni, R.A. (1992) "Top Management Team Deterioration as Part of the Downward Spiral of Large Bankruptcies," *Management Science*, 38: 1445–1466.

Henderson, R. and Mitchell, W. (1997) "The Interactions of Organizational and Competitive Influences on Strategy and Performance," *Strategic Management Journal*, 18 (Special Summer Issue): 5–14.

Hinings, C.R. and Greenwood, R. (1988) *The Dynamics of Strategic Change*, Oxford: Blackwell.

Hitt, M.A., Ireland, R.D., and Hoskisson, R.E. (2001) *Strategic Management: Competitiveness and Globalization (Concepts)*. 4th edn, Ohio: South-Western Publishing.

Hui, L.T. (2004) "Business Timeliness: The Intersections of Strategy and Operations Management," *International Journal of Operations and Production Management*, 24(6): 605–624.

Matthias, J. (2001) "Bakun: A Dam Controversy," *Asiafeatures.com*, 24 May.

Meyer, J.W. and Rowan, B. (1977) "Institutionalized Organizations: Formal Structure as Myth and Ceremony," *American Journal of Sociology*, 83: 340–363.

Meyer, J.W. and Scott, W.R. (eds) (1983) "Centralization and the Legitimacy Problems of Local Government," *Organizational Environments: Ritual and Rationality*, CA: Sage.

Miller, K.D. and Bromiley, P. (1990) "Strategic Risk and Corporate Performance: An Analysis of Alternative Risk Measures," *Academy of Management Journal*, 33: 756–779.

"New Hope in a New Home," *New Straits Times*, October 14, 2003.

North, D.C. (1990) *Institutions, Institutional Change and Economic Performance*, Cambridge: Cambridge University Press.

Oliver, C. (1997) "Sustainable Competitive Advantage: Combining Institutional and Resource-based Views," *Strategic Management Journal*, 18(9): 697–713.

Pushpanathan, S. (2003) "Appreciating, Understanding the ASEAN Concept," *The Jakarta Post*, 9 August.

Scott, W.R. (1987) "The Adolescence of Institutional Theory," *Administrative Science Quarterly*, 32: 493–511.

Scott, W.R. (2001) *Institutions and Organizations*, 2nd edn, Thousand Oaks: Sage.

Scott, W.R. and Meyer, J.W. (eds) (1983) "The Organization of Societal Sectors," *Organizational Environments: Ritual and Rationality*, CA: Sage.

Suchman, M.C. (1995) "Managing Legitimacy: Strategic and Institutional Approaches," *Academy of Management Review*, 20(3): 571–610.

Then, S. (2002) "NGO Cries Foul over Plans to Extract Timber from Bakun," *The Star Online*, 30 August.

Then, S. (2003) "Board: No Big Damage by Bakun Project," *The Star Online*, 28 September.

Wood, D.J. (1991) "Corporate Social Performance Revisited," *Academy of Management Review*, 16(4): 691–718.

Yong, O.K. (2003) "Towards an ASEAN Single Market and Single Investment Destination," *Address by Secretary-General of ASEAN at the Boao Forum for Asia Annual Conference*, Hainan Province, China, 2 November.

Part III

Regional Implications: Following or Leading?

8
Vietnam, Flying Geese, and the Globalization of China

Thomas D. Lairson

The integration of China into the world economy via FDI, as a platform for global production and exports and as a reservoir of global cash resulting from giant trade surpluses, is well-understood.[1] Also significant is consideration of the implications of economic changes in China for its Asian neighbors. Specifically, the process of China's movement from shallow to deep integration into the global economy may well affect its less well-developed Asian nations (Lardy, 2001; Zweig, 2002). Will China's development pattern follow that of most other Asian tigers, with rising costs leading to efforts to move up the value chain even while shedding production of labor-intensive activities? And will this lead to opportunities for nations in the region with lower-cost structures?

The globalization of China is more than economic opening and inflows of FDI.[2] As deep integration progresses, China becomes more susceptible to structural transformations in the global economy. One process common to development in much of Asia involves less-developed states advancing in the path of more advanced states. This "flying geese" pattern has been seen in the development of Japan, Korea, Taiwan, Hong Kong, Singapore, and Malaysia. For example, rising costs in Japan between 1955 and 1970 resulted and led Japanese firms toward globalization of their enterprises by moving labor-intensive operations offshore to Korea, Taiwan, and Hong Kong, thereby boosting management capabilities, technology, and economic growth in these nations. And Japanese firms were also pressed to move up the global value chain in order to maintain economic growth. In the 1980s, Japanese firms again launched a wave of FDI-related growth in Southeast Asia when currency exchange-related costs rose (Hatch and Yamamura, 1996, Encarnation, 1999). Economic growth in Korea, Taiwan, Singapore, and Hong Kong in the 1980s and 1990s produced rising costs mainly from increasing wages and led to outward FDI directed at China and other lower-cost Asian states such as Malaysia, Indonesia, and Vietnam. Can we expect that this same pattern will be followed in China and its lower-cost neighbors, such as Vietnam?

The economic resurgence of China has sometimes been noted as a threat to Southeast Asia (Ravenhill, 2006). Fears abound of a diversion of FDI and a competitive disadvantage in exports for these nations. A more optimistic perspective frequently offered focuses on the emergence of a division of labor that consigns smaller nations a role in providing raw materials and manufacturing inputs to China. The "flying geese" perspective provides an even more optimistic twist to these ideas by adopting a dynamic analysis of FDI and trade, seeing a complementarity in economic development based mainly on how shifting comparative advantage drives the foreign investment calculations of transnational corporations (TNCs). However, the processes of dynamic change identified by the FGM are inadequate for understanding not only the broad patterns across Asia over the past four decades but also Vietnam's present and future relationship to China. In particular, we must look beyond the simple market relationships identified in the FGM to the dynamic evolutionary processes involving the interaction of TNCs, the governments and firms in the poorest states, and global production, knowledge, and technology networks. It is in the operation of these networks and the relative capabilities and costs of various states where the dynamics of comparative advantage and flying geese are to be found.

A number of important questions are raised by this line of inquiry. To what extent and in what ways can we expect China-based firms to shift operations to Vietnam? Can Vietnam, which is a lower-cost alternative, benefit from China's growth? Are there good reasons to expect the creation of regional economic clusters focusing on China and including Southeast Asian nations? How do the forces of technology, global production networks, knowledge flows, and political and institutional capability affect this process?

This chapter examines these questions in light of recent developments in the global economy, including China's recent accession to the World Trade Organization (WTO), Vietnam's upcoming accession to the WTO, the Association of South East Asian Nations (ASEAN)–China free trade agreement (FTA), and continuing development of both China's and Vietnam's economy. Based on an analysis of changing cost structures and demographic trends, we predict much more rapid growth in Vietnam as a lower-cost alternative for much of the labor-intensive but low-wage production that has migrated to China in recent years. And this can come not only from decisions by traditional transnational firms, but also from the globalization of domestic Chinese firms sending FDI into Vietnam.

We begin with a theoretical examination of the FGM of economic growth and development across Asia follows, including comments about the limitations of the model. The position of the Chinese economy as it relates to regional comparative advantage is considered, along with how the emerging comparative advantages of Vietnam can attract new investment. We draw conclusions about the likelihood of shifting labor-intensive production from China to Vietnam.

Flying geese and economic restructuring in Asia

From the beginning of the industrial era more than two centuries ago, a sequential pattern of economic growth and development can be identified. Nations tend to follow each other in the processes of entry into industrialization and in the industrial sectors that are emphasized. During the 20th century, first Japan, then the little dragons, and later China and other Asian states entered into the industrial world and eventually into global markets as successful exporters. The "flying geese" model (FGM) is an effort to explain how and why this has happened. In particular, the model examines the evolutionary dynamics of the "geography of comparative advantage" and how this leads to the transmission of industrial capabilities from state to state (Ginzberg and Simonazzi, 2005).

The FGM of regional interdependence and structural evolution is actually several variations on a general theme. The earliest versions of the model focused on the impact of industrial imports from leading industrial nations into a less-developed nation and the subsequent efforts of that poorer nation to develop a local industrial base through import substitution. Over time, improvements in local competitiveness based on local developments leads to success in exports, usually back to the leading nation. Thus, this version of the FGM identifies a hierarchical set of arrangements in global markets generated by advantages in productive capabilities. The "lead goose" transmits these advantages to "follower geese" through trade and later serves as a market for the exports of these same products (Dowling and Cheang, 2000; Kojima, 2000; Ozawa, 2003). More recently, scholars have linked the political interests of American hegemony to the theory of product cycles to identify the mechanisms for shifting locations of production (Cumings, 1984). Other scholars have been more critical of the FGM, preferring to substitute technological change for product cycles and asserting the somewhat harsh limits to the developmental prospects for the follower states (Bernard and Ravenhill, 1995).

Recent work on the FGM has given way to a focus on the cost differences that emerge from the timing of economic development and the role of transnational corporations (TNCs). This new approach to the mechanisms linking development in different nations is consonant with other research examining the processes for the transmission of capabilities from leading to latecomer firms and on the prospects this has for upgrading across the value chain. The initial forms of the FGM saw the driving force for dynamic comparative advantage arising from the actions of local firms in less-developed nations. This approach is no longer adequate. Now, we need to consider in detail the origins of dynamic comparative advantage from the interaction of TNCs (which may originate from many lead states) with the local firms, governments, and institutions in follower states (Bell and Albu, 1999; Mytelka, 2000; Humphrey and Schmitz, 2002).[3] Further, these interactions take place within (and help constitute) global networks of production, knowledge, technology, and finance, which are the sources for the creation of capabilities in latecomer states that generate dynamic comparative advantages and make possible a rapid shift to the export of world-class products (Borrus *et al.*, 2000; Nolan, 2001; Dicken, 2003; Ernst, 2003; Luthje, 2004; Brooks, 2005). These global (and regional) production networks fragment the value chain into differentiated elements, locating the various parts in different nations where conditions best support the production or development of that element of the value chain. The organizing force for GPNs typically is a leading TNC able to define and integrate the system of design, production, marketing, and distribution across national boundaries (Prencipe *et al.*, 2003).

Perhaps the biggest factor in moving all states in East Asia – including China and Vietnam – into the global economy and up the value chain is the existence of global knowledge and technology networks and the connections of these networks to transnational firms and global markets. Together with the close connections to global investment networks based on foreign direct investment (FDI), follower/latecomer states and their firms have the opportunity for tapping into these networks to build and upgrade local knowledge and technology capabilities. Vietnam's and China's ability to make rapid progress in knowledge and technology upgrading is greatly facilitated by these global networks, which are the result of the massive waves of globalization over the past 50 years. These global knowledge and technology networks are embedded in the global migration of students and faculty, in the communication networks created by the Internet and global travel, in global consulting services, in the global army of expatriate managers, in transnational communities of highly educated knowledge workers (Saxenian, 2006), in systems of FDI flows (UNCTAD, 2005; Lall and Urata, 2003), and in global trade in products, services, and technology (Keller and Samuels, 2003). These networks provide an enormous resource for rapid upgrading and accelerate the capacity for nations to enter global markets and move up the value chain. But this process depends critically on the abilities of local firms and institutions to restructure local capabilities so as to attract FDI and absorb and enhance knowledge and technology flows (Chen, 2006).

The FGM engages a very important pattern in the structural transformation of the locus of production linked to dynamic changes in comparative advantage. The processes for generating this transformation have evolved over time. For countries such as Taiwan, Singapore, and Korea in the 1970s and 1980s, the basic pattern was for entry at low-end labor-intensive production, with significant exports as a basis for economic growth. This was made possible through efforts of the national government in creating local conditions and institutions able to tap into the global capabilities of transnational firms. FDI from these firms flowed into the follower nation in order to set up labor-intensive production.[4] Rising incomes for each of these nations led to an increasing share of national income for workers. As costs rose, the low-end labor-intensive elements of the value chain were relocated. For Korea and Taiwan, this happened as local firms engaged in FDI to Asian follower states such as China; for Singapore, this came as TNCs relocated labor-intensive elements of the value chain to Malaysia and Thailand. Nations that were originally followers became leaders. With several iterations of follower becoming leader, the role of TNCs, global/regional production networks, global knowledge networks, and global investment networks became even more pronounced. Today, in understanding the FGM we need to account for these arrangements in ways that take into account transnational firms operating global networks and latecomer states restructuring local capabilities to attract resources from these networks.

The restructuring of the geography of production comes in two linked forms: one based on actions by transnational firms (TNCs) and/or domestic firms in the lead goose and the other based on actions by domestic firms and governments in the less-developed nation. First, when TNCs operating in labor-intensive portions of the value chain are presented with nations in the same region with similar skills but different cost structures, these firms may shift operations from the higher- to lower-cost nation. Further, domestic firms in the higher-cost nation may similarly chose to go global to shift operations to the lower-cost nation.

However, the choices of TNCs can differ from domestic firms. TNCs are likely to have a larger global knowledge base and experience and may not see geographical proximity as so important, while domestic firms may see going global much easier if they move operations to a regional nation. One other calculation for TNCs is to diversify sources of supply, thereby reducing the risks of political or economic instability. But most important is that TNCs are usually the central actors in global production networks. This means they segment the supply chain and locate the various pieces in countries where the comparative advantages best match the needs of the supply chain fragment.

The second area of adjustment involves governments and firms in the follower goose. Having low wages is a necessary but not sufficient condition for attracting FDI from the lead goose or from other sources. Governments must structure the terms for entrance by TNCs and must create complementary capabilities that make the low wages in the country actually effective in generating comparative advantage. This can include development of transportation, communication, Internet infrastructure, and power capabilities. But typically this also extends to education, specialized training, local suppliers, political stability, and establishing favorable terms for importing components and other inputs.

In short, the government of the follower goose must create an effective local institutional and market environment and credibly demonstrate a commitment to continuing and augmenting this system into the foreseeable future. Local firms may need to provide components, services, other specialized products to TNC operations and may need help in upgrading to global standards of quality and time to market. The capabilities for this upgrading play an essential role in attracting FDI and sustaining economic growth. The comparative advantage of the follower goose comes from this combination of complementary assets that make its low wages effective in attracting FDI and as a platform for global production in a rapidly changing and evolving global market. And future prospects for this nation depend on the ability to continually upgrade these assets so as to adapt to changes in global markets. In the contemporary global and regional system, when the ensemble of complementary assets of the follower state begins to approximate that of the lead state and thereby establishes the capacity for entry into global production networks, resources in the form of FDI will flow from the leader to the follower.

As we have seen, the basic patterns of the FGM can be observed in Japan's relationship to Southeast Asia in the 1980s and in Korea's and Taiwan's relationship to China and Southeast Asia over the past 15–20 years. A very large fraction of FDI into China in the 1980s and 1990s came from the Chinese economic area including Taiwan, Hong Kong, and Singapore (Naughton, 1997). As late as 2001, nearly half of the inward FDI to China came from (or through) Hong Kong (OECD Observer, 2003). Taiwan, facing rising costs and falling profit margins, has made massive investments in China, locating well over half of its electronics manufacturing capability there. The total investment by Taiwan in China is over $100 billion.[5] The ability of the recently industrialized nations of East and Southeast Asia to globalize their economies via FDI is demonstrated by a quick look at the nation of origin of the 50 largest TNCs from developing countries.[6]

Trajectories of change in China

The FGM identifies important developmental trajectories that emerge as previously poor nations begin to achieve significant levels of economic wealth and income. Where is China in this process of development?[7] Perhaps the most striking feature of China's economic situation is, unlike any other large nation, that China's economy has a huge contingent of TNCs using this nation as a global production platform. Most of this production is at the low end of the value chain. It is labor-intensive and usually involves importing components and some form of assembly (Zheng and Wern, 2005).

China is much like Singapore, Hong Kong, and Malaysia in its reliance on transnational firms as a source of capital, production knowledge, and access to global markets. Additionally, China has come to depend on several Asian states for the import of components used in its assembly operations. These same nations, from which labor-intensive operations had moved to China, have shifted their area of specialization in regional production networks to higher value-added elements of the supply chain. As a consequence, intra-Asian trade reflects these regional production networks. More than 75 percent of the value added for processed exports from China comes from foreign sources (Gaulier *et al.*, 2005; Zheng and Wern, 2005).[8] Thus, China's globalization and economic growth to date are deeply connected to the evolution of regional production networks.

China is a key player in the creation of global and regional production networks. This system sets the standard for global competitiveness and has led to the creation of considerable global knowledge capabilities that define an important form of path dependence for developments in the region. Further, the impact of TNCs in developing China as a low-cost producer and assembler can have profound implications for other states in the region when the cost basis for these arrangements begins to change. Given the size of global and regional operations located in China, when the cost advantages of China start to end the effects for countries like Vietnam can be considerable.

One of the most important questions regarding China is how long this comparative advantage in labor-intensive manufactured goods will last. With 200–300 million rural workers not yet fully part of global production, can we expect this advantage to continue for many years to come? Our observations indicate the Chinese economy has begun to show signs of changes that will erode its cost advantages and thereby activate this system of flying geese. Two of the most important contributors to rising costs are efforts to upgrade China's position in global value and innovation chains through development of its education and scientific capabilities (Zhou and Leydesdorff, 2006) and efforts to address some of the negative externalities of growth, including income inequality, labor rights, and pollution (Barboza, 2006; Kahn, 2006).

The operations in science education are driven by the need to enter global knowledge networks as more of an equal and thereby raise China's position in global production networks beyond that of low-wage assembly and manufacturing. The Chinese government is committed to increasing R&D as a percent of GDP from about 1.4 percent now to 2.5 percent in the next 15 years.[9] The recent efforts to enhance worker welfare, including giving state-controlled unions the power "to negotiate worker contracts, safety protection and workplace ground rules," are designed to raise worker incomes and improve working conditions and thereby enhance the standing and legitimacy of the Communist Party. These are not surprising developments, given the already high levels of income in China's eastern cities and the need to more equitably distribute the benefits of economic growth. Other Asian nations experienced the same sorts of pressures and made adjustments as incomes rose. But, for our purposes, these actions will result in rising costs for business operations located in China. One estimate is the new labor laws alone will increase wages by 50 percent (Barboza, 2006).

Another side of the equation is China's potential role as a market for labor-intensive products. Accession to the World Trade Organization (WTO) leads to falling tariffs for China and declines in nontariff barriers (Lardy, 2002). China as a market for imports will expand as these barriers fall and as Chinese incomes rise. China as a consumption hub for production in Asia will expand and could draw in additional exports from the Association of South East Asian Nations (ASEAN).

The Chinese ability to move up the value chain is impeded by an unsustainable degradation of the environment and natural resources, savings rates that will have to fall, weakly developed domestic firms, a poorly functioning financial system, problems in moving goods across provincial borders, arbitrary rules by bureaucrats at all levels of the country, and a domestic industrial structure based largely on limited value-added production for global markets. Yet another barrier to China's ability to move up the value chain, especially in attracting FDI for production of high-value goods, is its dismal record in dealing with intellectual property (Song and Ee, 2005).

Can Vietnam fly with China?

Doi moi began to gain traction after 1990, and over the past 16 years Vietnam has been among the world's fastest-growing economies with an average growth of 7.5 percent per year. Even with the exceptionally rapid population growth, per capita income has more than doubled in that same period: from $250 to about $600 (International Finance Corporation Database). There are, however, wide disparities between urban and rural incomes. Although about 80 percent of Vietnam's population lives in rural areas, income levels in cities remain more than eight times that of the countryside. Nonetheless, the levels of absolute poverty in Vietnam have been cut by half to just over 25 percent of the population. Inflation has generally remained in single digits. In many ways, Vietnam's economy today has progressed about as far as China's had in the early 1990s.

In 2005 growth was 8.4 percent, placing Vietnam into the top ranks of nations. This growth has been driven largely by export expansion. After 1999, exports have represented more than 50 percent of GDP, compared to only 20 percent in 1989. The majority of exports are of manufactured goods and the majority of these are low-skilled labor-intensive products (Jenkins, 2004). The privatization of the Vietnamese economy, mainly in the reform of state-owned enterprises (SOEs), has made progress. However, this is one of the main arenas for conflict between reformers and conservatives and rapid change here remains elusive (Painter, 2003).[10] FDI has been vital to Vietnam's growth, bringing not only capital but perhaps more importantly knowledge, technology, and access to global markets. Nonetheless, Vietnam remains far behind the largest recipients of FDI (Table 8.1). By one measure, China receives about 30 times as much FDI as Vietnam. Though Vietnam has achieved considerable economic growth and foreign investment, there is much more unrealized potential.

Vietnam's economic prospects depend increasingly on its membership in the emerging regional free trade area in ASEAN (Wei-Yen, 2005). Not only does ASEAN contain enormous natural resources, there are also considerable knowledge, technology, and productive resources. These nations are at quite different stages of economic development, some very rich, some somewhat developed, and others – such as Vietnam – quite poor. Within the region, Vietnam can be seen as the low-cost production platform for an increasingly integrated Southeast Asian economic zone. Some of the most important assets of ASEAN include:

Table 8.1 Vietnam's FDI, selected years (in millions of US dollars)

	1990–2000 Average	2000	2002	2003	2004	2005
Inward FDI	1322		1,200	1,450	1,610	2,020
FDI stocks	1655 (1990)	20,596			29,115	31,135

Measuring FDI is very difficult and this leads to very different figures. This table presents data in the most conservative form. By contrast, using a more liberal measure for 2005, leads to a total of $6 billion (Luong, 2006, 149). For discussion of problems with FDI data, see (UNCTAD, 2005, 4–5).
Source: UNCTAD, *World Investment Report, 2006b*, Vietnam Country Fact Sheet.

Table 8.2 Inward FDI to ASEAN and China, 2001–2005 (in billions of US dollars)

	2001	2002	2003	2004	2005
ASEAN	18.46	13.82	18.45	25.65	38.1
China	46.9	52.7	53.5	60.6	53.3

Source: *ASEAN Statistical Yearbook*, 2005; UNCTAD.

- ASEAN has a GDP of $850 billion (non-PPP) (larger than India)
- ASEAN GDP at PPP is $2.4 trillion
- ASEAN per capita GDP: Nominal $1400; PPP $4200
- Population of ASEAN is 550 million
- Inward FDI to Southeast Asia in 2005 was $38 billion. China's inward FDI in 2005 was $53 billion (Bradsher, 2006).

Though China still dwarfs ASEAN in many ways, FDI levels are not that different (Table 8.2).

At present, an ASEAN free trade agreement (FTA) may not seem very important, as trade among ASEAN states is relatively small. But such a trade agreement can aggregate national markets into a much more viable regional market capable of generating two of the most important drivers of economic growth: specialization and economies of scale for producers for this market. Tariff barriers are relatively high among ASEAN states, thereby permitting significant gains from trade when these barriers are removed. As economic growth has improved, ministers from ASEAN states have recently made commitments to advance the date for achieving integration via a functioning FTA from 2020 to 2015 (Fuller, 2006).[11] Vietnam's leaders seem to have resolved many of the disputes in the government over the level of economic opening. The ASEAN FTA, combined with Vietnam's now successful WTO bid and likely permanent normal trade relations with the United States, has set them on a very clear path.

One of the most important economic questions for evaluating the effects of greater ASEAN–China trade is the degree of complementarity between the Chinese and Southeast Asian economies (Wong and Chan, 2003).[12] Studies of the ASEAN–China trade relationship often conclude that both tend to export similar goods and therefore should be seen as competitive and not complementary (Tongzon, 2005). However, this ignores the effect of regional production networks and the capacity of TNCs to align a regional division of labor with various elements of the supply chain for a single product.[13]

The existence of regional production networks, with China as the assembler of components produced in more advanced economies in East and Southeast Asia, is a result of the operation of the processes identified in a refashioned FGM. Trade relations between ASEAN and China focus on exporting commodities and components. In 2003, exports from ASEAN to China were $47.3 billion and imports from China were $30.9 billion. Total trade between China and ASEAN doubled between 2000 and 2003 and is growing at 25 percent annually (Park, 2005).[14] One important area for trade is the need for raw materials from Southeast Asia to support Chinese industrialization. However, after the Asian financial crisis of 1997–1998, trade in manufactured goods has increased, most of which takes place in these regional production networks organized by TNCs.[15] ASEAN states accounted for 9 percent of China's total imports in 2004 and more than two-thirds of this was in manufactured goods. Between 1997 and 2004, ASEAN exports of office machinery, telecommunications equipment, and electrical machinery rose from $2.6 billion to $32.2 billion. Clearly, a regional division of labor linking China and ASEAN states already exists (Ravenhill, 2006, 671–673). China has become the labor-intensive segment of a regional production network because of the combination of low labor costs and complementary assets that have attracted FDI from TNCs.[16]

An important question is whether China will be able to maintain or even expand its role as the primary global production base as an ASEAN–China FTA takes hold in coming years (Ong, 2003). What are the Vietnamese economic capabilities that can translate into a comparative advantage in relation to China and thereby lead to a flying geese arrangement? Perhaps surprisingly, given China's stature as the premier location for labor-intensive production, Vietnam has an emerging advantage here. Vietnam's population is 84 million, making it the eighth largest in the world, roughly the same size as Germany but with an enormous advantage in demographic trends. More or less continuous war from 1930 to 1975 was followed by a baby boom. Vietnam's population has increased by 40 million in the last 30 years and nearly 60 percent of its population is under 30. This large number of young Vietnamese creates demographic characteristics that favor location of manufacturing firms: a young work force with some English skills. More than 1.2 million new workers are entering the job market in Vietnam annually and most live within a reasonable commuting distance to urban areas where factories can be located.

China's one-child policy has led to a relative decline in the proportion of young workers, and this decline will accelerate in the next decade. This is especially pronounced for persons under 25 who make up a large part of factory labor. This shortage has begun to show up in rapidly rising wages, especially in regions such as Guangdong Province. There factories have many more jobs than workers and wages have recently jumped by 18 percent (Bradsher, 2006). China has often been seen as having a near-limitless supply of unskilled labor. The size of the Chinese population and raw numbers of unskilled workers seem to confirm this. However, policy changes by the Chinese government, the physical location of many of the remaining low skilled in the remote countryside, and demographic trends suggest this conclusion may be less valid in the future.

Vietnam's labor costs are below those in China and, combined with a decent infrastructure for communication, transportation, and power, this makes Vietnam a viable alternative to China. The regulatory environment is also becoming different with rising Chinese concern over the impact of the worst polluting industries creating new rules and restrictions. There is some reason to expect additional efforts to shift these industries to Vietnam and other lax regulators in Southeast Asia (Goodman, 2005). In addition, China's wage levels must be modified to reflect additional costs in welfare payments required for all firms. This can increase wage costs by as much as 60 percent. Vietnam can expect to benefit from the continuing disinvestment from China, which in 2004 was $13 billion, and from the Chinese government's "Go Abroad" policy, which promotes FDI by Chinese firms and reflects considerations found in the FGM (Wei and Wern, 2005, 24–26). One indicator of the emerging globalization of Chinese enterprises is the recent jump in outward FDI from China. In 2005, this amounted to more than $11 billion, up from $1 to $2 billion in previous years (UNCTAD, 2006a).

There is evidence – albeit anecdotal – that Vietnam has begun to benefit from these advantages. China is already Vietnam's largest trading partner with more than $7.5 billion in two-way trade. Chinese firms in recent years have operated through Hong Kong to establish relationships to develop Vietnam's energy capabilities. But investment has also been funneled into manufacturing in textiles and garments and to develop Vietnam as a base for production for the large potential Southeast Asian market. Japanese firms that have been longtime investors in China have begun exploring investment in Vietnam, not only to take advantage of cost differences but also to reduce the risks of political friction between China and Japan (Goodman, 2005). And Vietnam has developed a significant capability in the production of textiles and garments for export, a labor-intensive industrial sector traditionally reserved for nations with a comparative advantage in wage levels (Nadvi *et al.*, 2004).[17]

In early 2006, Intel, with its famously detailed analysis of location for its international manufacturing facilities, chose Vietnam (Ho Chi Minh City) over Thailand, Malaysia, and China for a testing and packaging plant. The level of political stability and education in Vietnam, in addition to wage levels, were central elements in the decision (Lee, 2006).[18] An even better example of Vietnam's links with global knowledge networks is with Cisco Systems, the world's leading company in networking for the Internet. Cisco has a strong role in Vietnam through its "Channel Partner Program," which works with local firms to upgrade capabilities and knowledge in supplying networking solutions. Cisco provides extensive training for these local Vietnamese firms and certifies the capabilities. This important knowledge transfer strengthens local firms and, depending on the nature of governmental efforts in promoting local knowledge networks, can diffuse to other firms in Vietnam (Cisco Systems, 2006).

There remain major issues in Vietnam that can slow down or even block the potential benefits from China's globalization. Vietnam's cost advantages in wages and an effective work force are partially offset by a somewhat ineffective government and the costs this imposes on firms. One example is in taxation, which plays a negative role because of arbitrary and inconsistent enforcement. This leads to a much higher effective tax rate, perhaps as much as five times higher than in Organization for Economic Cooperation and Development (OECD) countries.[19] The level of corruption in Vietnam is substantial, though differences with China may be small. The Vietnamese government plays a large role in national investment but uses SOEs as a major vehicle for this investment. Much more effective would be the creation of new institutions and firms, connected to global markets and to global knowledge, technology, and financial networks, and able to play a partnership role with private firms in Vietnam (domestic or transnational) to receive and use this investment. The Vietnamese government relies too heavily on these transnational firms, finding the political difficulty of strong, but private, domestic firms too great to launch a program to support and enhance these firms.

Conclusions

The processes of economic growth and structural transformation have been accelerated by globalization and now take place much more quickly than in even the recent past. This is the result of the emergence of global networks of knowledge, technology, finance, trade, and communication, which provide the resources for the extraordinary pace for economic change in nations such as China and Vietnam. When nations develop local institutions able to tap into, capture, disperse, and apply these resources, rapid economic growth is possible. As the process of coevolution of global networks and local institutions continues, such nations are themselves quickly subjected to structural transformation brought on by interaction with these networks.

China has been a follower goose for a relatively short time. Can we say that it has progressed to the point where it can function as a lead goose? If we think beyond national capabilities to global networks, the answer is surely yes. Because China is a major force in defining global and regional production networks, the restructuring of these networks is tantamount to the restructuring of China. Thus, it is within global production networks that decisions about location of production are made and where calculations of comparative advantage matter. And when cost calculations can be mapped onto alternative capabilities in nations like Vietnam, such flying geese restructuring will take place. The rising force of lower barriers to trade in the region will make the calculations of transnational firms heading global and regional production networks and Chinese firms participating in these networks much easier and will place Vietnam in a more central role. There are good reasons to expect that the patterns of the FGM that led to China's incorporation in regional and global networks will be, at least partly, replicated in Vietnam.

China's costs are beginning to rise and various decision makers already see the need to shift away from low-end production there. In addition, emerging regional trade agreements and WTO membership for both China and Vietnam produce credible commitments to market-enhancing local efforts that are irreversible and that create opportunities for a regional division of labor focused on regional and global markets. One form this division of labor could take with Vietnam is for China to develop a greater capacity for advanced component design and manufacture and for the assembly end of the supply chain to happen in Vietnam. A regional cluster linking Guangzhou and Haiphong is a potential development. Wage levels in Vietnam are about 30 percent below those in eastern China and transportation between Haiphong and these areas is relatively efficient and inexpensive. Perhaps the major unanswered question is whether Vietnam can create the system of dynamically evolving complementary local assets that will make it attractive to firms making these calculations? And a related question is whether Vietnam's government can provide the help in establishing local firms capable of taking on production for global markets, or whether must Vietnam rely on transnational firms (wherever they are from) to provide the production capabilities?

Vietnam's emergence at this point is not simply because it has a comparative advantage in wage levels; rather, it is the conjunction of an emerging combination of complementary assets in Vietnam with rising costs associated with a similar set of assets in China. These assets are the result of cooperative efforts of the Vietnamese government and existing TNCs operating in Vietnam. And, this set of assets has been constructed to match the needs of various sectors of GPNs, including regional units of these networks. It is within this system of arrangements that comparative advantages for Vietnam emerge and the patterns of flying geese develop.[20]

From the perspective of a theoretical analysis of this process, we need to recognize that comparative advantage is more than relative cost structures that emerge from relative natural endowments. Rather, comparative advantage is constructed out of the development of complementary local assets able to attract FDI from the main players in GPNs who offer the capital, technology, and knowledge that permit access to global markets. The FGM does have relevance to our analysis but we need to rework the theoretical understanding of the economic forces driving the processes of change. International trade theory and its derivative concept of comparative advantage must be replaced by a theory that considers not just the structuring force of global trade and FDI, but also the structure of trade itself (intrafirm trade/intra-GPN trade), the processes of production (GPNs), and the bases of production (technology and knowledge).[21] These forces now interact with the institutional capabilities and other complementary assets created by national and local governments and define systems of dynamic comparative advantage influencing the development prospects of many nations.

Notes

1. China's foreign exchange reserves have now topped $800 billion (Browne, 2006).
2. For detail on FDI into China, see Gallagher (2005) and Huang (2005).
3. John Dunning argues effectively that the determinants of comparative advantage have shifted to processes associated with the relationships of states and firms (Dunning, 1997a).
4. The role of FDI was less for Taiwan and even less for Korea than for Singapore. In Taiwan and Korea, government support for development of local firms and other institutions made it possible to tap into global knowledge networks as a basis for developing local production for distribution through global production networks.
5. Based on information provided during author conversations with government officials in Taiwan, 2003–2004. Also see Zheng and Wern (2005, 16–17).
6. Thirty-nine of these 50 firms are from East and Southeast Asia (UNCTAD, 2005).
7. An important overview of the Chinese economy is Ahmad (2004).
8. We will return to discussion of regional production networks and ASEAN later.
9. An indicator of the coming success in moving up the value chain is the rising productivity of Chinese workers. Recent evidence points to important productivity gains among private Chinese firms operating in technology industries. In 2005, these Chinese firms had roughly the same productivity as TNCs operating in China in the same industries (Dean, 2006).
10. One positive element of the SOE situation in Vietnam is that less than 10 percent of the Vietnamese workforce is in SOEs (Painter, 2003).
11. ASEAN statistics can be found at http://www.aseansec.org/13100.htm.
12. Political and strategic issues are also relevant. The Chinese government sees the budding relationship with ASEAN in economic and in strategic terms, and as a means to gain greater influence in the area at the expense of the United States. The strategic interactions between China and the United States relating to Southeast Asia are considered by Stuart-Fox (2004). For discussion of China–ASEAN relations, see Ba (2003) and Cheng (2001).
13. Further, much of the evidence for a competitive relationship for FDI comes from Malaysia. Here, government policy has been much less effective in helping firms there move up the value chain.

14. In the years after 1998, intra Asian trade has rise much faster than previously and much more rapidly than trade within Nafta countries.
15. Remember, many of these TNCs are based in Japan, Korea, Taiwan, and Singapore.
16. Though labor may represent only a small part of total value added, the competitive advantage of many firms depends on the ability to break out of the labor-intensive portion of the value chain and minimize costs by locating this element in the most cost-effective place.
17. Firms from Taiwan have engaged in several joint ventures, which provided critical managerial and technical skills, along with contacts to inputs suppliers and global buyers to create a shoe industry in China and in Vietnam. And, fears of potential restrictions on Chinese exports by Europeans led to the effort by Taiwanese firms to establish operations in Vietnam.
18. In November 2006, Intel decided to triple its intended investment in Vietnam to $1 billion. For discussion of the many dimensions in Intel's decision to locate a similar type of plant in Costa Rica, see Spar (1998).
19. International Finance Corporation, Doing Business Database, http://www.doingbusiness.org/ExploreEconomies/Default.aspx?economyid=202. Also see rankings at http://www.doingbusiness.org/EconomyRankings/Default.aspx?direction=asc& sort=1. Also see World Bank and International Finance Corporation (2006).
20. The importance of created assets in comparative and competitive advantage is emphasized by Porter (1990).
21. This is a variation of an analysis of international trade theory in Dunning (1997b).

References

Ahmad, Sameena. 2004. "Behind the Mask," *The Economist* (March 18).
ASEAN Statistical Yearbook. 2005. Jakarta. Available at: http://www.aseansec.org/18175.htm
Ba, Alice D. 2003. "China and ASEAN," *Asian Survey*, 43.4 (July/August): 622–647.
Barboza, David. 2006. "China Drafts Law to Empower Unions and End Labor Abuse," *New York Times* (October 13, 2006): A1, C6.
Bell, Martin and Michael Albu. 1999. "Knowledge Systems and Technological Dynamism in Industrial Clusters in Developing Countries," *World Development*, 27(9): 1715–1734.
Bernard, Mitchell and John Ravenhill. 1995. "Beyond Product Cycles and Flying Geese: Regionalization, Hierarchy, and the Industrialization of East Asia," *World Politics*, 47 (January): 171–209.
Borrus, Michael, Ernst, D., and Haggard, S. (eds). 2000. *International Production Networks in Asia*, London: Routledge.
Bradsher, Keith. 2006. "A Younger India is Flexing Its Industrial Brawn," *New York Times* (September 1): A1, C5.
Brooks, Stephen G. 2005. *Producing Security*, Princeton: Princeton University Press.
Browne, Andrew. 2006. "China's Reserves Near Milestone, Underscoring Its Financial Clout," *The Wall Street Journal* (October 17): A1.
Chen, Yun-Chung. 2006. "Changing the Shanghai Innovation Systems: The Role of Multinational Corporations' R&D Centres," *Science, Technology and Society*, 11(1): 67–107.
Cheng, Joseph Y.S. 2001. "Sino-ASEAN Relations in the Early Twenty-first Century," *Contemporary Southeast Asia*, 23.3 (December): 420–451.
Cisco Systems. 2006. http://newsroom.cisco.com/dlls/global/asiapac/

Cumings, Bruce. 1984. "The Origins and Development of the Northeast Asia Political Economy: Industrial Sectors, Product Cycles, and Political Consequences," *International Organization*, 38(1): 1–40.

Dean, Jason. 2006. "China Tech Firms Gain Ground," *The Wall Street Journal* (December 1): B2.

Dicken, Peter. 2003. *Global Shift*, New York: Guilford.

Dowling, Malcolm and Chia Tien Cheang. 2000. "Shifting Comparative Advantage in Asia: New Tests of the 'Flying Geese' Model," *Journal of Asian Economics*, 11: 443–463.

Dunning, John. (ed.) 1997a. "Globalization, Technological Change and the Spatial Organization of Economic Activity," *Alliance Capitalism and Global Business*, London: Routledge, 180–206.

Dunning, John. (ed.) 1997b. "What's Wrong – and Right – with Trade Theory?" *Alliance Capitalism and Global Business*, London: Routledge, 119–145.

Encarnation, Dennis. (ed.) 1999. *Japanese Multinationals in Asia*, Oxford: Oxford University Press.

Ernst, Dieter. 2003. "Global Production Networks and Industrial Upgrading – A Knowledge-centered Approach," in Gary Gereffi, (ed.) *Who Gets Ahead in the Global Economy?* Baltimore: Johns Hopkins University Press.

Fuller, Thomas. 2006. "Southeast Asia Group Seeks to Accelerate a Trade Zone," *New York Times* (August 23): C4.

Gallagher, Mary Elizabeth. 2005. *Contagious Capitalism: Globalization and the Politics of Labor in China*, Princeton: Princeton University Press.

Gaulier, Guillaume *et al.* 2005. "China's Integration in East Asia: Production Sharing, FDI and High-Tech Trade," CEPII, Working Paper No 2005–09 (June).

Ginzberg, Andrea and Annamarie Simonazzi. 2005. "Patterns of Industrialization and the Flying Geese Model: The Case of Electronics in East Asia," *Journal of Asian Economics*, 15, 1051–1078.

Goodman, Peter S. 2005. "China Ventures Southward: In Search of Cheaper Labor, Firms Invest in Vietnam," *Washington Post*, (December 6): D1.

Hatch, Walter and Kozo Yamamura. 1996. *Asia in Japan's Embrace*, Cambridge: Cambridge University Press.

Huang, Yasheng. 2005. *Selling China: Foreign Direct Investment During the Reform Era* , Cambridge: Cambridge University Press.

Humphrey, John and Hubert Schmitz. 2002. "How Does Insertion in Global Value Chains Affect Upgrading in Industrial Clusters?" *Regional Studies*, 36(9): 1017–1027.

International Finance Corporation, *Doing Business Database*. http://www.doingbusiness.org/ExploreEconomies/Default.aspx?economyid=202.

Jenkins, Rhys. 2004. "Vietnam in the Global Economy: Trade, Employment and Poverty," *Journal of International Development*, 16: 13–28.

Kahn, Joseph. 2006. "China Makes Commitment to Social Harmony," *New York Times* (October 12): A14.

Keller, William and Richard Samuels. 2003. *Crisis and Innovation in Asian Technology*, Cambridge: Cambridge University Press.

Kojima, Kiyoshi. 2000. "The 'Flying Geese' Model of Asian Economic Development: Origin, Theoretical Extensions, and Regional Policy Implications," *Journal of Asian Economics*, 11, 375–401.

Lall, Sanjaya and Shujiro Urata. (eds.) 2003.*Competitiveness, FDI and Technological Activity in East Asia*, Cheltenham: Edward Elgar.

Lardy, Nicholas R. 2001. *Integrating China into the Global Economy*, Washington: Brookings Institution Press.

Lardy, Nicholas R. 2002. "The Economic Future of China," speech at the Asia Society (April 29). available at http://www.asiasociety.org/speeches/lardy.html

Lee, Don. 2006. "Manufacturers Taking Flight – to Vietnam: The country is luring companies with generous incentives and lower costs than China," *Los Angeles Times* (August 18): A1.

Luong, Hy V. 2006. "Vietnam in 2005," *Asian Survey*, 46.1 (January–February): 148–154.

Luthje, Boy. 2004. "Global Production Networks and Industrial Upgrading in China: The Case of Electronics Contract Manufacturing," East-West Center Working Papers, No. 74.

Mytelka, Lynn. 2000."Local Systems of Innovation in a Globalized World Economy," *Industry and Innovation*, 71 (June): 15–32.

Nadvi, Khalid, John T. Thoburn, Bui Tat Thang, Nguyen Thi Thanha, Nguyen Thi Hoa, Dao Hong Le, and Enrique Blanco De Armas. 2004. "Vietnam in the Global Garment and Textile Value Chain: Impacts on Firms and Workers," *Journal of International Development*, 16: 111–123.

Naughton, Barry (ed.) 1997. *The China Circle: Economics and Electronics in the PRC, Taiwan, and Hong Kong*, Washington: Brookings.

Nolan, Peter. 2001. *China and the Global Business Revolution*, New York: Palgrave.

OECD Observer. 2003. (September).

Ong, Eng Chuan. 2003. "Anchor East Asian Free Trade in ASEAN," *The Washington Quarterly*, 26.2 (Spring): 57–72.

Ozawa, Terutomo. 2003. "Pax American-led Macro-clustering and Flying-geese-style catch-up in East Asia: Mechanisms of Regionalized Endogenous Growth," *Journal of Asian Economics*, 13: 699–713.

Painter, Martin. 2003. "The Politics of Economic Restructuring in Vietnam: The Case of State-owned Enterprise 'Reform,' " *Contemporary Southeast Asia*, 25.1 (April): 20–43.

Park, Donghuan. 2005. "The ASEAN-China Free Trade Area: A Critical Assessment," paper presented at the 30th Annual Conference of the Federation of ASEAN Economic Association, Manila (November 24–25).

Porter, Michael. 1990. *The Competitive Advantage of Nations* , New York: Free Press.

Prencipe, Andrea, Davies, A., and Hobday, M. (eds.). 2003. *The Business of Systems Integration*, Oxford: Oxford University Press.

Ravenhill, John. 2006. "Is China an Economic Threat to Southeast Asia?" *Asian Survey*, 46(5): 653–674.

Saxenian, AnnaLee. 2006. *The New Argonauts* , Cambridge: Harvard University Press.

Song, Tan Kim and Khor Hoe Ee. 2005. "China's Changing economic Structures and Its Implications for Regional Patterns of Trade Production and Integration," paper presented at the 30th annual conference of the Federation of ASEAN Economic Associations (November 24–25).

Spar, Debora. 1998. *Attracting High Technology Investment: Intel's Costa Rican Plant*, Washington: World Bank, 1998.

Stuart-Fox, Martin. 2004. "Southeast Asia and China," *Contemporary Southeast Asia*, 26(1): 116–139.

Tongzon, J. 2005. "ASEAN-China Free Trade Area: A Bane or Boon for ASEAN Countries?" *World Economy* 28(2): 191–210.

UNCTAD. 2005. *World Investment Report: Transnational Corporations and the Internationalization of R&D*. New York: United Nations Publications.

UNCTAD. 2006a. China Fact Sheet, 2006. http://www.unctad.org/wir

UNCTAD. 2006b. *World Investment Report. 2006.* Vietnam Country Fact Sheet.

Wei-Yen, Denis Hew. 2005. *Roadmap to an ASEAN Economic Community*, Singapore: ISEAS Press.

Wong, John and Sarah Chan. 2003. "China-ASEAN Free Trade Agreement," *Asian Survey*, 43.3 (May/June): 507–526.

Yam, Tan Kong. 1997. "China and ASEAN: Competitive Industrialization through Foreign Direct Investment," in Barry Naughton (ed.) *The China Circle: Economics and Electronics in the PRC, Taiwan, and Hong Kong*, Washington: Brookings, 111–135.

Wei, Zheng Kit and Ong Jia Wern. 2005. "China's Rise as a Manufacturing Powerhouse: Implications for Asia," paper presented at the 30th Annual Conference of the Federation of ASEAN Economic Associations (November 24–25).

World Bank and International Finance Corporation. 2006. *Doing Business 2006*, Washington DC.

Zhou, Ping and Loet Leydesdorff. 2006. "The Emergence of China as a Leading Nation in Science," *Research Policy*, 35: 83–104.

Zweig, David. 2002. Internationalizing China: Domestic Interests and Global Linkages, Ithaca: Cornell University Press.

9

Paths to Globalization: The Korean *Chaebol* and Chinese State-owned Enterprises

James P. Johnson

For thousands of years, China and Korea have coexisted as neighbors. At times, Chinese influence was very strong, allowing Chinese concepts and philosophies to permeate the Korean peninsula – at least among the educated elite. At other times, especially during periods of turmoil, Korean dynasties shunned contact with China, earning Korea the sobriquet of "the Hermit Kingdom." But in the mid-20th century, China and Korea found themselves in similar circumstances: both had experienced a brutal occupation by Japan followed by internal strife and were left destitute; radical Communists had taken control of mainland China and half of Korea; and for the governments of both China and South Korea, the major challenge was how to feed their people and restore their economy. Over the next 50 years, these two neighbors followed separate paths of development but by 2005 China, with a population of 1.2 billion, had become in purchasing power parity (PPP) terms the world's second largest economy behind the United States, while South Korea, with a population of 48 million, ranked 13th, on par with Mexico, Canada, and Spain. Two principal features of the current economic structure of South Korea and China are their heavy dependence on international trade and preferential treatment afforded certain domestic firms, especially in the earlier stages of economic development. In 2001 the value of South Korea's merchandise exports was equivalent to 37.7 percent of GDP, compared with 10 percent of GDP in the early 1970s (Economist 2006a); in China, it was 23 percent in 2001, but growing fast to 35.8 percent in 2004,[1] mainly as a result of China's entry into the World Trade Organization in 2001. In South Korea, business conglomerates (*chaebol*) helped to drive economic development, while state-owned enterprises (SOEs) in China have had a special place in that country's economy.

What is of special interest to business theorists is how these two neighbors succeeded in developing their economies, what similarities and differences explain their growth trajectories, and what challenges they face as they strive to maintain or improve their ranking among the world's major economies. To answer these questions, we examine the cultural underpinnings of their economies and the political context of their economic development, within the theoretical framework of resource-based theory and institutional theory. The chapter is structured as follows: first, we examine the cultural similarities and differences between China and South Korea; we then trace the economic development of each country over the past 50 years; then, using resource-based theory and institutional theory we discuss the growth and development of Korean *chaebol* and Chinese SOEs that have emerged onto the global stage. We conclude by examining the challenges that face these firms in the early part of the 21st century.

The cultural roots of economic structure

Religion is at the core of much of a nation's cultural values, and China and South Korea have shared similar religious-based values for over a thousand years. It is difficult to categorize religious beliefs in China since, under the Communist system, organized religious worship was discouraged. Buddhist practices are still widespread, as is Islam in the western provinces, but the philosophies that underpin Chinese culture are Confucianism and Taoism, both of which are not religions per se but guides to living a moral life. Many Chinese also have a belief in the spiritual world, but their religious belief does not include the concept of a single deity. As in much of eastern Asia, there is no strong pressure to adhere to a single religious belief, so individuals are free to select from a variety of beliefs and teachings. In addition, there are ancient folk religions that include ancestor worship, shamanism, and the veneration of local deities, often associated with mountains or forests; astrology and *feng shui* are also common practices.

The Koreans adopted many Chinese beliefs; the authoritarian, male-dominated teaching of Confucius is reflected in the paternalistic and male-dominated Korean culture, as is the country's emphasis on education and respect for ancestors. Confucian teaching continues to shape contemporary South Korean society and it is evident in the nation's moral code and its legal system, as well as in interpersonal relationships and communication patterns. For example, the rules of decorum demand formality in speech and behavior when dealing with nonfamily members, if only to show respect for other people and thus make for better social relations. Hard work, obedience to elders, protection of the family, and correct behavior among family members are very much Korean values. In business contacts, personal relationships are extremely important and Koreans depend on their network of informal contacts – *in-mak*, a network of relationships that stem from connections with family, school, university, military service, and work. Korean Buddhism, however, followed its own path and is characterized by an emphasis on the similarities rather than the differences among Buddhist schools and among other religions (Cho, 1998). A unique feature of Buddhist temples in Korea is a side chapel dedicated to a mountain spirit, usually depicted as an old man with a pet tiger. It is a symbol of native shamanistic beliefs and has no connection with the original teachings of Buddhism.

Figure 9.1 Flag of the Republic of Korea

Also, a fundamental Korean ideal is a sense of harmony and balance in everything, and nowhere is this better represented than in the flag of South Korea (Figure 9.1).

The central circle is divided into two. The red part at the top is *yang*, the positive force that represents fire, day, light, and all things constructive. The blue part at the bottom represents the passive side of the cosmos – water, night, death, and rest. The two are joined perfectly into a whole. The bars in the four corners of the flag also represent harmony and balance. The three unbroken bars at the top left mean "heaven." The broken bars diametrically opposite it are "earth." The bars at the top right, two broken and one solid, mean "water" while those in the bottom left mean "fire." According to this belief, the universe is balanced in this way (Hidden Korea, 2006).

When we examine Hofstede's (1980) dimensions of culture, we see that China and South Korea differ significantly on four of the five values (Figure 9.2). China scores higher on power distance, masculinity, and long-term orientation, and South Korea scores higher on uncertainty avoidance.

At first glance, it may seem surprising that South Korea differs so much from its neighbor. However, South Korea's cultural profile is different from that of all other Asian countries but is similar to that of Latin American countries. The explanation could be in the high percentage of Koreans that are Christian and that, over time, Christian values have influenced residual Asian values. In the 20th century, Christian missionaries were very active in South Korea, especially after the Korean War, and Christians are now estimated to comprise about 50 percent of the population (World Press, 2006).

Both China and South Korea score low on individualism, reflecting their Confucian roots. In both countries, particularism – a focus on the interests of one's own group – is an important cultural value that has developed from Confucian principles; in the business world, personal relationships form the basis for doing business. In China, one must develop *guanxi*, a network of relationships that provide reciprocal favors; in Korea, it is *in-mak*. However, there is a misunderstanding in the West about the nature of *guanxi* in China.

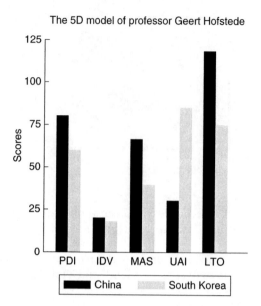

The 5D model of professor Geert Hofstede

Figure 9.2 Comparison of cultural values

In the 1980s and much of the 1990s, the influence of the Chinese government in business was pervasive. There were numerous procedures and regulations that managers had to comply with and, in order to cut the bureaucratic red tape, many Chinese tapped into their *guanxi* to find ways to shortcuts around the bureaucracy. This *guanxi xue* often overstepped legal boundaries and brought the notion of *guanxi* into disrepute among foreigners, who frequently perceived it as a form of corruption. As government influence over business declined in the late 1990s, *guanxi xue* became less of an issue in China, except in SOEs – an issue that we will discuss further below. In the following sections, we trace the economic development of South Korea and China in the late 20th century and examine the emergence of *chaebol* in South Korea and SOEs in China.

Economic expansion: South Korea

At the close of the Korean War in 1953, South Korea's economy was devastated. The 1950s were years of economic hardship and political corruption but, in 1961, a military coup brought General Park Chung-Hee to power. South Korea then experienced almost 20 years of rapid industrialization under the harsh, autocratic rule of President Park until his assassination in 1979. Park's government encouraged private enterprise and, by providing incentives to export a wide range of goods, the economy blossomed. Incentives included preferential treatment in obtaining low-interest bank loans from state-owned banks, import privileges, permission to borrow from foreign sources, and tax benefits. Some of the businesses that benefited from these incentives later became *chaebol* – family-owned business conglomerates with interrelated ownership and management (Library of Congress, 1990).

The *chaebol* played a crucial role in South Korea's economic development, and institutional theory (Oliver, 1991) provides an explanation for why conglomerates (a term that includes *chaebol* in Korea and *keiretsu* in Japan) can thrive in a developing economy. When national institutions are weak or lacking, conglomerates serve as their own intermediaries and are able to internalize transactions, thus reducing transaction costs. For example, when an efficient stock market is lacking, conglomerates can transfer funds from one subsidiary to another to provide capital funding; if the domestic legal system is inefficient or corrupt, the conglomerate's reputation can substitute for contracts; where the educational system is poor, conglomerates can select promising candidates and train them in-house or overseas. Two important differences exist between the *chaebol* and the Japanese *keiretsu*; first, the *chaebol* were not permitted to own private banks, and the Korean government could direct banks to allocate funds in those areas that it favored; second, *chaebol* were family-owned businesses that, even today, are largely controlled by their founding families (Economist, 2006a).

The combination of *chaebol* and preferential government loans, which continued through the 1980s and 1990s, meant that the *chaebol* could make almost risk-free investments in capital-intensive industries such as petrochemicals, steel, shipbuilding, cars, and semiconductors. At the same time, by forming joint ventures with foreign multinationals, the *chaebol* were able to acquire much-needed foreign product and process technology that allowed South Korea to develop its industrial economy in a very short period. Thus, by seeking and acquiring specialist resources, *chaebol* such as Samsung, Hyundai, and Daewoo, were developing internal resources and capabilities that were later to give them a competitive edge against global competitors. According to the resource-based view of the firm (Barney, 1991; Peteraf, 1993), a firm's unique resources and capabilities provide the basis for its strategy, which should allow the firm to best exploit its core competencies relative to opportunities in the external environment. Sustainable competitive advantage is achieved by continuously developing existing resources and creating new resources and capabilities in response to rapidly changing market conditions. This was what the *chaebol* strived to do during the 1980s and 1990s, first into assembly and light industries, then heavy industries and chemicals, then into more capital-intensive and technologically advanced sectors, and more recently into the service sector.

For example, let us trace the development of the Korean semiconductor industry. In the mid-1960s, US firms such as Fairchild and Motorola began to assemble transistors in Korea in order to take advantage of the country's low-cost labor and its openness to foreign investment; later, Japanese firms (Toshiba, Sanyo, NEC) formed joint ventures with Korean firms for the same purpose. In the mid-1970s, other Korean firms entered the market by operating simple assembly plants of semiconductor products, but fierce competition in the small domestic market enabled only a few firms to survive. By the end of the 1970s, Samsung and Lucky-Goldstar (later LG) had established firm positions in the semiconductor industry through mergers and acquisitions of both domestic firms and joint ventures that had gone out of business (Wang, 2002). At the same time, government-imposed trade barriers insulated these firms from foreign competition. Soon, the *chaebol* were investing heavily in production equipment and R&D; because of their diversified businesses, they could afford to sustain financial losses in the semiconductor business in the short to medium term, but at the same time they were further developing their internal resources. By the mid-1980s, they were moving up the value-added chain and manufacturing memory chips to their own design while other businesses in their *chaebol* were finding uses for semiconductor goods, expanding the reach of the *chaebol* into other sectors of the Korean economy. Samsung has now become the global number 2 in production of mobile phones and is developing a global reputation for quality and innovation in consumer electronics; LG, meanwhile, has become the global number 1 in television shipments, with Samsung at number 2 (DigitalTV DesignLine, 2006).

Export-led industrialization helped South Korea's GNP to grow over 8 percent per year, from US$2.3 billion in 1962 to US$204 billion in 1989; GNP per capita annual income grew from US$87 in 1962 to US$4830 in 1989 (Library of Congress, 2006). By 1990, South Korea was among the "Asian Tigers" whose economic growth astounded the rest of the world. The *chaebol* were now financially independent and secure, thereby eliminating the need for further government-sponsored credit and assistance and in the 1990s they also began to produce for a growing domestic market. Once an isolated nation of farmers, South Korea is now a nation with the world's highest rate of Internet access, a global leader in semiconductor production, and a global innovator in consumer electronics (Library of Congress, 2006).

Economic expansion: China

When the Chinese Communist Party (CCP) came to power in 1949, its primary aims were to restore centralized control and establish China's economic and political independence. However, Mao Zedong did not want China to be beholden to the Soviet Union and insisted on seeking a separate, uniquely Chinese way of resolving social and political problems. What resulted were disastrous experiments such as the Great Leap Forward, designed to propel China's industrialization, and the Cultural Revolution, which delayed China's economic progress by a generation. While 1950–1979 was generally a time of economic expansion among the capitalist nations, it was a period of economic stagnation for China. By 1978, Chinese living standards were far below those of most other Asian countries and, because of the inefficient command economy and the "iron rice bowl" policy, the average Chinese firm had 11 times more workers than in Japan (Foy and Madison, 1999).

That year, Deng Xiaoping initiated an economic reform program designed to help modernize the nation's economy. Similar to the short-lived "socialism with a human face" introduced in Czechoslovakia in 1968, these reforms were dubbed "socialism with Chinese characteristics"; they included the establishment of township–village enterprises (TVEs), agricultural reforms that allowed farmers to sell surplus crops for cash, the establishment of four "special economic zones" in the coastal regions to attract foreign investment, and the reallocation of state resources away from the military and inefficient sectors of heavy industry and toward more efficient sectors of the Chinese economy (Morrison, 2006). These reforms paved the way for China's rapid economic growth over the next 28 years, and initially China's SOEs were to be the engines of the new economic policy.

SOEs had been the foundation of China's industrial economy under the CCP from 1950 to 1978, since they conformed to the Marxist dictum of concentrating the factors of production in the hands of the people. Furthermore, the strict social and political hierarchy introduced by the CCP conformed to Confucian norms: the party assumed the role of the head of the household, to whom the people owed loyalty and obedience; in return, the party would take care of their needs and direct their daily life. By 1978, nearly three-quarters of China's industrial production was produced by SOEs, operating according to centrally planned output targets. Private enterprises and foreign-invested firms were almost nonexistent (Morrison, 2006). A major result of the reforms was a decrease in state control of the economy: the contribution of SOEs to China's industrial output dropped from 77.6 percent in 1978 to 28.5 percent in 1999, while privately owned industry increased from almost zero to 33 percent (Table 9.1). From 1979 to 2005 China's real GDP grew at an average annual rate of 9.7 percent (Morrison, 2006); however, cooperative TVEs in labor-intensive industries and foreign invested companies (FIEs), not SOEs, were the main drivers of China's economic growth (Baek, 2005). They were generally perceived to be cumbersome, inflexible, inefficient, and overmanned, and the Chinese government recognized the need for reform of the SOEs (Xinhua, 2003).

Table 9.1 Composition of national industrial output (percent)

Ownership	1978	1985	1990	1999
SOE	77.6	65	54.6	28.5
Collective	22.2	32	35.6	38.5
Private	0.2	3	9.8	33

Source: Statistical Yearbook of China; China Economic Information Network (www.cei.gov.cn).

Table 9.2   China's merchandise world trade, 1979–2005 (in billions of dollars)

Year	Exports	Imports	Trade balance
1979	13.7	15.7	−2.0
1980	18.1	19.5	−1.4
1985	27.3	42.5	−15.3
1990	62.9	53.9	9.0
1995	148.8	132.1	16.7
2000	249.2	225.1	24.1
2001	266.2	243.6	22.6
2002	325.6	295.2	30.4
2003	438.4	412.8	25.6
2004	593.4	561.4	32.0
2005	762.0	660.1	101.9

Source: International Monetary Fund, *Direction of Trade Statistics*, and official Chinese statistics.

During the late 1990s and early 2000s, China's economy experienced rapid export-led growth of between 8 percent and 12 percent per year (Table 9.2). China's SOE reforms had also made some progress: by 2002, more than half of China's 159,000 SOEs had launched their enterprise reforms, with some enterprises suffering long-term losses and in heavy debt, and some going out of business. However, that year, 11 Chinese SOEs entered the Global Top 500 list in 2002 (Xinhua, 2003).

In 2005, China became the second largest economy in the world after the United States when measured on a PPP basis, and the Chinese government now has a goal of quadrupling GDP by 2020 and more than doubling the per capita GDP (Library of Congress, 2006). The presence of state-owned multinational giants from China is now a hot topic in the business press. Just as for the Korean *chaebol*, the success of these firms is due partly to institutional forces and partly to the need to acquire resources overseas – especially for companies in the energy sector. For example, the China National Offshore Oil Company (CNOOC), 70 percent state-owned, has expanded aggressively overseas in search of energy resources, mainly through alliances and joint venture partnerships, and in 2001 its shares were listed on the Hong Kong and New York stock exchanges, where it can better compete for investors' favors. By 2006, CNOOC had signed 172 petroleum contracts and agreements with 75 foreign oil companies from 21 countries and regions (CNOOC, 2006).

Chaebol and SOEs: the next stage

There is no doubt that South Korea and China have made impressive gains in economic performance in recent decades. However, both countries have reached a stage of development at which they must question the continued use of favored firms. In the case of South Korea, the Asian financial crisis of 1997–1998 was the catalyst for change. In 1995, the top 30 *chaebol* produced 16 percent of South Korea's GDP and accounted for 50 percent of exports; the top four groups at the time – Hyundai, Samsung, Daewoo, and LG – dominated the economy, producing 9 percent of GDP in 1995. With easy, cheap loans from complacent banks, the *chaebol* were swamped in debt, much of it short-term, when the Thai *baht* collapsed in July 1997. As exports to neighboring Asian countries dried up, these companies were unable to meet their financial obligations and South Korea's financial system began to break down. The government stepped in swiftly and decisively. Many of the banks were nationalized and restructured and then privatized. The banks were encouraged to lend to small and medium-sized firms, as well as to consumers, which stimulated domestic spending. As part of an agreement with the International Monetary Fund (IMF, 1999), the Korean government agreed, among other things, to oversee the restructuring of the top five *chaebol* and to privatize a number of state-owned firms. Subsequently, half of the top 30 *chaebol* in 1996, including Daewoo, went bankrupt and were broken up; the others divested many of their businesses to become more focused, restructured, and improved their financial position (Economist, 2006a).

As the institutional environment changed in South Korea and the globalization of markets continued apace, some *chaebol* recognized that the types of resources that they needed to be competitive in the future had shifted. They understood the need to shift away from a focus on low-cost manufacturing and borrowed technology to investments in greater value-added activities, such as design, brand building, and advertising. For example, Lucky Goldstar rebranded itself as LG, while Samsung Electronics ditched its lackluster subbrands, such as Plano, Tantus, and Yepp, in favor of a single master brand. At the same time, Samsung increased the number of its design staff in Seoul, opened design centers overseas to be closer to its global customers and to stimulate new ideas, flattened the corporate hierarchy by encouraging designers to pitch ideas directly to top executives, and focused on becoming the world leader in mobile phone handsets (*Business Week*, 2004). In 2004, Samsung won 33 design awards at top design contests in Europe, North America, and Asia. Today, Korean brands such as Samsung, Hyundai, and LG are developing global reputations for design, functionality, and quality.

But the restructuring of the *chaebol* is not yet over. The Korean government has announced its intention to introduce legislation to (1) make Korean firms more accountable to outside shareholders; (2) close tax loopholes that allow the avoidance of gift and inheritance taxes by the families that own the *chaebol*; (3) prevent industrial firms from owning financial subsidiaries that might invest in the firm's own shares (Economist, 2003). In April 2006, the powerful chairman of Hyundai was arrested on charges of embezzlement and breach of fiduciary trust, an act that signaled that the Korean government is serious in its bid to curb the excesses of the *chaebol*.

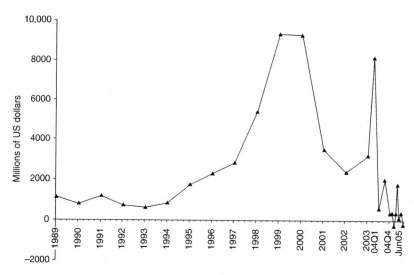

Figure 9.3   Inward FDI to South Korea
Source: Noland (2005).

There are also institutional barriers to structural reform that have a negative impact on South Korea's ability to attract much-needed foreign direct investment (FDI). First, the labor market in South Korea is very inflexible and labor relations are volatile, a situation that deters foreign investment and encourages Korean firms to set up operations overseas. Second, South Korea's legal system makes foreign executives criminally liable for a broader range of activities than in many other countries, which also deters FDI. Third, Noland (2005) reports that an overwhelming majority of Koreans evince a strong xenophobic streak and think that their culture should be protected against foreign influence – an attitude that, as Noland points out, could be a red flag for foreign investors. In fact, the initial flow of inward FDI that followed the post-1997 reforms was not sustained over subsequent years (Figure 9.3).

Finally, South Korea's educational system has been criticized for being too rigid, emphasizing rote learning instead of fostering the kind of creative thinking that can lead to product and process innovation in a knowledge-based economy. Without these reforms, it is unlikely that the success of a handful of Korean firms will be replicated.

In China, too, despite the impressive growth in its economy, there are still major obstacles to the reform of SOEs. According to Wu Jingliang (2000):

> Although the state sector produces only about one third of overall GDP, it is still the major user of scarce economic resources. Reform of state-owned enterprises (SOEs) has been far from satisfactory, and the old system maintains its influence and continues to impede the establishment and perfection of the new market economic system. Therefore, we cannot say that the

market has started to operate as the primary allocator of economic resources. For example, the state sector, although contributing to only one third of China's GDP, consumes two thirds of the country's capital resources.

Wu identifies the major obstacle as the unwillingness of CCP members to relinquish control of the economy, in the fear that doing so will result in the CCP losing political and social control of the country. Furthermore, SOEs put a heavy strain on China's economy since over half are believed to lose money and are supported by subsidies, mainly through loans from state banks (Morrison, 2006), which diverts scarce resources from potentially more efficient and profitable enterprises. Although committed to reducing trade barriers under the terms of its membership of the World Trade Organization, the Chinese government is reluctant to do so in many industries because the poor financial condition of many SOEs might result in widespread job losses, creating greater social and political pressures on China's leadership (Morrison, 2006).

Even where foreigners are invited to invest in Chinese firms, as in the public offering of the Industrial and Commercial Bank of China (ICBC), they must be wary because in the Chinese economy political considerations often come first, information is unreliable, and the banking system is still far from transparent (The Economist, 2006b). Although partnerships with SOEs may still offer foreign investors the quickest way to enter China, especially in industries with high barriers to entry, China must quickly modernize the SOEs in order to continue to attract FDI. As long as China's leaders continue to distrust market institutions, they will continue to support the existence of SOEs, especially in "pillar" industries related to energy, telecommunications, and national security.

On the surface, China's privately owned firms seem to be doing a better job of responding to the needs of the global market. Haier in domestic appliances, Lenovo in personal computers, Huawei in electronics, and Baosteel in heavy industry have all forged a global reputation in their respective industries. However, their success has been primarily in emerging markets or in manufacturing products for niche markets; they are not yet "world-class" companies and it is not evident that they are capable of competing head-to-head with bigger multinational rivals. In addition, it is not clear to what extent these firms are truly independent of the state since China's regulatory system is not transparent and state-controlled agencies are thought to be major shareholders of many privately held Chinese firms.

Conclusions

There seems to be a strong similarity between Korea's growth trajectory in the 1980s and 1990s and the trajectory that China seeks to follow today with its emphasis on a combination of SOEs in heavy engineering and consumer products. There is a danger that lack of regulatory control and too close a relationship between industry and government might lead to *chaebol*-type excesses in China's economy:

> Like the bosses of South Korea's *chaebol* before them, Chinese managers respond to regulatory inconsistency and opacity by pursuing short-term returns and excessive diversification rather than by investing in long-term technological development. Most are unwilling to develop "horizontal" networks with customers, suppliers and trade bodies – which in other countries establish technology standards and foster confidence in long-term research. In China, a company's best defense against corruption and the direct political linkages that benefit rivals is often to avoid business collaboration entirely and instead build vertical links up the Communist Party hierarchy and curry favor with local bureaucrats.
>
> (The Economist, 2005)

China's leaders today face a variety of challenges to the nation's future economic development. They have to maintain a high growth rate, deal effectively with the rural workforce, improve the financial system, continue to reform the SOEs, foster the productive private sector, promote better international cooperation, and change the role of the government in the economic system (LOC, 2006). However, instead of following the Korean model of incremental globalization and organic growth, Chinese firms need to leapfrog the incremental stages via the acquisition of the strategic resources that they will need in order to compete in the 21st century – skills in innovation, marketing, branding, distribution, human resources, etc. At the same time, Chinese firms need to use inward FDI to learn critical management skills from their foreign partners and to acquire key technologies – but they must do so within the confines of intellectual property protection regulations imposed by the World Trade Organization.

The role of academics and practitioners in this situation should be one of lobbying and persuasion to promote the changes that are long overdue – to convince their Chinese partners and Chinese officials of the need to follow through with the reforms that have already been approved but delayed.

Note

1. My own calculations from World Trade Organization data.

References

Baek, Seung-Wook (2005). "Does China Follow 'the East Asian Development Model'"? *Journal of Contemporary Asia*, 35 (4): 485–498.
Barney, J. B. (1991). "Firm resources and sustained competitive advantage". *Journal of Management*, 17: 99–120.

Business Week (2004). Samsung design. November 29. http://www.businessweek.com/magazine/content/04_48/b3910003.htm

Cho, Sungtaek (1998). "Buddhist philosophy, Korean". In E. Craig (ed.), *Routledge Encyclopedia of Philosophy*. London: Routledge. http://www.rep.routledge.com/article/G201SECT12

CNOOC (2006) China National Offshore Oil Company: Exploration and Production. http://www.cnooc.com.cn/yyww/gsjj/ywbk/228462.shtml. Accessed 17 October 2006.

DigitalTV DesignLine (2006). TTE tumbles from top TV spot as LG, Samsung surge ahead. September 26, Segundo, CA. http://www.digitaltvdesignline.com/news/showArticle.jhtml?articleID=193005663

Foy, Colm and Madison, Angus (1999). "China: A world economic leader". *OECD Observer*, 215 (January). http://www1.oecd.org/publications/observer/215/e-foy.htm

Hidden Korea (2006). *Hidden* Korea. PBS Online. http://www.pbs.org/hiddenkorea

Hofstede, Geert (1980). *Culture's Consequences*, Newbury Park, CA: Sage.

IMF (1999). Korea Letter of Intent and Memorandum of Economic Policies, November 24. http://www.imf.org/external/NP/LOI/1999/112499.HTM

Library of Congress (1990). *A Country Study: South Korea*. http://memory.loc.gov/frd/cs/krtoc.html

Library of Congress (2006). Country Profile: China. http://lcweb2.loc.gov/frd/cs/profiles/China.pdf

Morrison, Wayne M. (2006) "China's economic conditions". Federation of American Scientists, Congressional Research Services Brief No. RL33534. July 2006.

Noland, Marcus (2005). "Foreign investors are a progressive force". *Korea Times*, September 22. http://www.iie.com/publications/opeds/noland0905.pdf

Oliver, Christine (1991). "Strategic responses to institutional processes". *Academy of Management Review*, 16: 145–179.

Peteraf, Margaret A. (1993). "The cornerstones of competitive advantage: A resource-based view". *Strategic Management Journal*, 14: 179–191.

The Economist (2003). Unfinished business: Reform of the chaebol is only halfway there. Survey of South Korea, April 17. http://www.economist.com/surveys/displaystory.cfm?story_id=E1_TGJSSGS

The Economist (2005). China: Struggle of the champions. January 6. http://www.economist.com/business/displaystory.cfm?story_id=E1_PVPVRTR

The Economist (2006a). South Korea: Country Briefing. http://www.economist.com/countries/SouthKorea/profile.cfm

The Economist (2006b). China's biggest bank: A dragon stirs. October 12. http://www.economist.com/research/articlesBySubject/displayStory.cfm?subjectid=478048&story_id=8031185

Wang, Yunjong (2002). Investment liberalization success story: The case of Korea. New York: United Nations Online Network in Public Administration and Finance (UNPAN). http://unpan1.un.org/intradoc/groups/public/documents/APCITY/UNPAN014167.pdf

World Press (2006). *South Korea: Facts*. http://www.worldpress.org/profiles/Korea_south.cfm

Wu Jingliang (2000). China's economic reform: Past, present and future. *Perspectives*, 1 (5). www.oycf.org/perspectives/5_043000/china.htm

Xinhua (2003). "Measures to promote SOE reform." Xinhua News Agency November 20. http://www.china.org.cn/english/2003/Nov/80450.htm

10
Domestic Interfirm Networks and the Internationalization of Taiwanese SMEs

Thomas C. Lawton and Ku-Ho Lin

Introduction

In countries like Taiwan, small and medium enterprises (SMEs) have, for some time, collectively accounted for the majority of international trade activity. Taiwanese SMEs have displayed a high – and growing – propensity to internationalize. Since the early 1980s, more than one in four Taiwanese SMEs have been involved in international trade and 10 percent have established overseas productions or business units (SMEA, 2002). Many internationalized in conjunction with their domestic networking partners and tended to duplicate the existing network structure in the host markets (Chung, 1997). Such an approach to internationalization, based on extended domestic interfirm relationships, has become a major trend in the internationalization of Taiwanese SMEs.

Research into the effects of interfirm networks on the internationalization process focuses on partnerships with already internationalized firms or relationships with firms and subsidiaries in foreign markets. Less attention is given to the influence of domestic interfirm relationships in the context of internationalization processes. This chapter investigates this less explored theme and contributes to our understanding of the role that domestic interfirm networks play in the internationalization process of SMEs. We identify the determinants of domestic interfirm network utilization in the internationalization process of Taiwanese SMEs in the automobile, electronics, and textile industries. We argue that internationalizing through domestic interfirm networks is directly associated with firms' limited nonfinancial resources, perceived uncertainties and risks associated with internationalization, and dependence on home partners. The technology level of firms and deficiencies in local knowledge and experience do not have significant effects on firms' decisions to utilize domestic interfirm networks in the internationalization process.

Internationalization through an interfirm network

Networking has been a characteristic of Taiwanese SMEs in domestic operations. Such a characteristic can also be found in the internationalization of these firms (Chen, 1998; 2003). Personal relationships and family ties are regarded as a main feature of Taiwanese business. These traditional business networks are usually utilized to help the firms enter into foreign markets and get absorbed into local networks (Chen and Chen, 1998; Chen, 2003). However, these networks usually erode as the firm's internationalization activities increase. An important reason is that these relationships are unable to raise the capital required for increasing fixed investment and technological outlays (Ernst, 1997). Furthermore, such networks also tend to be location specific and hence are less useful as a means of expanding international activities (Chen and Chen, 1998).

Taiwanese SMEs in an interfirm network usually chose to internationalize with their existing partners in the same production networks and tend to duplicate the network structures developed at home in the host markets abroad (Chung, 1997; SMEA, 2001). Such "herd internationalization" (Tseng, 1995) has become a characteristic of the internationalization of Taiwanese SMEs. By internationalizing within the network, Taiwanese SMEs could enjoy several competitive advantages, including production costs, production efficiency, and flexibility, which would disappear if the firms sever themselves from the network (Lee, 2002). Furthermore, the SMEs also benefited from the logistical support, market information, and technological assistance provided by existing networks when the internationalization process first occurred (Chen, 1998).

Various network relationships have existed among Taiwanese SMEs. Among these interfirm networks, the Center-Satellite (C-S) systems have been found to be extremely successful in accelerating the internationalization of Taiwanese SMEs (Wu, 1996; Ernst, 1997; Wu, 2003). When a member firm has internationalized to an overseas market, it usually exerts a pressure on its C-S partners to follow suit and then move their networks offshore (Lee, 2002). Over half of the Taiwanese C-S systems have internationalized to overseas markets via such an approach.

The group-form internationalization of manufacturing SMEs usually has been explained in terms of the Japanese *Keiretsu* model (Johansson and Vahlne, 1990; Dunning, 1993). The model assumes that SMEs operate as dependent suppliers to large, established multinational corporations. Thus, internationalization of SMEs is driven completely by the larger firm. However, the Taiwanese C-S system is not entirely the same as the Japanese *Keiretsu*. The leading firms in the C-S systems usually do not possess such a strong dominant power as the Japanese *Keiretsu*; thus the affiliates in the systems possess more flexibility in participating in the international activities and the operations in both home and host markets (Luo and Yeh, 2001). In addition, the internationalization decisions of the C-S systems are usually made mutually by the affiliates (Tsai and Yu, 2000). When the center or larger firms intend to internationalize to other markets, they usually invite or suggest the affiliate firms go together as a means of sharing the internationalization costs and risks. Another important reason for the center firms to invite the affiliates to enter a foreign market together is to avoid the firm's specific techniques being acquired or learned by local firms (Gereffi and Pan, 1994). The majority of affiliates in the C-S system would follow the center or larger firm's movements and internationalize with the whole system (Lee, 2002).

The determinants of corporate internationalization decisions

A number of approaches have emerged to explain the determinants of SME internationalization. Traditionally, the internationalization models of SMEs explained the firm's internationalization decisions in terms of deficiencies in external resources (Chen, 1995; Crick and Spence, 2005) and internal resources (Ernst, 1997; Mentzer *et al.*, 2000), or the lack of international experience and knowledge (e.g., Madhok, 1997; Petersen and Pedersen, 1999; Zaheer *et al.*, 1999). However, each of these studies explains the firm's internationalization decisions through a specific perspective and tends to ignore other factors. All determinants should not be discussed separately, as they usually influence the firms' internationalization strategies in an interactive manner (Ahokangas, 1998). Our study incorporates the key factors addressed in the main internationalization models so as to present a more realistic and comprehensive overview of corporate internationalization decisions. Beginning with resources, we shall now treat the five key factors in succession.

(1) Resources
In the resource perspective it is pointed out that a firm's own internal resources and the external resources within the network determine the course of the firm's internationalization (Chen, 1995; Crick and Spence, 2005). SMEs have traditionally been considered weak contributors to internationalization due to financial and managerial constraints (Martinez and Jarillo, 1989; Oviatt and McDougall, 1999). As resource deficiency is a main characteristic of SMEs, we argue that internal resource constraints, including financial and nonfinancial aspects, can be one of the main determinants of a firm's decision to internationalize through its domestic interfirm networks. By internationalizing via its interfirm network, the firm can acquire the external resources that are controlled within the network and, which in turn, help the firm to reduce transaction costs in a new geographical market.

(2) Knowledge and experience
The role of domestic interfirm networks in local and international knowledge acquisition has been underaddressed in prior studies because the network members are usually deficient in international experience and knowledge. This study argues that domestic interfirm networks can be utilized as a vehicle for knowledge acquisition in host markets. By learning through interfirm networks, firms can reduce the perceived uncertainties of foreign markets without having to wait until their own market knowledge has reached

the required level (Forsgren, 2001). Sharma and Blomstermo (2003) argue that networks may influence the internationalization process of firms, as they can receive more, better, and earlier knowledge, compared to their competitors. The information benefits generated through participating in an interfirm network are specific and difficult to imitate for firms outside the network. While internationalizing with other network members, a firm can obtain local knowledge not only by learning on its own but also from its network partners. Such an approach may help the firm accumulate local knowledge more effectively than when it internationalizes alone.

(3) Environmental uncertainties and risks
Some commentators argue that a firm does not internationalize if the perceived risk is higher than a preconceived tolerable level (Forsgren, 2001). Prior studies have pointed out that interfirm networks could be an important way to help SMEs reduce the perceived uncertainties and risks of internationalization (Wuand Huang, 2002; Kirby and Kaiser, 2003). Lambe and Spekman (1997) argue that an uncertain market environment usually encourages foreign firms to form network partnerships in the market. Such relationships offer higher levels of coordination, greater stability, and enhanced flexibility to cope with the uncertainties of the environment.

(4) Technology level
Internationalization can be an essential means by which firms with advanced or proprietary technology can achieve the necessary sales volumes before the technology becomes obsolete or imitated by other firms. When facing a highly competitive environment in the overseas market, technological changes are usually uncontrollable for individual firms. Under this uncertainty, SMEs may utilize their domestic interfirm networks in order to obtain more advanced technologies, or to keep their existing technologies within their organization or network (Mentzer *et al.*, 2000).

(5) Degree of interdependence
Johnsen and Ford (2000) point out that the interdependence of relationships in business networks causes a firm to consider the impact and influences of external parties in the network when it designs and implements an internationalization strategy. The influence of the interfirm network in shaping a firm's internationalization process has been discussed previously (Johansson and Mattson, 1988). However, the effect of the nature and level of interfirm relationships (i.e., the degree of interdependence) on the firm's internationalization decisions has had little attention. The degree of interdependence has a critical role in affecting a firm's intentions when forming strategic partnerships to pursue internationalization (Mentzer *et al.*, 2000), as well as impacting the firm's profitability in the host market (Blankenburg-Holm *et al.*, 1996). We therefore propose that different levels of interdependence with domestic business partners will influence a firm's internationalization decisions.

Exploring the internationalization of Taiwan's SMEs

We focused our empirical research on three industrial sectors: automobiles, electronics, and textiles. In foreign direct investment activities in the Asian region, these three sectors have been the most prominent manufacturing sectors (UNCTAD, 1995). Taken together, they accounted for nearly 50 percent of world merchandise trade in 1994 and 60 percent of Asian exports (WTO, 1996). In Taiwan, electronics, textiles, and automobiles (including its related manufacturing sectors) have also been the top manufacturing sectors for international business, accounting for over 22 percent of the total amount of outward investment from 1952 to 2005 (Investment Commission, MOEA, 2004). Furthermore, annual export figures for the three sectors, taken together, account for almost 70 percent of the total export of Taiwan (Department of Statistics, MOEA, 2004).

We surveyed a sample of 1198 companies across the three sectors mentioned. The total number of valid replies was 191, making a response rate of 15.94 percent. In order to investigate the determinants using predictive powers, regression analysis is employed in this research (Field, 2000). A dichotomous categorical dependent variable is employed in this regression (i.e., to internationalize through the domestic interfirm networks versus other forms of internationalization). As such, binary logistic regression is an appropriate approach for this analysis (Field, 2000). Such an approach has been adopted by prior internationalization studies (Pan *et al.*, 1999). In this binary model, firms internationalizing through domestic interfirm networks (the C-S systems) are coded as "1" and the others are coded as "0."

The baseline model of the logistic regression can be written as follows:

$$P \text{ (internationalize through domestic interfirm networks} = 1) = 1/\{1+e^{-y}\}$$

where $y = f$ (ownership type, firm size, firm age, degree of dependence with business partners, home market factors, host market factors, organizational factors, internal competence factors, and internal constraint factors).

Several demographic variables and the other 22 possible influential factors obtained from the literature review are entered as explanatory variables in the regression model. In order to check if there are any possible problems of multicollinearity, a correlation analysis was conducted. Since the explanatory variables are ordinal level, Spearman's test is conducted for the correlation examination. The correlation matrix of the explanatory variables is presented in Appendix 1. The correlation matrix shows that several weak and moderate correlation relationships exist among several exploratory variables. None of the correlation coefficients in this test was greater than 0.50, while a correlation coefficient above 0.60 is considered rather high (Pallant, 2001). These weak or moderate correlations among the variables would not generate serious collinearity problems, indicating the results are not affected by these correlation relationships (Benito *et al.*, 1999).

This study defines a firm's degree of internationalization by using an indicator, i.e., the intensity of foreign sales to total sales (FSTS), or foreign revenue

Table 10.1 FSTS intensity of respondents

FSTS intensity	Total		C-S group		Non-C-S group	
	n	Percent	*n*	Percent	*n*	Percent
25% or less	42	22	12	14	30	28
26–50%	54	28	21	25	33	31
51–75%	58	30	32	38	26	25
76–100%	37	20	20	23	17	16
Total	191	100	85	100	106	100

to total revenue (FRTR), which is used commonly in previous studies (Hassel *et al.*, 2003). Of importance to this study is the average FSTS of the firms in the first 5 years of internationalization. Table 10.1 presents the FSTS intensities of the entire sample, as well as compares the distributions between the C-S and the non-C-S firms.

According to the result, the firm's FSTS intensities of the C-S and non-C-S groups show around 61 percent of the C-S firms had more than 50 percent FSTS intensities, which indicates these firms had over half of their revenue from overseas markets in their initial internationalization stage. The non-C-S group, on the other hand, had 40 percent of the firms in this category; 72 percent of the non-C-S group had more than 25 percent FSTS intensities. Both groups showed a high level of internationalization in the firm's initial stage, which indicates that the internationalization of Taiwanese firms was not only a switch of production bases, the firms also expanded their business in overseas markets.

In discussing the factors affecting decisions on approaches to internationalization, the literature suggests that the external and internal environments both contain motivations and constraints to the firm's internationalization. These factors, together, usually affect the firm's internationalization decisions (Ahokangas, 1998).

Earlier we considered whether financial and nonfinancial resources impacted on the decision to internationalize through the domestic inter-firm networks. We predicted that firms with reduced levels of resources (both financial and nonfinancial) would tend to internationalize with the domestic interfirm networks. The results showed that the shortages of financial resources tended to be less influential in the firm's choice of internationalizing through the domestic interfirm networks. The comparison between the two groups also showed no significant difference in their awareness of the level of financial constraints. The investigation concerning the influence of nonfinancial resource constraints, i.e., the general knowledge of international operations and cross-boundary management skills, showed a different result. Compared to the financial constraints, the internationalization decisions of both groups tended to be more influenced by their shortage levels in these nonfinancial resources. The statistical test results also showed a positive association between the nonfinancial resource shortages and the choice of internationalization with the domestic interfirm networks.

Therefore, the empirical results tend to support the argument that the deficiency of nonfinancial resources may result in different internationalization approach choices, but there was insufficient evidence to support the prediction in respect to the influence of financial shortages on the firm's choices of internationalization approach.

We also explored the influence of market knowledge and international experience on the firm's internationalization decisions. Knowledge and experience of international business are arguably beneficial to the firms' internationalization process. Pedersen and Shaver (2000) argue that firms will start to internationalize after accumulating enough knowledge and experience in the home market. The obtained knowledge and experience can reduce the ambiguity and complexity when pursuing foreign markets (Zaheer, 2002). By combining the view of the stages model and network model, the study assumed that a higher deficiency in local and international market knowledge is a determinant when deciding to internationalize through domestic interfirm networks.

Our results further confirmed that shortages of knowledge and experience are the main internal constraints for both the C-S and non-C-S groups in influencing their internationalization decisions. The results also showed that the C-S group was more affected by these shortages. However, the results lacked sufficient evidence to show that knowledge and experience deficiency is a significant determinant leading the firms to choose different internationalization approaches.

We examined how firms' perceptions of the risks and uncertainties of internationalization affected their internationalization decisions. More specifically, this study hypothesized that firms with an increased awareness of the environmental uncertainties and risks of the host markets would tend to internationalize through domestic interfirm networks. High levels of uncertainty about host markets encourage firms to embed themselves in network partnerships, which may offer higher levels of coordination, greater stability, and also flexibility to cope with the uncertainties of the environment (Lambe and Spekman, 1997). Our empirical survey showed that the C-S group on average perceived higher levels of uncertainty and risk toward internationalization. It was also a determinant for the firms to internationalize through domestic interfirm networks. The result implied that cooperating with other firms might be an approach to managing internationalization risks and uncertainties. Higher perceived risks and uncertainties may result in the firms internationalizing through domestic interfirm networks.

In addition, we tested the relationship between the firm's technology level and its intention to pursue internationalization through domestic interfirm networks. Lacking technical capability is one of the greatest obstacles to SME internationalization. The firms with significant technical advantages are more likely to be able to internationalize independently (Brush and Vanderwerf, 1992). Therefore, we argued that firms with lower technology levels are more likely to adopt a cooperative approach with their interfirm networks in internationalizing. The results of statistical tests showed no significant evidence to support the proposition. The technology level showed a similar influence on both groups; it is also not a significant factor in determining the firms' internationalization approaches. Although it is pointed out that interfirm networks can be utilized by the firms in their internationalization process in order to obtain more advanced technologies, or to keep their existing technologies within their organizations (Mentzer *et al.*, 2000), these functions were not evident in this study.

Finally, we examined whether the firm's degree of interdependence will affect its internationalization approach. A firm's degree of dependence on its main business partners in the home market has a critical influence on a firm's intention to form partnerships in its internationalization process (Mentzer *et al.*, 2000). This study thus assumed that the firms with higher degree of dependence on their main home partners would tend to internationalize through domestic interfirm networks. The results showed that the C-S group had a higher level of customer concentration than the other group in the domestic market, indicating that the C-S group possesses higher levels of dependence on their main partners. This study recognized that the dependence degree positively associated the firm's decisions to internationalize through the domestic interfirm networks. We used the degree of customer concentration (i.e., the percentage of a firm's annual sales from its top three customers in the domestic market) to indicate the interdependence of the firm with its domestic partners. Higher customer concentration translates as higher interdependence between firms.

Conclusion

This study confirmed that "acquiring nonfinancial external resources" and "reducing internationalization risks and uncertainties" were the determinants that caused firms to internationalize through domestic interfirm networks. High uncertainties about host markets encourage the firms to embed themselves in network partnerships, which may offer higher levels of coordination and greater stability and also flexibility to cope with the uncertainties of the environment (Lambe and Spekman, 1997). The survey result implies that cooperating with other firms can be an approach to managing internationalization risks and uncertainties. The higher the perceived risks and uncertainties, the more likely it is that firms will internationalize through domestic interfirm networks. In addition, strong dependency on business partners is also a significant factor in firms' internationalization decisions. The dependency within an interfirm network leads a company to internationalize together with its domestic partners in order to maintain interfirm relationships, reduce investment costs, and avoid competition in the initial stage. On the other hand, internationalization opportunities provided by the domestic partners is also an important reason for firms to internationalize through the networks. Previous work has illustrated that participating in an interfirm network benefits a firm's internationalization process in several ways, e.g., acquiring external resources (Coviello and Munro, 1997), acquiring local knowledge (Gulati, 1999), and obtaining more advanced technologies (Mentzer *et al.*, 2000). We found no significant effect in respect to the firm's technology level and selection of internationalization approaches. Furthermore, internationalization knowledge and experience sharing, assumed by the network approach to be the main functions of interfirm networks, was not sufficiently evident in our findings. The results reflected the fact that most Taiwanese SMEs internationalized in an unprepared manner (SMEA, 1999). These firms usually did not obtain sufficient local knowledge (social, economic, cultural, regulatory, and so on) before they internationalized. Such an unprepared state may result from resource constraints, the unavailability of information channels, and insufficient time to prepare for internationalization.

A group approach to internationalization is common among Taiwanese SMEs. In this research, the overall results showed the positive effect of domestic interfirm networks on corporate internationalization. The study suggests that a firm and its environment should not be regarded as separate entities. SMEs may shape their corporate environment by interacting with other firms. Domestic interfirm networks also play a certain role in creating a bridge between SMEs and host market in terms of knowledge acquisition and the capturing of business opportunity. The competitive advantages generated within the networks – such as long-term cooperative relationships, lower investment costs, unsolicited contract demands, and technical integration – lead the firms to internationalize with their existing domestic partners. These alternative advantages may provide an explanation for the firm's internationalization together with domestic partners who do not possess international knowledge and experience. Based on the findings of our research, we suggest that the senior management teams of SMEs should not only focus on the firm's internal constraints to internationalization but also look to its network for resources and opportunities to internationalize. We further suggest that long-term relationships in domestic interfirm networks can increase the internationalization capabilities of SMEs.

Acknowledgments

An earlier version of this chapter was presented at the Academy of International Business annual meeting, Beijing, China, June 23–26, 2006. Our thanks to all our session participants and to the anonymous referees for comments received. Thomas Lawton would also like to thank Ms Vicky Nicholson for her administrative support in preparing the final version of this chapter.

Appendix 1 Correlation Matrix of the Explanatory Variables

	1	2	3	4	5	6	7	8	9	10	11	12	13	14	15	16	17	18	19	20	21	22	23	24	25	26
Ownership Type	1.000																									
Firm Size	.054	1.000																								
Firm Age	.137	.033	1.000																							
Interdependence	.085	.154*	-.031	1.000																						
Follow customer/partners	.083	.069	.040	.152*	1.000																					
Follow competitor's move	.051	.036	-.002	.063	.166*	1.000																				
Approach overseas markets	-.010	.045	.018	.178*	.152*	.187*	1.000																			
Taiwanese government's policy	-.095	-.024	-.053	.052	.130	-.103	-.010	1.000																		
Local government promotions	.029	-.004	-.074	.031	.134	.217**	.169**	.371**	1.000																	
Recession of home economy	-.150	.020	-.023	.116	-.177*	.249*	.238*	.131	.185**	1.000																
Saturation in home market	-.010	-.086	.084	.046	.065	.248*	.313**	.265**	.260**	.118	1.000															
Potential overseas markets	.068	.075	-.061	.026	.170	.254**	.218**	.028	.208	.123	.019	1.000														
Lower costs	-.079	-.066	-.040	-.003	-.049	.101	.301*	.020	.231**	.509*	.147*	.228*	1.000													
Better condition that Taiwan	.012	.020	.056	.009	.156	.248*	.030	.080	.315**	.297**	.229**	.230**	.408**	1.000												
To achieve globalisation	.121	.024	-.101	-.248*	-.011	.159*	.058	-.066	.207*	.010	.024	.387**	.261**	.296**	1.000											
To achieve economies of scale	-.047	.067	.054	-.011	.149	.098	.276**	.105	.299**	.242**	.267**	.325**	.208**	.244**	.350**	1.000										
Possess advanced technology	-.028	-.033	-.206	.145	.077	.030	.262**	.291**	.181*	.176	.311*	.109	.301**	.031	-.019	.235	1.000									
Limited non-financial resource	.085	.009	-.082	.088	.001	-.039	.253*	-.020	.053	.170	.126	.204**	.208**	-.085	.047	.317**	.157**	1.000								
Lack of knowledge	-.031	-.202	-.058	.077	-.059	-.040	.084	.050	-.005	.276*	.137	.101	.226*	-.080	.010	.252**	.273**	.482**	1.000							
Lack of international experience	.021	-.054	-.136	.065	.010	-.089	.165*	.090	.050	.195	.112	.107	.161	-.107	.067	.334**	.361*	.413**	.222	1.000						
Unavailability of channels	.053	-.045	.037	.051	.063	.012	.064	.017	-.055	.147	-.003	.134	.128	-.061	-.037	.193*	.193**	.232**	.466**	.438**	1.000					
Cultural distance as a barrier	-.090	.018	-.060	.196*	.063	-.055	.208*	.226	.183	.402	.227	.107	.297	.138	-.023	.350	.379	.382*	.418*	.464*	.508**	1.000				
Investment risks and uncertainties	-.009	-.104	-.142*	.207**	.008	-.131	.231*	.098	.083	.261**	.099	.012	.366*	.060	.021	.249	.406	.435	.473*	.408*	.380**	.427**	1.000			
Lack of financial resources	-.041	-.097	-.149	.068	-.081	-.110	.168*	.116	.069	.248**	.169	.006	.357**	.120	-.005	.347	.373	.379	.401	.453	.438	.510	.508**	1.000		
Difficulties in forming partnership	.053	-.147	.157	.132	.182*	-.094	.159*	.017	.023	.109	.092	.137	.203	-.023	-.039	.191	.231	.379**	.408**	.392**	.500**	.344*	.416	.465	1.000	
Guaranteed demands	.104	-.019	.085	.163	.127*	-.068	.309	-.081	-.123	.280**	.129	.121	.266	.017	.026	.059	.194**	.333**	.341	.378*	.370**	.466**	.452**	.428**	.429**	1.000

* Correlation is significant at the .05 level (2-tailed).
** Correlation is significant at the .01 level (2-tailed).

References

Ahokangas, P. (1998), "Internationalization and Resources," [www document], Vaasa University Digital Collection, available on: http://www.tritonia.fi/vanha/ov/acta64/acta64.html. (accessed May 12, 2004).

Benito, G.R., Pedersen, T., and Petersen, B. (1999), "Foreign operation methods and switching costs: Conceptual issues and possible effects," *Scandinavian Journal of Management*, 15: 213–229.

Blankenburg-Holm, D., Eriksson, K., and Johansson J. (1996), "Business network and cooperation in international business relationships," *Journal of International Business Studies*, 27(5): 1033–1054.

Brush, C.G. and Vanderwerf, A. (1992), "A comparison of methods and sources for obtaining estimates of new venture performance," *Journal of Business Venturing*, 7(2): 157–170.

Chen, H. and Chen, T.J. (1998), "Network linkages and location choice in foreign direct investment," *Journal of International Business Studies*, 29(3): 445–468.

Chen, T.J. (2003), "Network resources for internationalization: The case of Taiwan's electronics firms," *Journal of Management Studies*, 40(5): 1107–1130.

Chung, C. (1997), "Division of labor across the Taiwan strait: macro overview and analysis of the electronics industry," in B. Naughton (ed.), *The China Circle: Economics and Electronics in the PRC, Taiwan and Hong Kong*, Brookings Institution Press: Washington, DC, pp. 164–209.

Coviello, N.E. and Munro, H. (1997), "Network relationships and the internationalization process of small software firms," *International Business Review*, 6(4): 361–386.

Crick, D. and Spence, M. (2005), "The internationalization of high performing UK high-tech SMEs: A study of planned and unplanned strategies," *International Business Review*, 14: 167–185.

Department of Statistics, MOEA, Taiwan (2004), online database, available on: http://2k3dmz2.moea.gov.tw/gnweb/statistics/, (accessed October, 2004).

Dunning, J.H. (1993), *Multinational Enterprises and the Global Economy*, Essex, Addison-Wesley Publishers Ltd.

Ernst, D. (1997), "What permits David to defeat Goliath? The Taiwanese Model in the computer industry," International Business Economics Research Chapter Series, No. 3 Farkas, AJ, Aalborg University, Denmark.

Field, A. (2000), *Discovering Statistics using SPSS for Windows*, Sage, London.

Forsgren, M. (2001), "The concept of learning in the Uppsala internationalization process model: A critical review," *International Business Review*, 11(3): 257–277.

Gereffi, G. and Pan, M.L., (1994), "The globalisation of Taiwan's garment industry," in E. Bonachin (ed.), *Global Production: The Apparel Industry in the Pacific Rim*, Philadelphia, Temple University, pp. 126–146.

Gulati, R. (1999), "Network location and learning: the influence of network resources and firm capabilities on alliance formation," *Strategic Management Journal*, 20(5): 397–420.

Hassel, A., Hpner, M., Kurdelbusch, A., Rehder, B. and Zugehör, R. (2003), "Two dimensions of the internationalization of firms," *Journal of Management Studies*, 40(3): 701–719.

Investment Commission, MOEA, Taiwan (2004), *Report of the Outward Investments of ROC Enterprises*, Taipei, MOEA.

Johansson, J. and Mattson, L.G. (1988), "Internationalization in industrial systems – a network approach," in N. Hood and J.E. Vahlne (eds.), *Strategies in Global*

Competition, reproduced in P.J. Buckley and P.N. Ghauri (eds.) (1999), *The Internationalization of the Firm: A Reader*, Academic Press: London, pp. 287–314.

Johansson, J. and Vahlne, J.E. (1990), "The mechanism of internationalization," *International Marketing Review*, 7(4): 11–24.

Johnsen, R.E. and Ford, D. (2000), "Establishing an international network position: findings from an exploratory survey of UK textile suppliers," [www document], IMP 2000 Conference chapter, available on http://www.bath.ac.uk/imp/trackd.htm, (accessed June 02, 2004).

Kirby, D.A. and Kaiser, S. (2003), "Joint ventures as an internationalization strategy for SMEs," *Small Business Economics*, 21(3): 229–242.

Lambe, C.J. and Spekman, R.F. (1997), "Alliances, external technology acquisition, and discontinuous technological change," *Journal of Product Innovation Management*, 14(2): 102–116.

Lee, W.H. (2002), "Internationalization strategy of SMEs," in R.H. Lang *et al.*(eds.), *Business Strategy of Small and Medium sized Enterprises*, Taipei, National Open University Press, pp. 361–385.

Luo, J.D. and Yeh, K. (2001), "From family business to business family: A comparative analysis of production networks in Taiwan's garment and PC industries," *Hong Kong Journal of Sociology*, 3: 71–94.

Madhok, A. (1997), "Cost, value and foreign market entry mode: The transaction and the firm," *Strategic Management Journal*, 18: 39–61.

Martinez, J.I. and Jarillo, J.C. (1989), "The evolution of research on coordination mechanisms in multinational corporations," *Journal of International Business Studies*, 20(3): 489–514.

Mentzer, J.T., Min, S., and Zacharia, Z.G. (2000), "The nature of inter-firm partnering in supply chain management," *Journal of Retailing*, 76(4): 549–568.

Oviatt, B.M. and McDougall, P.P. (1999), "Accelerated internationalization: Why are new and small ventures internationalizing in greater numbers and with increasing speed?" in R. Wright (ed.), *Research in Global Strategic Management*, JAI Press, Stamford, CT.

Pallant, J. (2001), *SPSS Survival Manual*, Buckingham, Open University Press.

Pan, Y., Li, S., and Tse, D.S. (1999), "The impact of order and mode of market entry on profitability and market share," *Journal of International Business Studies*, 30(1): 81–104.

Pedersen, T. and Shaver, J.M. (2000), "Internationalization revisited: the big step hypothesis," Working Chapter Series, Department of International Economics and Management, Copenhagen Business School, available on: http://swoba.hhs.se/cbsint/abs/cbsint2000-005.htm, first viewed in May 2004.

Petersen, B. and Pedersen, T. (1999), "Fast and slow resource commitment to foreign markets: What causes the difference?" *Journal of International Management*, 5(2): 73–91.

Sharma, D. and Blomstermo, A. (2003), "The internationalization process of born globals: A network view," *International Business Review*, 12: 739–753.

Tsai, M.T and Yu, M.C. (2000), "Strategic alliances of Taiwanese firms in China: Case studies," in Y.W. Wu (ed.), *Case studies of the Internationalization of Taiwanese Firms*, Taipei, Hua-Tai Press Ltd., pp. 375–402.

Tseng, S. (1995), "Herd Behavior in Investment and Informational Cascades," Research project report, National Science Council, Taiwan (NSC 84-2415-H-008-002).

United Nations Committee on Trade and Development (UNCTAD) (1995), *World Investment Report*, Geneva, United Nations.

Wu, R.I. and Huang, C.C. (2002), "Entrepreneurship in Taiwan, turning point to restart," Research chapter of Entrepreneurship in Asia program, The Maureen and Mike Mansfield Foundation, available on http://www.mcpa.org/programs/program_pdfs/ent_taiwan.pdf, (accessed May 17, 2004).

Wu, U.M. (ed.) (2003), *Taiwanese Business Groups*, Taipei, National Open University Press.

Wu, W.I. (1996), "The internationalization process of SMEs: a comparison study of Taiwan, Japan and South Korea," *Management Journal of Fu-Zen University*, 5(2): 75–102.

Zaheer, S., Albert, S., and Zaheer, A. (1999), "Time scales and organizational theory," *Academy of Management Review*, 4: 725–741.

11
The Globalization of Northeast China's MNCs: A Study of the Electronics Industry

Jun Kurihara

Introduction

This chapter examines global strategies of the electronics multinational corporations (MNCs) in Northeast China and discusses policy implications for the region. First, it discusses that the region's electronics industry possesses completely different features compared with its counterparts located in other regions including Beijing, Shanghai, and Guangdong. Second, the chapter identifies global strategies for multilingual language IT-enabled services (ITES) in Dalian and region-wide revitalization of traditional state-owned enterprises (SOEs). Third, the chapter presents policy recommendations for Northeast China where the Chinese government places its emphasis on economic development in the globalization age.

No one would deny that the Chinese economy has achieved a marked progress since the beginning of its liberalization efforts in 1978. On December 12, 2005, however, everybody was surprised at the news released by the Paris-based Organization for Economic Cooperation and Development (OECD): "China Overtakes US as World's Leading Exporter of Information Technology Goods."[1] During the past quarter century, experts who have closely monitored China's rapid economic development in the information and communications technology (ICT) industry have come to understand that inward foreign direct investment (FDI) from Taiwan, Japan, and the United States has played a large role in China in producing and exporting their products. Recently, however, the picture of China's ICT industry has dramatically changed and become more complex. In addition to foreign companies that are doing businesses in China, Chinese ICT companies have become large enough to engage in cross-border merger and acquisition (M&A) deals including the TCL/Thomson case in November 2003 and the Lenovo/IBM case in December 2004. In other words, China's outward FDI, as well as inward FDI, has become of great importance when we think about China's future economic development with a "tail-wind" of the so-called "Going Global" government policy.[2] In this connection, experts were again impressed by the announcement made on September 6, 2006, by the Chinese government (the Ministry of Commerce (MOFCOM) and the National Bureau of Statistics of China (NBS)) that China's outward FDI for 2005 registered 12.3 billion US dollars by increasing 123 percent from the previous year.[3]

According to the annual report of the United Nations Conference on Trade and Development (UNCTAD), the level of China's outward FDI (flow base) has been growing dramatically, far exceeding that of India. The substantial increase in FDI has been triggered by China's insatiable hunger for energy and other national resources abroad. As for the stock base FDI, China is still far behind compared with Brazil and Russia, among the so-called four BRIC countries (Brazil, Russia, India, and China) (Table 11.1). Recent activities of China's MNCs, however, might change the entire picture of the world's FDI map before long. Mr Zhao Chuang, Deputy Director of MOFCOM's Department of Foreign Economic Cooperation, was reported to have said that the outstanding of China's outward FDI, about 50 billion US dollars at the end of 2005, will continue to increase by 6 to 7 billion US dollars. Like other economic activities in China, outward FDI also witness its regional and industrial divergence. Chinese MNCs located in five provinces (Zhejiang, Shandong, Fujian, Jiangsu, and Heilongjian) and Shanghai City account for 62.9 percent of the entire outward FDI for year 2005. Active M&As, according to MOFCOM, were tried by Chinese MNCs in industries such as (a) textile and apparel, (b) electronics, (c) information technology, and (d) natural resources.

Table 11.1   Outward FDI of major countries (billions of US dollars)

	2003	2004	2005	2000	2005
	Flow base			Stock base	
World	561.1	813.1	778.7	6,471.4	10,671.9
Developed economies	514.8	686.3	646.2	5,578.3	9,271.9
United States	129.4	222.4	−12.7	1,316.2	2,018.2
Japan	28.8	31.0	45.8	278.4	370.5
EU	286.1	334.9	554.8	3,050.1	5,475.0
Germany	6.2	1.9	45.6	541.9	967.3
France	53.1	57.0	115.7	445.1	853.2
United Kingdom	62.2	94.9	101.1	897.8	1,238.0
Developing economies	35.6	112.8	117.5	871.0	1,273.6
China	−.02	1.8	11.3	27.8	46.3
Hong Kong China	5.5	45.7	32.6	388.4	470.5
Taiwan province	5.7	7.1	6.0	66.7	97.3
Brazil	0.2	9.8	2.5	51.9	71.6
India	1.3	2.0	1.4	1.9	9.6
Russia	9.7	13.8	13.1	20.1	120.4

Source: UNCTAD (2006), pp. 299–306.

Northeast Chinese MNCs: An intra-China comparison

Having reviewed the aforementioned marked "rise" of Chinese MNCs, Western and Japanese experts are now concerned with Chinese MNCs in the future – (1) Is the "rise of Chinese MNCs" a threat to Western and Japanese MNCs?[4]; (2) What kind of competition and collaboration will emerge between Chinese MNCs and Western and Japanese MNCs? In order to shed light on these questions, this chapter examines several specified regions and industries. Several strategies taken by Chinese MNCs are well understood – (a) strategy for the establishment of distribution networks in host countries, (b) strategy to build production facilities for new markets, (c) strategy to secure resource development for material and energy, (d) strategies for technology acquisition and brand formation.[5] Strategies of (a), (b), and (d) are all associated with electronics companies, while the strategy of (c) is closely tied with MNCs in industries including oil refining and steel.[6] China's electronics MNCs, amidst intensified competition both in their domestic and overseas markets, are forced to brace themselves for sophistication in strategies especially for technology acquisition and brand formation.

Based upon in-depth interview surveys in Japan, China, and the United States, this chapter addresses prospective corporate strategies for electronics companies and policy implications in Northeast China. In early 2005, the author conducted an extensive survey of economic development strategies for Northeast China (Liaoning, Jilin, and Heilongjiang provinces) and reported the results and policy implications in March 2005.[7] The 2005 report, based on the survey, tells the following three things – (1) uneven economic development in China, (2) a lack of industrial agglomeration in Northeast China (especially in the electronics industry), and (3) the region's strengths.

First, any student of the Chinese economy would realize that a vast tract of the Chinese continent gives us a wide variety of features of economic activities among regions. For this reason, we are forced to face a difficulty that is indigenous to China. In order to get a clearer picture of the Chinese economy, we should narrow our focus while taking into account the possibility of comparing our focal point with the other parts of the Chinese economy. Accordingly, the chapter examines Northeast China's electronics industry with frequent reference to the other parts of China (the Beijing- and Tianjin-led Northern Coastal Region, the Yangzi Delta, and the Zhujiang Delta (Guangdong)).[8] Second, Northeast China's electronics industry has a relative weak position vis-à-vis other regions (Table 11.2). In other words, the region's electronics industry is very vulnerable to intra-China economic competition regarding industrial agglomeration.[9]

Northeast China's relatively weak position, however, does not necessarily provide a pessimistic view for the future. First, several research results suggest that Chinese MNCs located in the North Coastal Region and the Zhujian Delta find it difficult to implement viable strategies to compete with their Japanese and South Korean counterparts in terms of brand building as well

Table 11.2 Major characteristics of China's electronics industry (2004)

| | Number of companies | | Number of employees | | Major statistics of electronics industry | | | | | |
| | | | | | Sales (Yuan) | | Profit (Yuan) | | R&D personnel | |
	Number	percent	1,000	percent	Billions	Percent	Billions	Percent	Number	Percent
All China	2,385	100	1,600.1	100	1,334.4	100	56.3	4.2	121,918	100
By company size										
Large-sized	287	12.0	861.4	53.8	1,166.9	87.5	45.5	3.9	74,940	61.5
Medium-sized	554	23.2	444.0	27.7	122.9	9.2	9.2	7.5	25,366	20.8
Small-sized	1,544	64.7	294.7	18.4	44.6	3.3	1.6	3.6	21,612	17.7
By type of major equity holder										
SOEs	117	4.9	70.1	4.4	12.7	1.0	0.3	2.5	3,925	3.2
HK and TW	415	17.4	362.6	22.7	245.3	18.4	7.3	3.0	16,140	13.2
Foreign	530	22.2	629.4	39.3	794.8	59.6	37.5	4.7	33,498	27.5
By region										
Northeast	66	2.8	29.7	1.9	19.4	1.5	0.1	0.3	2,013	1.7
Lioaning	48	2.0	23.4	1.5	18.0	1.3	0.3	1.9	1,683	1.4
Jilin	8	0.3	4.9	0.3	1.0	0.1	(0.3)	n.m.	155	0.1
Heilongjiang	10	0.4	1.4	0.1	0.4	0.0	0.0	7.1	175	0.1
N. Coastal	454	19.0	152.1	9.5	221.7	16.6	15.8	7.1	18,174	14.9
Beijing	282	11.8	62.4	3.9	69.4	5.2	2.4	3.5	9,210	7.6
Tianjin	69	2.9	39.7	2.5	102.7	7.7	12.1	11.8	2,828	2.3
Hebei	23	1.0	10.5	0.7	2.4	0.2	0.1	4.1	282	0.2
Shandong	80	3.4	39.5	2.5	47.2	3.5	1.2	2.5	5,854	4.8
Yanzi Delta	848	35.6	518.2	32.4	500.4	37.5	17.6	3.5	32,506	26.7
Shanghai	160	6.7	116.6	7.3	233.3	17.5	5.9	2.5	8,094	6.6
Jiangsu	395	16.6	298.3	18.6	209.0	15.7	8.3	4.0	14,592	12.0
Zhejiang	293	12.3	103.4	6.5	58.1	4.4	3.3	5.7	9,820	8.1
Zhujian Delta	530	22.2	573.8	35.9	458.3	34.3	19.8	4.3	43,951	36.0
Others	487	20.4	326.3	20.4	134.5	10.1	3.0	2.3	25,274	20.7

Note: The percentage shown in the statistics of the profit denotes the profit/sales ratio.
Source: NBS. (2006) pp. 12–16, 30–45, 53–55, 65–75, 132–153, and 164.

as product quality and productivity. For example, Haier, the Qingdao-based largest electronics MNC in China, is now facing a dilemma of preponderance in the domestic marketplace and struggling in the overseas marketplace.[10] Some analysts, based upon the above Haier case, conclude that it would be unwise of Chinese MNCs to adopt "self-sufficient" brand strategies that had been adopted by their Japanese and South Korean counterparts.[11] In this vein, the 2004 Lenovo/IBM deal was a wise policy adopted by the Beijing-based Lenovo Group. To date, Lenovo, instead of building its own brand, has demonstrated its savvy strategy to save its financial and human resources without delay. This type of strategy, however, does not necessarily lead to success. The Huizhou-based 25-old TCL, the world's largest TV producer, bought ailing European TV makers (German Schneider in 2002, and French Thomson in 2003). The bold move, though much applauded at that time, has not yet made TCL's businesses profitable as of mid-2006 without achieving its dream of becoming a Chinese Sony or Samsung.[12]

In addition to brand building, quality control and productivity are still make Chinese MNCs fall behind their Japanese counterparts. A comparative study in productivity between Chinese and Japanese MNCs illustrates a huge difference in process technology and resultant differences in flexibility and productivity (Table 11.3).

Table 11.3 A comparison in production technology for air conditioner factories between Chinese and Japanese MNCs (2004)

Comparison	Chinese MNC (Haier), Qingdao	A Japanese MNC, Thailand
Production lines	Belt-conveyer type production	Cell production
Number of types produced	8	7 (expandable to 300)
Differentiation among production lines	No	Yes
Product quality examination	3 times	1 time after production
Production per line/day	1,657	1,672
Changeover in production	30 minutes	Less than 5 minutes
Employees per line	35	23
Production units per day	4,971	8,360
Production workers per day	210	230
Productivity: production units per worker	23.7	36.3

Source: Amano, T. (2005) p. 130.

Northeast China: strategies to turn weaknesses into strengths

Northeast China's electronics industry, compared with other major industrial clusters, has a lamentable level of industrial agglomeration. The chapter, however, provides us with a third finding – despite its weakness regarding industrial agglomeration, Northeast China has its own strengths: (1) a rapidly growing software industry, (2) its geographical vicinity (especially with respect to Japan and South Korea), and (3) the strength of traditional SOEs and the region's academic institutions.

Dalian: a Chinese "multilingual" Bangalore

First of all, China's software industry has mushroomed for the past 5 years, with an average annual growth rate of over 40 percent, and reached the level of its production of 390 billion yuan (48.8 billion US dollars) and its exports of 3.6 billion US dollars, a 28.2 percent increase from the previous year.[13] Though the leading areas in the industry are Beijing, Shenzhen, and Shanghai, Dalian has a comparably strong group of software-related institutions. And therefore Dalian, as a prospective site for IT outsourcing (ITO) and business process outsourcing (BPO), is now riveting the attention of Japanese MNCs.[14] According to the Liaoning province Government, however, the Japanese shares of FDI in terms of the value implemented and the number of establishments are not necessarily high compared with other foreign countries. The average figures for years 2001–2003 were 18.4 percent and 19.3 percent, respectively.[15] The comparable figures for predominant players – Hong Kong and South Korea combined – were 44.3 percent and 46.3 percent, respectively.[16] The figures for the United States during the same period were 10.9 percent and 13.0 percent, respectively.

Despite the smaller share of the entire FDI in Liaoning province, Japanese MNCs have an extremely important role in economic development of Northeast China. First, the Japanese shares of activity associated with exports and imports are extremely high among foreign companies. Japanese MNCs' shares of exports and imports for the year 2003 were 35.3 percent and 31.2 percent. The figures for Hong Kong-based companies were 4.2 percent and 0.7 percent. And the figures for South Korean companies were 14.7 percent and 5.8 percent. The figures for the US-based companies were relatively high – 10.7 percent and 15.4 percent. These figures have given us the following conclusions. First, Japanese MNCs, though their FDI value and the number of offices are relatively small, are operating in manufacturing activity closely associated with exports and imports. Second, Hong Kong-based and South Korean MNCs are engaged in economic activity closely related with the local economy including consumer-oriented businesses and distribution activity. Accordingly, the region's economic development will be closely related with future behavior of Japanese MNCs when the region wants to increase the values of exports and imports, and enhance the level of living standards by introducing an economically efficient management style in the region.[17]

A second role played by Japanese MNCs is to nurture tomorrow's Chinese MNCs in the software industry. It should be noted that Dalian, unlike India's Bangalore, tries to develop Japanese-speaking talents.[18] Therefore, Japanese MNCs, along with their US and South Korean counterparts, could help Dalian become a multinational software site that would give birth to Chinese MNCs. Currently, from the viewpoint of Japan's electronics MNCs, Northeast China is a region for industrial machine and software but not for sophisticated electronic components. Accordingly, the region is not necessarily a predominantly attractive region compared with the other Chinese regions or alternatively prospective footsteps outside Japan. Table 11.4 shows a regional distribution in China of factory establishments implemented by Japanese electronics-related companies for the immediately recent years during the author's survey in the 2005 report. Investment in the fields of optoelectronics and sophisticated electronic components has been concentrated in the Tianjin-centered Northern Coastal Region, the Yangzi Delta, and the Zhujiang Delta. Accordingly, Northeast China has been relatively neglected from the perspective of location strategies of Japanese electronic components companies.

Individual MNCs echo the geographical pattern given in Tables 11.5 and 11.6.

While Matsushita/Panasonic has a large number of establishments in the Yanzi Delta, the Northern Coastal Region, and the Zhujiang Delta, in Northeast China it has only four establishments, and all of them are located in Dalian; Mitsubishi Electric has only one establishment in Northeast China.

In sharp contrast to Northeast China being regarded as a prospectively second or third manufacturing site for Japanese electronics MNCs, neighboring regions including South Korea, Taiwan, and Thailand still present a highly attractive business environment.[19] Especially, Thailand attracts the attention of the majority of Japanese electronics MNCs. In this connection, a JETRO analyst made an intriguing comparative analysis between newly industrialized economies (NIES), ASEAN's four countries (ASEAN-4), and China based upon her own interview survey in 2004.[20] The analysis suggests that despite a rapid increase in FDI in recent years, Japanese accumulated FDI in China is relatively small – in the electronics industry as a whole, as at the end of 2002, the figures for NIES, ASEAN-4, and China were 714.4 billion yen, 982.3 billion yen, and 515.7 billion yen, respectively. In other words, the combined figures for NIES and ASEAN are over three times as large as that of China. Accordingly, Northeast China, as a prospective site for production is still at the risk of being overshadowed by regions outside China. This analyst further suggests in her study that Japanese MNCs are now expanding their production facilities in the Yangzi Delta and Zhujiang Delta regions on the ground that these regions are close to Chinese domestic markets and suitable for exploiting external effects of agglomeration that already exist in the region.[21]

166

Table 11.4 Japanese electronics MNCs: recent trends in geographical distribution in China (2004–2005)

Regions	Companies (product segments) (number)	Location
Northeast China	Super Solution Technologies (Software) (3)	Dalian, Liaoning
	Fuji Electric (Breakers) (6)	Dalian, Liaoning
	Mitsubishi Electric (Industrial machine) (8)	Dalian, Liaoning
	OKK (Machining Center) (14)	Dalian, Liaoning
	Omron (Healthcare Products) (41)	Dalian, Liaoning
	Fuji Electric Systems (Control Devices) (58)	Jilin
Northern Coastal Region	Renesas Technology (Semiconductor) (46)	Haidian, Beijing
	Fujinon (Optical Parts) (66)	Tianjin
	Toyoda-Gosei (Mobile phone-related plastic products) (102)	Tianjin
	Taiyo Yuden (Electronic Components) (165)	Tianjin
Yangzi Delta	Optrex (Mobile, Car Navigation) (14, 47)	Zhangjiagang, Jiangsu
	Renesas Technology (Semiconductor) (46)	Suzhou Industrial Park, Suzhou, Jiangsu
	Sumitomo Chemical (IT-related materials) (50)	Wuxi, Jiangsu
	Japan Aviation Electrics Industry (JAE) (Connector) (85)	Wuxi, Jiangsu
	Omron (Sensor) (91)	Shanghai
	Nitto Kogyo (Electronic Components) (210)	Jiaxing, Zhejing
	Kyokuto Electric (Electronic Components) (219)	Shanghai
	Iwatani (Suzhou ISR e-Films Co., Ltd) (Optical Films) (273)	Taicang, Jiangsu
	Sanyo Electric (Condensors) (275)	Suzhou, Jiangsu
Zhujiang Delta	Hitachi Global Storage Technologies (HDD) (29)	Shenzhen
	Mitsui High-tech (Semiconductor Parts) (44)	Dongguang, Guangdong
	Otax (Connectors) (305)	Shenzhen
	Oki Electric (Printers) (306)	Shenzhen
	Nissei Electric (Electronic Components) (310)	Zhongshan, Guangdong

Note: Numbers denote the designated number of the original source.
Source: JETRO. (2005) "Nippon Kigyo no Taichu-Shinshutsu Jokyo 2004-nen 4-gatsu – 2005-nen 1-gatsu (Japanese Companies' New Establishments and Expansion in China, April 2004–January 2005)," *Chugoku Keizai (Chinese Economy)* (April) pp. 165–185.

Table 11.5 Matsushita/Panasonic: geographical distribution in China (2006)

Regions	Matsushita/Panasonic establishments	Province/city
Northeast China	China Hualu Panasonic Avc Networks Co., Ltd (Dalian)	Liaoning
	Panasonic Storage Battery (Shenyang) Co., Ltd	Liaoning
	Panasonic Automotive Systems Dalian Co., Ltd	Liaoning
	Panasonic Communications (Dalian) Co., Ltd	Liaoning
Northern Coastal Region	Beijing Matsushita Color CRT Co., Ltd	Beijing
	Panasonic Putian Mobile Communications Beijing Co., Ltd	Beijing
	Panasonic Electronic Devices (Beijing) Co., Ltd	Beijing
	Qingdao Matsushita Electronic Components Co., Ltd	Shandong
	Panasonic Welding Systems (Tangshan) Co., Ltd	Hebei
	Panasonic Electronic Devices Film Capacitor (Beijing) Co., Ltd	Beijing
	Panasonic Electronic Devices (Tianjin) Co., Ltd	Tianjin
	Panasonic AVC Networks Shandong Co., Ltd	Shandong
	Panasonic Ecology Systems Beijing Co., Ltd	Beijing
	Panasonic Electronic Devices (Qingdao) Co., Ltd	Shandong
	Panasonic Lighting (Beijing) Co., Ltd	Beijing
Yangzi Delta	Panasonic Home Appliances Washing Machine (Hangzhou) Co., Ltd	Zhejiang
	Panasonic Battery (Shanghai) Co., Ltd	Shanghai
	Panasonic Home Appliances Microwave Oven (Shanghai) Co., Ltd	Shanghai
	Shanghai Matsushita Electronic Instrument Co., Ltd	Shanghai
	Panasonic Motor (Hangzhou) Co., Ltd	Zhejiang
	Panasonic Semiconductor (Shanghai) Co., Ltd	Shanghai
	Panasonic Home Appliances Refrigerator (Wuxi) Co., Ltd	Jiangsu
	Panasonic System Solutions Suzhou Co., Ltd	Jiangsu
	Panasonic Refrigeration Devices (Wuxi) Co., Ltd	Jiangsu
	Panasonic Home Appliances & System (Hangzhou) Co., Ltd	Zhejiang
	Panasonic Home Appliances Rice Cooker (Hangzhou) Co., Ltd	Zhejiang
	Panasonic Plasma Display (Shanghai) Co., Ltd	Shanghai
	Panasonic Battery (Wuxi) Co., Ltd	Jiangsu
	Panasonic Home Appliances (Hangzhou) (Export Processing Zone) Co., Ltd	Zhejiang
	Panasonic Semiconductor (Suzhou) Co., Ltd	Jiangsu

Table 11.5 (Continued)

Regions	Matsushita/Panasonic establishments	Province/city
	Universal Communication Technology (Hangzhou) Co., Ltd	Zhejiang
	Panasonic Motor (HA) (Hangzhou) Co., Ltd	Zhejiang
	Panasonic Factory Solutions Suzhou Co., Ltd	Jiangsu
	Panasonic Home Appliances (Hangzhou) Co., Ltd	Zhejiang
	Panasonic Home Appliances (Hangzhou) Precision Machining Co., Ltd	Zhejiang
Zhujiang Delta	Panasonic Wanbao Home Appliances Electric Iron (Guangzhou) Co., Ltd	Guangdong
	Panasonic Motor (Zhuhai) Co., Ltd	Guangdong
	Panasonic Wanbao Compressor (Guangzhou) Co., Ltd	Guangdong
	Panasonic Home Appliances Air-Conditioning (Guangzhou) Co., Ltd	Guangdong
	Panasonic Ecology Systems Guandong Co., Ltd	Guangdong
	Panasonic Electronic Devices (Jiangmen) Co., Ltd	Guangdong
	Panasonic Battery (Zhuhai) Co., Ltd	Guangdong
	Panasonic Communications Zhuhai Co., Ltd	Guangdong
Others	Panasonic AVC Networks Xiamen Co., Ltd	Fujian
	Panasonic Manufacturing (Xiamen) Co., Ltd	Fujian
	Panasonic Carbon (Anyang) Co., Ltd	Henan

Source: Panasonic. (2006) [web document] http://panasonic.net/corporate/ global_network/cn/.

Table 11.6 Mitsubishi Electric: geographical distribution in China (2006)

Regions	Matsushita/Panasonic establishments	Province/city
Northeast China	Mitsubishi Electric Dalian Industrial Products Co., Ltd	Liaoning
Northern Coastal Region	Mitsubishi Electric (China) Co., Ltd	Beijing
	Mitsubishi Soyea Mobile Communication Equipment Co., Ltd	Beijing
	Mitsubishi Electric (H.K.) Ltd (Beijing Office)	Beijing
	Baoding Tada Cooling Equipment Co., Ltd	Hebei
	Baoding Baoling Transformer Co., Ltd	Hebei
	Shandong Hualing Electronic Co., Ltd	Shandong
Yangzi Delta	Mitsubishi Electric (China) Co., Ltd	Shanghai

	Mitsubishi Soyea Mobile Communication Equipment Co., Ltd	Zhejiang
	Mitsubishi Electric (H.K.) Ltd (Shanghai Office)	Shanghai
	Mitsubishi Electric Shihlin Automotive Changzhou Co., Ltd	Jiangsu
	Mitsubishi Electric Air-Conditioning & Visual Information System Ltd	Shanghai
	Mitsubishi Electric Automation (Shanghai) Ltd	Shanghai
	Shanghai Mitsubishi Elevator Co., Ltd	Shanghai
	Shanghai Mitsubishi Engineering & Technology Co., Ltd	Shanghai
	Shanghai Mitsubishi Electric & Shangling Microwave Oven and Electric Appliance Co., Ltd	Shanghai
	Shanghai Mitsubishi Electric & Shangling Air-Conditioner and Electric Appliance Co., Ltd	Shanghai
	Keling Electric (Shanghai) Co., Ltd	Shanghai
Zhujiang Delta	Mitsubishi Electric (H.K.) Ltd (Guangzhou Office)	Guangdong
	Mitsubishi Electric (Guangzhou) Compressor Co., Ltd	Guangdong
	Guandong Ryoden Lift & Escalator Co., Ltd	Guangdong
Others	Xi Dian Mitsubishi Electric Transmission & Distribution Products Development Co., Ltd	Shanxi
	Xi Ling Electric Power Products Manufacturing Co., Ltd	Shanxi
	XD-Mitsubishi Electric Switchgear Co., Ltd	Shanxi

Source: Mitsubishi Electric. (2006) [web document] http://global.mitsubishielectric. com/ company/ offices/asia.html.

Although Dalian does not invite much attention from overseas manufacturers, the city can attract the best cream of China's human resources because of its economic attractiveness. An intra-China comparison in employee compensation gives us an impression that Dalian competes with Shenzhen and exceeds Beijing and Shanghai in terms of total compensation (Table 11.7). The author's interview surveys confirm that Dalian-located software educational institutions are attracting the attention of smart students from all of China. Furthermore, compared with other regions, Dalian is geographically close to Japan, South Korea, as well as Beijing.[22] Accordingly, many of Dalian people are well accustomed to first or second foreign languages (English, Japanese, and Korean). For this reason, some interviewees gave the author an impression that Dalian is a Chinese Bangalore, specifically speaking, not just the English-speaking people's Bangalore, but a Chinese "multilingual" Bangalore.

Dalian Software Park (DLSP) illustratively provides an impression of a Chinese "multilingual" Bangalore. In 1988, DLSP was established and designated as one of the ten national software bases by the State Development

Table 11.7 Comparison of first-year programmers' compensation in major ITO cities (2005, Beijing = 100)

	Dalian	Beijing	Shanghai	Hangzhou	Shenzhen	Chengdu	Xi'an	Wuhan
Total	123	100	103	89	123	84	75	86
Salary	80	72	72	64	96	62	56	64
Social benefits	43	28	31	25	28	22	19	22

Source: A.T. Kearney. (2005) p. 14.

Planning Commission. In the park, the private-run Dalian Dongruan Information Technology College attracts excellent students despite more expensive tuitions. According to the DLSP, 326 enterprises have settled in; among major foreign MNCs are GE, IBM, HP, Dell, Matsushita, Sony, Toshiba, Accenture, and SAP to name but a few.[23]

As a "multilingual" Bangalore, Dalian provides a window of opportunity to develop mutlilingual software. As an example, on March 25, 2005, Matsushita/Panasonic made an announcement that it would launch its first car navigation system into the Chinese market. Year 2008 is now expected to witness China's automobile sales exceeds in number that of Japan. And a growing number of Chinese drivers could be promising and prospective customers if Matsushita/Panasonic provide a "killer" or popular software system. One element of Panasonic's "killer" system could be "bilingual," i.e., Mandarin and Cantonese. Incidentally, Panasonic's navigation system is being developed through the network of Panasonic Automotive Systems Dalian. As another example, on June 22, 2006, Beijing Oracle Software Systems announced its plan to establish an Oracle Global Support Center (GSC) in Dalian. As one of 18 GSC around the globe, the Dalian GSC is expected to serve as a multilingual service desk to provide local-language technical assistance to Oracle customers in mainland China, Taiwan, and South Korea.[24] The US MNC looks to the DLSP's competitive advantage by describing that "Dalian's rising reputation as a preferred customer support hub stems largely from the city's attractive environment in terms of infrastructure, multilingual talent, government support and intellectual property protection."

HiSoft: A Dalian-born Chinese MNC

Among Chinese software companies at their nascent stages, experts are concerned with the marked growth of a software company, HiSoft Technology International Ltd. As a comprehensive IT service provider being established in 1996, it has grown large enough to possess 1800 system engineers with its international financial backing including JAFCO, Intel Capital, Granite Global Ventures, and the International Finance Corporation (IFC).[25]

Table 11.8 Short history of a Dalian-born MNC: HiSoft

	Milestones
1996	Founded as Dalian Haihui Sci-Tech Co., Ltd
1998	Formed a Joint Venture, JBDK, with Japan's JBCC (IBM, Japan)
2002	Established Offices in Tokyo and OsakaAppointed as the first Global Development Center of General Electric (GE)
2003	Established a US subsidiary in Atlanta
2004	Received Financial Support from JAFCO, Intel Capital, Granite Global, and the IFC
2005	Merged with Teksen Horizon Systems and Ensemble International Ltd

Source: HiSoft. (2005).

The company, being nurtured by Japanese and American electronics companies, started overseas businesses in Japan in 2002, and in the United States in 2003. Furthermore, in 2005, HiSoft acquired two Beijing-based software companies – Teksen Hrizon Systems and Ensemble International Ltd (Table 11.8).

Currently, HiSoft has overseas establishments in Japan (Tokyo and Osaka), the United States (Atlanta, Danbury, and Boston), and Canada (Montreal). In the meantime, the company is developing its businesses with its Chinese customers that would need international expertise (e.g., China Life Insurance). As a result, the company has expanded

Strategies to reutilize traditional strengths of SOEs

Northeast China has long been known as China's center of state-owned heavy industry. The region also has a constellation of excellent universities. In Dalian, there are many nationally known universities including Dalian University of Technology (DUT), Dalian Jiaotong University, Dalian Maritime University (DMU), the Dalian University of Foreign Languages, and the Dongbei University of Finance and Economics (DUFE). Liaoning University (LNU) and Northeastern University (NEU) are located in Shenyang. In Jilin province, the gigantic Jilin University (JLU) dominates Changchun that is dreaming of becoming China's Detroit. At the same time, there are some technologically fledging companies in Changchun Optoelectronic Industry Park.[26] Furthermore, in Harbin, the Harbin Institute of Technology (HIT), the Harbin Engineering University (HEU), and Heilongjing University (HLU) are located. The HIT is known as its high-technology research projects include China's first simulation computer, the first intelligent chess-playing computer, the first CMOS chip IC card of original design, and the first giant computer-aided real-time three-dimensional constructing system.

Thus, Northeast China can possess a wide variety of its own MNCs, if the region can introduce new institutional frameworks to exploit SOE's industrial might and the region's research and educational assets. In this connection, it should be noted that Japanese MNCs located in this region, again,

Table 11.9 Regions Expected to Expand the Relationship with Suppliers in China (2004) (Percent of the Japanese MNCs' respondents)

	Dongbei region (Dalian, etc.)	Huabei region (Beijing, Tianjin)	Huadong region (Shanghai, etc.)	Huanan region (Shenzhen, etc.)
Operating in Northeast Asia	10.9	8.3	17.9	24.3
Operating in South Korea	9.4	3.1	6.3	6.3
Operating in Taiwan	15.7	15.7	17.1	27.1
Operating in Hong Kong	3.3	3.3	18.3	58.3
Operating in China	11.4	8.1	19.2	18.9
Operating in ASEAN	2.3	2.5	4.5	10.2

Note: Italics denote figures that are referred to in this section.
Source: JETRO. (2004) 'Chugoku no Gaikyo (China: An Overview),' p. 38.

play another large role. They can help SOEs by an active interplay with them through forming technological alliances, and through privatization. Many of Japanese MNCs sends their technical staff members to the region regularly in search of prospective strategic technological alliances (STAs). In forging STAs with local SOEs, however, foreign MNCs with more active R&D operations want to lessen the economic and technological burden to "teach" local SOEs.[27] In general, SOEs are regarded as organizations that are unbearably slow to move. Accordingly, further efforts to precipitate the privatization of SOEs and to make them more adjustable to the market mechanism would be the most effective measure to enhance product quality in Northeast China.

In addition, Japanese MNCs want to strengthen their ties with South Korea because of the region's geographical vicinity. Table 11.9 shows the percentage of the total respondents among Japanese MNCs that are operating in Asia with regard to the question: "Which part of China would you expect to be in order to expand your supplier relationship?" Interestingly, Japanese MNCs operating in South Korea hope to expand their supplier relationships in Northeast China. Nonetheless, the number of Japanese MNCs operating in South Korea is quite limited. Accordingly, prospective Chinese MNCs in the region should explore the possibility to expand the relationship with South Korean MNCs as well as Japanese MNCs.

Policy implications

Every national and regional leader tries to have Northeast China transformed to be the fourth area after the Yangzi Delta, the Zhujiang Delta, and the Northern Coastal Region.[28] In October 2003, the 16th National Congress of the Communist Party of China (CPC) endorsed the "Rejuvenate the Northeast Initiative." To date, recent efforts have been successful. Further efforts,

Table 11.10 Comparison among Dalian, Shenyang, Beijing, and Shanghai

Cities/Areas	Population Million	GDP Billions of yuan	GDP per capita Yuan	GDP per capita US$	Industrial production Billions of yuan
Dalian	5.6	163.2	29,143	3,520	154.7
Shenyang	6.9	160.3	23,268	2,810	106.4
Combined Dalian-and-Shenyang	12.5	323.5	25,902	3,128	261.1
Beijing	11.5	366.3	31,880	3,850	103.2
Shanghai	13.4	625.1	46,614	5,630	286.6

Note: Calculated with the rate of US$1 = 8.28 yuan.
Sources: Statistical Yearbooks of Dalian, Shenyang, Beijing, and Shanghai, (2003).

however, are expected along with the case of the "Great Western Development Initiative." The region, therefore, needs policy realignments. The following arguments try to identify key concepts for policy formulation.

Time to build a combined "Greater Dalian-and-Shenyang Zone"

Setting aside the past and present condition of competing and complementary relationships between Dalian and Shenyang, it is now high time for the two cities to revitalize the entire Liaoning province as Northeast China's leading area like Beijing, Shanghai, and Guangdong. Table 11.10 shows a comparison of the key statistics in Dalian, Shenyang, Beijing, and Shanghai. Table 11.10 indicates that neither Dalian nor Shenyang can match the impressive figures of Beijing and Shanghai, especially in terms of population, GDP, and industrial production. The figures of a combined Greater Dalian-and-Shenyang Zone (GDSZ), if materialized, could match those of Beijing and Shanghai.

Establishment of a more consolidated Liaoning headquarters

To materialize the GDSZ, a new, quick, and bold decision-making process should be established. Accordingly, related government organizations, including the Liaoning Province Development and Reform Commission, the Dalian Municipal Government, and the Shenyang Municipal Government, are expected to work out well-harmonized plans for a GDSZ in a close relationship with the State Council's Office of the Leading Group for Revitalizing Northeast China and Other Old Industrial Bases. These plans are expected to include, first of all, a scheme to improve the traffic networks between the two cities. Dalian has the largest port facilities in the province, while

Shenyang the largest airport facilities. There should be synergy effects if the two cities are to be connected. Therefore, closer physical links should be established. Currently, it takes around 3.5 hours to move between the two cities by car; however, according to the author's interview survey, it sometimes takes a longer time for various reasons including various administrative procedures. Therefore, policy measures to improve traffic conditions should be reexamined and formulated. Second, government resources to invite FDI and privatize SOEs should be combined. This effort would reduce the risks of wasting financial, human, and time resources by avoiding dual investment and of losing competitiveness against the other regions including Beijing, Shanghai, and Guangdong. The Dalian Municipal Government is exerting efforts to invite FDI by strengthening the consulting functions (a) to invest from abroad, (b) to swiftly process the necessary documents, (c) to collect feedback information, (d) to train personnel, and (e) to form a special zone targeting small- and medium-sized companies to produce components. Such activities should be conducted along with the Shenyang Municipal Government.

Second leading area's contribution

In addition to the swift development of the leading area in Northeast China, there should be complementary and reinforcing policy measures and the development of neighboring provinces in harmony with the leading area. As the second leading areas, Tianjin in the Northern Coastal Region and Zhejiang province in the Yangzi Delta demonstrate their sustained economic prosperity. On the other hand, Northeast China's second leading area cannot be clearly identified as such between Jilin and Heilongjiang. Being unable to identify is not necessarily wrong. It might be a good phenomenon if the two provinces are competing with each other for the betterment of economic activity. However, the current competition between the two is at best presenting little difference among them. In other words, while Tianjin and Zhejiang provinces are helping as well as competing with their own leading areas (Beijing and Shanghai), Northeast China's second leading area (Jilin or Heilongjian) has nothing to do with economic development and prosperity of the leading Liaoning province. In the meantime, there has been a clear recognition for many years that economic development of Northeast China needs integration and coordination of economic policies throughout Northeast China. The State Council's Leading Group of Revitalizing the Northeast Region and Other Old Industrial Bases, set up in December 2003 with Premier Wen Jiabao as its head, has reiterated for the past years about (1) restructuring of SOEs, (2) technical upgrading, (3) enhancement of investment both domestic-originated and from abroad throughout the region. And, in April 2004, in order to precipitate the movement toward integration and coordination of region-wide economic policies, a specially designated Office for the Leading Group was set up within the State Development Planning Commission (NDRC) with NDRC's Vice-Chairman Zhang

Guobao as its head. Despite the aforementioned efforts, further policy integration and coordination should be imperative with a clearer intention and announcement of the government. Accordingly, furthering the idea behind past efforts, more integrated and coordinated development policies (ICDPs) should be formulated in line with a consolidated Liaoning headquarters.

Conclusions

This chapter has tried to identify corporate strategies and policy measures to nurture Chinese MNCs in Northeast China. For better or worse and like it or not, many MNCs are exposed to global megacompetition. Northeast China, accounting for one-tenth of the nation's GDP with a population of 107 million, is expected to transform itself into a more efficient and competitive region in the age of globalization. China's entry into the World Trade Organization (WTO) and the advent of the Internet are now forcing such transformation at a more rapid pace than ever. Under these circumstances, Northeast China, where SOEs still dominate its economy, is forced to revitalize its corporate activity (a) with further FDI and (b) with further privatization of SOEs, both of which would enhance their economic efficiency and strengthen the corporate structure to meet the challenges of global megacompetition.

Economic policies to nurture Chinese electronics MNCs in Northeast China are (a) to precipitate the region's leading area – a closely combined Dalian-and-Shenyang area as a GDSZ – to attract the attention of prospective investors, and (b) to devise more integrated and coordinated development policies throughout Northeast China as "ICDPs" to achieve sustainable and stable growth of the leading area and lead to a clearer division of labor within the region.

Of greater importance is, as Sunzi's *Art of War* suggests, to implement swiftly these rightly chosen policies by taking advantage of rising momentum at a lightening speed. Accordingly, Northeast China should take full advantage of the coming of the globalization and information age to nurture the region's electronics MNCs. Accordingly, policy-makers and corporate strategies in the region should take to heart the oft-quoted epigram attributed to the British scientist Charles Darwin: "It is not the strongest of the species that survive, nor the most intelligent but the ones most responsive to change." The best timing for revitalizing Northeast China might be swiftly and mercilessly passing. Without agile and valiant handling, the region will experience the same destiny as in the past decade.

Notes

1. See OECD (2005).
2. Though seminal research works emerged during the early 1990s (e.g. Liu, Y. (1992) *Zuoguogongshi yu Zhongguo Qiyeguojihua* (*Multinational Corporation and Internationalization of Chinese Enterprises*). Beijing: China Trust Press, and Li, J. and Cao, F.

(1996) *Zhongguo Qiye de Guaguojingying* (*Multinational Operation of Chinese Enterprises*). (Beijing: China Planning Press), analytical studies have come out since the beginning of the century.

3. See MOFCOM (2006), "Statistic Bulletin on Direct Overseas Investment of China 2005 Jointly Issued by MOFCOM and NBS," [www.document] http://english.mofcom.gov.cn/aarticle/newsrelease/significantnews/ 200609/20060903072019.html.

4. As for materials describing Western perspectives, see, for example, "The State's Long Apron Strings," *Business Week* (August 22, 2005), p. 74; See, also, "Global Growth Wisdom as China Business Summit 2006 Ends," *Info-Prod Research* (Wire feed information) (September 11, 2006).

5. See, for example, Wu, F. (2005) and IBM Global Institute for Business Value. (2006).

6. As for the recent overseas activities of China's MNCs, see, for example, IBM Global Institute for Business Value. (2006), and Lunding, A. (2006).

7. See Kurihara, J. (2005).

8. As for the grouping of the regions, have a look at Table 11.2.

9. As for intra-China economic competition, see, for example, Zhang D. (2005).

10. See, for example, Amano, T. (2005) and Wu, F. (2006).

11. See, for example, Gao, P. *et al.* (2003).

12. See, for example, Wu, F. (2006), and TCL's website, http://www.tcl.com.cn/ main_en/.

13. See, for example, Institute of Scientific & Technical Information of China (ISTIC) (2006) "The Software Industry of China Earned 390 Billion yuan in 2005." [www document] http://english.chinainfo.gov.cn/ViewInfoText.jsp?INFO_ID =725&COLUMN_ID=02&KEYWORD=.

14. In May 2006, the Dalian Office of the Japan External Trade Organization (JETRO) released a directory of IT companies and related educational institutions located in the Dalian area. The directory provides detailed information on 30 software companies, 12 ITO business companies, 6 game-specializing software companies, and 14 educational institutions. See, as for the detail, JETRO. (2006).

15. As for the case of Dalian itself, Japan's preponderance is undeniable.

16. The shares of FDI implemented and the number of establishments for Hong Kong were 32.6 percent and 19.3 percent, respectively, while those figures for South Korea were 11.7 percent and 22.9 percent.

17. According to the author's interview survey, the economic impact of Japanese companies is of great significance especially in Dalian. As of 2001, Japanese companies account for 50.1 percent of industrial production, 78.7 percent of corporate profits, 48.0 percent of corporate tax revenue, and 46.6 percent of the number of employees in the corporate sector.

18. As for the agglomeration of Bangalore, see, for example, Okada, M. (2005) "Bangalore's Software Cluster," in A. Kuchiki and M. Tsuji (eds.) *Industrial Clusters in Asia: Analyses of Their Competition and Cooperation*, New York, Palgrave Macmillan.

19. As for detail explanations, see, for example, Kurihara, J. (2005).

20. Hinata, H. (2004) "Nikkei Denki Meka no Tai-chu Toshi to Higashi Ajia Kokusaibungyo (Japanese Firms' Foreign Direct Investment in China and a New Division of Labor within East Asia)," *Chugoku Keizai* (*Chinese Economy*) (January). pp. 70–83.

21. *op. cit.*, pp. 76–77.

22. In A.T. Kearney. (2005) there appears a comment "Dalian is only three hours to Japan, two hours to Seoul and one hour to Beijing."

23. See DLSP. (2006) [web document] http://www.dlsp.com.cn/english/About%20-Dlsp/aboutdlsp.asp.
24. See Oracle. (2006) "Oracle Announces Plan to Establish Global Support Center in China. Multi-lingual service desk to provide technical assistance to customers in North Asia" (June 22, 2006) [web document] http://www.oracle.com/ corporate/press/2006_jun/chinalglobalsupportcenter.html.
25. The documents prepared by HiSoft Technology International Ltd (2005).
26. Representative companies, though their size are very small, are Lanser Displaytech Inc., Changchun UP Optotech Co., Ltd, Changchun Optics Medical Apparatus Co., Ltd, Changchun Optics Medical Apparatus Co., Ltd (CNI), and Changchun Fangyuan Opto-Electronic Technology Co., Ltd (Fytech).
27. Generally, foreign MNCs in China have more active R&D operations; see Table 11.2.
28. As for the latest statement of a high-ranking official of the Chinese central government as of the end of March, see the formal statement appeared in the material: Zhang, G. (2005) "Speech by Zhang Gaobao, Chairman of State Council's Office of the Leading Group for Revitalizing Northeast China and Other Old Industrial Bases," (March 2, 2005) [web document] http://www.china.org.cn/e-news/news050302.htm.

References

Amano, T. (2005) "Chugoku Kaden Sangyo no Hatten to Nihon Kigyo: Nitchu Kaden Kigyo no Kokusai Bungyo no Tenkai (China's Growing Home Appliance Industry and Responses of Japanese Companies: A New Japan-China Division of Labor)." *Kaihatsu Kinyu Kenkyushoho* No. 22. Research Institute for Development and Finance, pp. 116–134.

Kearney, A.T. (2005) "The Changing Face of China: China as an Offshore Destination for IT and Business Process Outsourcing." [web document] http://www.atkearney.com /main.taf?p = 5,3,1,90. 2005.

Chinese Government, National Bureau of Statistics (NBS). (2006) *Gongye Qiye Keji Tongji Nianjian (Statistical Yearbook of Industrial Companies and Their Science and Technology Activities)*. Beijing: NBS.

IBM Global Institute for Business Value. (2006) "Going Global: Prospects and Challenges for Chinese Companies on the World Stage." [web document] http://www-935.ibm.com/services/us/index.wss/ibvstudy/imc/a1024122?cntxt=a1000074.

Japan External Trade Organization (JETRO). (2006) "Dairen-shi IT Kigyo oyobi Kanren Kyoiku Kikan Risuto (Directory of IT Companies and Related Educational Institutions in Dalian)." [web document] http://www.jetro.go.jp/biz/world/asia/cn/northeast/pdf/cisis2006.pdf.

Kurihara, J. (2005) "Economic Development Strategies for Northeast China: A Study of the Electronic Components Industry." Mimeo.

Organisation of Economic Cooperation and Development (OECD). (2005) "China Overtakes U.S. as World's Leading Exporter of Information Technology Goods." [web document] http://www.oecd.org/document/51/0,2340,en_2825_293564_35834236_1_1_1_1,00. html.

United Nations Conference of Trade and Development (UNCTAD). (2006) *World Investment Report 2006*. [web document] http://www.unctad.org/en/docs/wir2006_en.pdf

Part IV

Case Studies: Selected Industry Sectors

12
China Shifts into Gear in the Global Auto Market

Marc Fetscherin and Marc Sardy

Introduction

Cars have always played a role as a symbol of independence for people from all walks of life. The automobile industry also plays a role in the development and sustainability of economic growth. While it is most closely associated with North America, Europe, Japan, and Korea, China as the new player is set to join the global playground.

In 2001, as China entered the World Trade Organization (WTO), automobile production in China soared. For the first time in history, in 2004, a Chinese auto company appeared in the list of the Global 500. Shanghai Automobile Industry Corporation was ranked 461st on the list for its sales income at about 12.30 billion USD in 2003. Automobile production in China was about 6 million vehicles in 2006 for the domestic market. This makes China the third largest automobile market in the world, surpassing Germany and very soon also Japan. Nevertheless, today less than 2.4 percent of the population of China have automobiles. The growth rate in automobile sales is expected to be between 8 percent and 10 percent per annum through 2010 (N., 2005a). Some estimates of growth suggest that the Chinese automobile market will exceed the US market by 2015 (N., 2005b). However, the demand is variable by segment and type of car (premium versus mainstream versus low cost), as well as by location (urban versus rural).

Currently, China's automobile industry is a largely home-grown fragmented business, and is likely to undergo consolidation. In 2006, there were more than 120 automobile manufacturers, with 12 major players (N., 2006a). Automobile companies in China fall into two categories: small local manufacturers and large national ones. Local manufacturers make and market cars within their region, often within their local community. These small companies may produce as few as a thousand cars per year that are generally limited to their local market. The national players make and market cars in multiple regions within China. Many of them also have international manufacturing partners through joint ventures (JVs). There are about 30 such partnership arrangements in place with foreign auto manufacturers. These partnerships are about access, where Chinese companies get access to international expertise and skills and foreign auto manufacturers get access to the huge and growing Chinese market. Initially these JVs were very constrained by government regulation. For example, the foreign partners could purchase no more than 50 percent of assembly operations. To further complicate JVs, government regulations restricted partnership arrangements to assembly of only one model of car, or production of only one type of part. They were also restricted on their partnership arrangements and could, at most, JV with only two Chinese companies. These restrictions have been loosened in the last few years (Ravenhill, 2006).

Domestic Chinese automobile market

The Chinese automotive industry celebrated its 50th anniversary in 2003. In terms of quality, product features, and R&D however, it is still in its infancy when compared to global competitors. Much production over the last four decades was for military and commercial vehicles. Private car production in China is relatively new and emerged largely by the mid-1990s. By the end of the 1990s, automobile production in China was still below 1 million vehicles per year. In 2002, Chinese auto output hit 3 million vehicles and in 2006 it is expected to be about 6 million vehicles compared to the US auto market with over 16.9 million automobiles annually (Griswold and Ikenson, 2006). However, unlike the Chinese market and its double-digit growth, the US market has, for the first time, faced a decline in total units sold between 2005 and 2006 of about one half million vehicles. The growth in demand for Chinese automobiles within China can be attributed to many factors such as heavy foreign direct investment (FDI) for producing cars in China, liberalization of trade policy such as reduction of import taxes, expansion to new regions in China, and increase in per capita wealth. This growth rate has outpaced many of the developed more mature automotive markets. Table 12.1 shows the sales for the years 1994 to year 2004 (Luo, 2005).

Although growth throughout the 1990s was a respectable 14 percent, China's 2001 entry into the WTO brought changes in trade policy that dramatically increased growth in the industry. For example, the gradual elimination of quotas, licenses, or tariffs on imported vehicles went from

Table 12.1   Number of vehicles per segment (in millions)

Year	1995	1996	1997	1998	1999	2000	2001	2002	2003	2004
Truck	0.60	0.63	0.57	0.74	0.84	0.86	0.89	1.09	1.12	1.51
Bus	0.22	0.19	0.27	0.32	0.42	0.58	0.72	0.86	1.00	1.24
Cars	0.34	0.38	0.49	0.51	0.57	0.61	0.70	1.09	2.07	2.32
Total	1.15	1.20	1.33	1.56	1.84	2.05	2.31	3.05	4.19	5.07

70 percent in 2001 (80 percent for cars with engines over 3.0 liters) to 30 percent in 2005 and by July 2006 had further fallen to 25 percent (Ravenhill, 2006). Japanese and Western firms armed with billions of dollars of investment capital seized the opportunity to enter the formerly closed Chinese market through partnerships and JVs in order to access this growing market. Currently, these JVs control about 90 percent of China's passenger car market. The Chinese government ruled in its automobile industry policy that foreign auto companies can only make engines and finished cars in China together with Chinese national manufacturers, and that foreign companies are not allowed to hold the majority of shares in a JV (Luo, 2005). The left side of Figure 12.1 illustrates some of the partnership arrangements between national government-owned automotive companies and their JVs. The right side lists the local government-owned independent automotive companies as of 2005.

Most of the early partnerships were arranged solely with the large national manufacturers, which are partially owned or supported by the national Chinese government. In 2005, there were 28 separate JVs and wholly owned

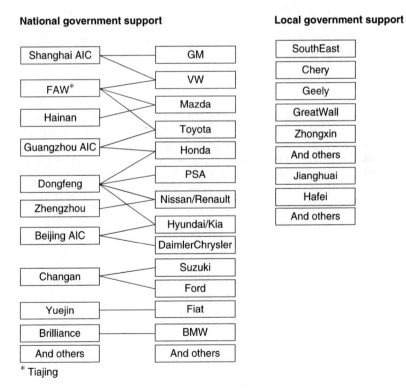

Figure 12.1 Major players in the Chinese automobile industry

Chinese companies producing more than 120 models, with an average annual volume per model of fewer than 30,000 units. Most plants are currently running at substantially less than 50 percent of capacity, despite the increasing demand (Ravenhill, 2006).

Chinese automobile companies going global

While most of China's automobile production has been manufactured for the domestic market there has also been rapid growth in exported automobiles to the international market. The Chinese automobile export market is still in its infancy. According to a study by Deloitte, the main reason why Chinese firms are not yet exporting is that their products have not yet been modified to meet international market standards. Furthermore, most Chinese automobile manufacturers lack effective distribution channels to connect with the international markets. Hence, the key success factors for exporting vehicles into international market are quality improvement, meeting safety standards and emission standards, sales and distribution networks, and establishing after-sales service and maintenance networks (N., 2006). Nevertheless, even with these challenges, in 2005, for the first time, there was a trade surplus for assembled vehicles. According to the China Association of Automobile Manufacturers, in 2005 the country exported about 170,000 vehicles, an increase of over 100 percent, while it imported about 160,000 units, a rise of about 10 percent from the previous year. Although the number of exports is still small compared to overall national sales, analysts expect the trade surplus in vehicles as likely to continue (Dyer, 2006). In 2005, export value reached USD 1.6 billion, a growth rate of 157 percent over the previous year. Exports were shipped to 179 countries. Destination regions ranked by volume were Asia, Africa, Europe, and South America. Of the 170,000 units, trucks made up nearly 100,000 units, with 90 percent of them being lightweight trucks. However, exports of sedans grew rapidly to reach more than 30,000 units, with a sales growth of more than 200 percent over the previous year. Most of these exports were Chinese domestic branded vehicles, many of which were sold to countries in the Middle East and the developing world (N., 2006). Malcolm Bricklin has said he will import cars made in China by the Chery Automobile Co. to the United States in 2008 or 2009 (N., 2006a).

The story is quite different for the JV between national players and foreign automobile companies, where the majority of their production is aimed at the domestic market. However, this might change soon as Honda established a facility in Guangzhou in mid-2003 to target European and Asian markets and began exporting cars to Germany in mid-2005. The German company VW exported 300 Chinese Polo models to Australia in 2003 (Brough, 2005). These initiatives, while small in volume, have tested the international market for Chinese-assembled vehicles. The tests have had mixed results and the sales volume has remained low due to concerns of poor quality control (Ravenhill, 2006). Foreign partners are wary of exporting Chinese cars to developed markets for many reasons. Chinese cars may cannibalize their production base in overseas markets (e.g., Chinese-made Mercedes cars exported to Europe), labor unions may oppose imports on grounds of unfair labor practices, or consumers and especially politicians may oppose imports on protectionist grounds. An odd paradox of Chinese automobile manufacturing is that some high-quality parts are not available in the local market and it may be potentially more expensive to assemble cars in China than in higher labor cost markets where the parts are accessible (Brough, 2005). Nevertheless, exporting automobiles would provide a solution to filling the excess capacity of automobile manufacturers and building economies of scale that would make Chinese manufactures more competitive in the global market. Therefore, it seems likely that over the next few years, the bulk of assembled vehicles for export from China would come from Chinese independent companies rather than international JVs. It is not a question of "whether" Chinese automobile manufacturers will export to international markets but more of "where" and "when."

Challenges facing Chinese manufacturers

The high cost of reaching consumers in more sophisticated markets make higher margins essential and are only possible if they improve their quality standards, develop international relationships, improve logistics, lower production costs, meet safety and emission standards, set up sales and distribution networks, and build after-sales service and maintenance networks. Another important factor is funding for R&D. Currently less than 1 percent of their sales volume is invested in R&D compared to between 3 and 5 percent for their corresponding competitors. This can have devastating results. For example, not long after Land Wind, produced by the Jiangxi-based Jiangling Holding Co., entered the European market, it was plagued by controversy regarding poor safety standards (Jianhua, 2006). The ambitious Chery car company has also met with setbacks in its expansion in Malaysia, where not only were the sales of Chery's complete cars banned, so were the sales of locally assembled Chery cars with imported parts. While this ban might also be the result of lobbying by the Malaysian's automobile manufacturers like NAZA[1] or Proton,[2] history has shown that poor-quality automobiles damage the brand image and destroy market share and markets. Customers may be tolerant of low-cost, low-quality electronics and consumer products, but might be more reluctant to accept this for expensive products like cars. Another challenge to exporting is the currency issue. While strengthening currency might seem good for China in the short run, in the long run it will make Chinese labor and Chinese-produced goods more expensive, potentially making them less competitive on a cost basis. This is especially true if the Chinese yuan appreciates with respect to the US dollar. Finally, these Chinese low costs are being challenged by a new generation of low-cost subcompacts developed by Japanese and Korean companies. Both have significant experience in developing high-quality low-cost vehicles that are performing well in this traditional entry-level export market segment. Nissan, Toyota, and Hyundai all have a reputation for products of good value. Their cars are not as inexpensive as the Chinese cars and they offer quality and fuel-efficient cars for USD 10,000–12,000 (N., 2006a).

What does history tells us? Parallels with the American automobile industry

The development of China's automobile industry development has some parallels with the US automobile industry. The first US car produced hit the road in the late 1880s. It would be about 30 years before automobile production would begin to take off. Sales of early automobiles remained at relatively low levels of around 4000 cars by 1900 (14 years after the first motorized tricycle) but by 1915 sales had grown to about 900,000 in total. This rapid growth was driven by the changes in production and mass assembly pioneered by Henry Ford. During this period, the number of automobile firms exploded to over 70 firms in the United States alone. Economic prosperity during the 1920s drove automobile sales up to 2.5 million cars by 1925. As incomes rose, the automobile became more affordable and more Americans rushed to purchase their own vehicles. The 1930s and the Great Depression saw a precipitous decline in automobile demand from a high of 3.5 million to about 1.1 million by 1933. This precipitous decline forced the consolidation of a very fragmented industry. In the 1970s and 1980s competition from European and Japanese automakers, combined with soaring oil prices, severely weakened the American automobile industry. None of the big four automakers (GM, Ford, Chrysler, AMC) were prepared to make the inexpensive, higher-quality, fuel-efficient cars that their foreign rivals produced. The big four were married to built-in obsolescence as a manufacturing strategy over total quality manufacturing. The cycle time for redesigning the automobile product line would take 5 years and the protectionist policies created in Washington made American auto manufacturers less efficient and less competitive. Although, in the early 1980s US quotas on Japanese automobile imports enabled the American auto manufacturers to keep their market share and profits high, the quotas did not lead to the substantial productivity improvements needed to make them competitive against the increasing Japanese threats.

Today, only two of the major US auto manufacturers, GM and Ford, have survived. Chrysler, the third of the major US automakers, was acquired in 1998 by Daimler. Nevertheless, the US automobile industry remains one of the largest drivers of the American economy. With 16.7 million cars sold annually it is still the largest single market for automobiles.

Will Chinese automobile companies follow the Japanese and the Koreans?

To date the development of Chinese automobile industry has been similar to the development that took place in Japan over the past 50 years. In postwar 1950s Japan, much of the manufacturing was plagued with quality problems. American-driven postwar procurement policies established by Douglas MacArthur supported Japanese industries throughout reconstruction after World War II. In the 1950s much of the developed world avoided Japanese products; they were synonymous with poor quality. Early efforts to build Japanese industrial vitality came in the form of an invitation to a little-known academic W. Edwards Deming. His early speech on Total Quality Management (TQM) and his 16 point plan for management supported his guarantee to turn around the quality problem within 5 years sold Japanese firms on the process of TQM. Within 10 years, Japanese products were no longer synonymous with poor quality. Throughout the 1970s and 1980s Japanese product quality displaced their Western counterparts as the badge of excellence. Today, the quality gap is narrower but it is still a source of competitive advantage for Japanese manufacturers.

Western automakers have a long-held belief that their markets are protected by high barriers to entry and that they know what their consumers want. At the same time, some even announced an end to the run of success by Japanese automakers due to growing protectionisms, saturated domestic market for Japan, and appreciation of the yen making exports more expensive. Optimism, blinded by nationalism, has made researchers and auto manufacturers unaware of the increasing threat posed by Japanese manufacturers. They even went so far as to suggest that Japanese firms would never enter the sedan or large car market with which American auto manufacturers were so well associated.

In retrospect, this was all wishful thinking. The Japanese auto manufacturers entered international markets and grew to dominate almost all automobile segments from the low-end to the luxury brands like Lexus, Acura, and Infiniti.

All of the Japanese automobile entrants into the American market have grown organically, by building their own sales and distribution networks and by not relying on Western partners. Japanese firms ultimately built or acquired assembly facilities in the United States to shelter themselves from currency exchange rate risks and to stave off formal protectionist tariffs.

Korean entry into the Western markets was initially a victim of bad timing. At the time Korean auto manufacturer Hyundai began to pursue entry into US markets, protectionist quotas and nationalist sentiment made for difficult entry (Helm, 1985). However, the Korean exporters made some effective adjustments by entering Western markets through less competitive neighboring markets. Korean manufacturer Hyundai was the top-selling car brand in Canada before they entered the US market (Stern, 1986). Hyundai has grown since the 1980s and is currently the seventh largest auto manufacturer in the world.

Table 12.2, adapted from Luo (2005), compares a Japanese, a Korean, and a Chinese company in terms of ownership, motivation for going global, product development process, product strategy, the environment of the domestic market, and domestic competition.

Table 12.2 Comparison of Japanese, Korean, and Chinese automobile companies

	Toyota	Hyundai	Chery
Ownership	Private	Private	Public
Motivation	To produce indigenous cars	To produce indigenous cars	To produce indigenous cars
Product development	Reverse engineering ↓ Independent Development	JV Joint development ↓ Independent development	Reverse engineering ↓ Joint development ↓ Independent development
Product strategy	Bottom-up (from economic cars to full line)	Bottom-up (from economic cars to full line)	Bottom-up (from economic cars to full line)
Market environment	Middle domestic demand for economic segment 1964 Tokyo Olympic Games	Small domestic demand 1988 Seoul Olympic Games	High domestic demand for all segments 2008 Beijing Olympic Games
Domestic competition	Middle competition Honda, Nissan major competitor	Low competition Daewoo is major competitor (KIA owned by Hyundai)	High competition

The lesson learned for existing competitors is to never underestimate the new, low-cost competitors, since low-cost leads to scale advantages and lower cost per unit of R&D expenditures. When managed well, in the case of Japan and South Korea, these advantages lead to higher-quality products across all product segments over time. The intensity of industry competition has only increased over the past three decades. South Korean manufacturers benefited from the rising yen and the accompanying increase in costs of Japanese vehicles. Despite these similarities, Chinese automotive companies are facing very strong competitors globally and they will not have the easy ride of their Japanese and Korean competitors.

Chinese automobile market makers and takers

The key players are split between local independent players and national players that have strategic a JV with international automobile companies. These independent local automobile manufacturers, which did not exist a decade ago, include successful regional companies such as Chery from Anhui province, Geely from Zhejiang province or Great Wall, and Zhongxing from

Hebei province. These firms are not only selling cars to the huge, rapidly growing domestic market, but they are also exporting. For example, Chery, which had sold fewer than 90,000 vehicles in 2004, has emerged as one of China's leading car exporters. Chery boasts distributors in 32 countries and is planning to generate 40 percent of its sales from exports by the year 2010. In a remarkably short time, firms like Chery have demonstrated the ability to combine local and foreign parts and designs to successfully bring to market a wide range of new models, with exterior designs from Italy and engines designed in England, Austria, and Germany. With increasing concern about enforcement of intellectual property rights (IPR), they are also developing their own or acquiring it legitimately through overseas acquisitions as in the case of Nanjing Automobile Group, which recently acquired MG-Rover. Unlike JV partners, the independent brands are not limited by the impact of export restrictions and have used overseas sales as a means of offsetting the impact of increased competition of the domestic market (Ravenhill, 2006). For example, in the first half of 2005 Great Wall exported nearly 4000 vehicles. Changan exported 700 SUVs to Europe, and became the first Chinese auto company to do so.

On the other hand, there are the national automobile manufacturers that have JVs with foreign companies to access management expertise, technology skills, as well as a brand name. Some of these Chinese firms are producing their own local brand in small quantities and selling these cars out of the "backdoor" of their factory. For the foreign JV partners, it enables them to have local production and prevent importation constraints.

Table 12.3 outlines the main Chinese automobile manufacturer in terms of total unit sales and passenger car sales for 2004.

In 2004, the top five companies (FAW, SAIC, Dongfeng, BAIC, and Changan), all of whom have JVs with foreign partners, together controlled almost 70 percent of total sales. This suggests that the current Chinese automobile market is more of an oligopoly.

Figure 12.2 plots the number of passenger car sales in 2004 on the vertical line and the number of JVs on the horizontal line

On the left side of the figure are the independent local manufacturers that have no JVs with foreign partners. These companies are selling their own brand to the domestic or international markets. Together, they hold about 10 percent of the total passenger car segment (and 5 percent of total sales); each sells between 30,000 and 105,000 units. In the middle and on the right side of the figure are the few big national players. These firms often have more than one JV and sell more vehicles than their independent local competitors. They control about 90 percent of the Chinese passenger automobile market.

The picture becomes even clearer when we further analyze passenger car sales by splitting the total passenger car sales into those produced under their own brand name and those produced under the brand name of their JV partners (see detailed table in the appendix). Figure 12.3 shows the number

Table 12.3 Top Chinese automobile manufacturers (Luo, 2005)

Companies	Total sales (unit) 2004	Passenger car sales (units) 2004
FAW	1, 013, 300	620, 886
SAIC	848, 542	617, 257
Dongfeng	503, 308	212, 383
BAIC	530, 993	173, 924
Changan	504, 805	157, 171
GAIC	209, 551	202, 066
Brilliance	99, 572	19, 690
Geely	105, 879	105, 879
Chery	86, 568	86, 568
Southeast	60, 069	28, 693
Jianghuai	127, 607	0
Yuejing	95, 275	26, 553
Jiangling	74, 715	0
Great Wall	55, 091	55, 091
Zhongxing	28, 114	0
Others	726, 611	13839
Total	5, 070, 000	2, 320, 000

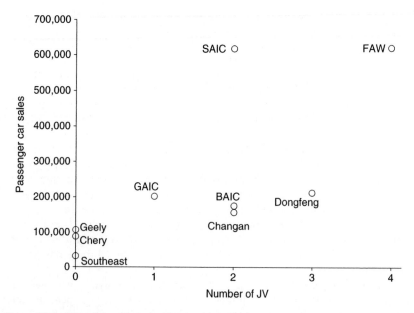

Figure 12.2 JV and total passenger cars sales (2004)

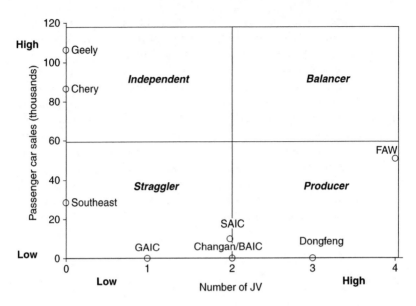

Figure 12.3   Strategic directions for Chinese automotive companies

of JVs per Chinese automobile manufacturer and the number of passenger car sales under their own brand.

Four different types of groups can be distinguished. The first group consists of local *independent* companies such as Geely and Chery, which do not have any JV partners and are selling their own branded products. The second group consists of companies having many JVs in place and selling only their JV partner's brand. They are acting as the *producer* for their JV partners and do not sell their own product. The third group consists of companies that do have a few JVs in place and are also selling their own brand but in small quantities. They are "straggling," as they seem to have neither enough sales volume from JV partners to profit from economies of scales nor shared benefits. It would appear that those companies need to focus more on JVs in order to increase capacity and lower production costs, acquire management expertise and technical skills, or to focus on becoming an independent automotive company and increase their production and sales of their own brand. The fourth group consists of those companies that have many JVs in place but are also selling their own brand in larger quantities. They have to carefully *balance* their own interests and positioning of their brand against the interests and positioning of their JV partners.

Our figure also illustrates that if a Chinese automobile company chooses to have a JV with a foreign company, it is more prone to solely produce the "global brand" and less likely to produce its "own brand." FAW seems to be the exception since they sell both their own brand and global brands. Due to the scarcity of available data on local manufacturers, our figure does not show the many other small car manufacturers in China. However, much like the US auto market of the 1920s, there will probably be an economic shakeout in the near future that will lead to a consolidation.

The question remains which of these strategic directions, building own brand, or becoming a producer of well-known global brands, or balancing both, will lead to success for Chinese auto manufacturers. As long as Chinese companies focus on the growing domestic market both approaches might work. However, the question remains what happens as domestic competition strengthens and more Chinese automobile manufacturers have to export or sell their products to international markets? It is inevitable that they will expand beyond their borders. Their success depends on the speed with which they can react to their customers, to their competitors, and to their international business environment.

Conclusion

When considering the direction that Chinese automobile manufactures will take over the next decade, it is fairly clear that their initial focus will be on China, a market with enormous growth potential and tremendous opportunity for sales. It is quite probable that the economies of scale and manufacturing insights gained from JVs in the local market will help China become an effective global competitor. How Chinese automobile manufacturers deal with quality issues and brand perception may determine how effectively and how quickly they become global competitors. They will also have to work within the constraints that result from China's success as a global manufacturer and net exporter. As China continues to succeed in a range of different products, the currency will strengthen and Chinese products will become more expensive. How the automobile manufacturers deal with these currency fluctuations will set the ground rules for their international success. It is clear that the export of Chinese brands is more likely to take place amongst firms that are manufacturers of their own brands rather than those producing products for their JV partners. While there are some signs that firms with JV agreements in place are producing their own brands and may also begin to export, it is most likely that early exports of Chinese cars will be small cars competing primarily on price.

Our data and analyses provide an early indication of the strategic directions that Chinese automotive companies may pursue; further analyses are necessary to fully understand the internationalization process and strategic directions as well as the scope and scale of Chinese auto manufacturers in the global automotive industry.

Notes

1. http://www.naza.com.my/.
2. http://www.proton-edar.com.my/.

References

Brough, P., 2005. China Automotive and Components Market 2005, KPMG.
Dyer, G., 2006. Figures show China as net vehicle exporter. In: *Financial Times*, London (UK), p. 9.
Griswold, D. and Ikenson, D., 2006. Blowing Exhaust: Detroit's Woes Belie a Healthy U.S. Auto Market. In: *Free Trade Bulletin* No. 22, Center for Trade Policy Studies, Cato Institute.
Helm, L., Nakami, L., Soo, J.J., Holstein, W.J., and Terry, E., 1985. The Koreans are coming: South Korea bets its future on export drive aimed at the US. In: *Business Week*, pp. 46–53.
Jianhua, F., 2006. Getting out of First Gear, Chinese auto industry drives into a future featuring innovation and the will to take on the international market. Beijing Review Online, http://www.bjreview.com.cn/06-10-e/bus-01.htm.
Luo, J., 2005. The Growth of Independent Chinese Automotive Companies. In: International Motor Vehicle Program. MIT, http://imvp.mit.edu/downloads/The%20Growth%20of%20Independent%20   Chinese%20Automotive%20Companies-05.06.pdf.
N., N., 2005a. Driving China: The New Automotive Frontier, Interview with Clarke, Troy E. and Mei, Wei Cheng. Georgetown, *Journal of International Affairs* 6 (2), 61–71.
N., N., 2005b. Picturing China's Automotive Future. The UMTRI Research Review, 36 (4), 1–3.
N., N., 2006a. Can China Gear Up to Sell Its Cars to U.S. Consumers? Quality Is Key. In: Knowledge@wharton.
N., N., 2006b. Future drivers of the China automobile industry. In: Special report for Boao Forum for Asia Annual Conference, Deloitte.
Ravenhill, J., 2006. The Growth of the Chinese Automobile Industry and its Impact on Production Networks.
Stern, J., 1986. Say what? Valley foreign-car dealerships bracing for the Korean invasion of the 1980s. *Phoenix Business Journal* 6 (14), 1.

13
Huawei Technologies: The Internationalization of a Chinese Company

Matthew S. Simmons

> This is a significant innovation.... We are excited to bring this groundbreaking 3G technology to our customers – another world-first for us.
> PCCW Hong Kong Executive Director, Mr Alex Arena, on mobile
>
> TV services enabled by Huawei's CMB Technology
> (Huawei Corporate Website, 2006)
>
> We're a very low-profile company. We'll be more open from now on because our ambition is to be a global company.
> Richard Li, Huawei spokesman (Hennock, 2005)

Fiscal year 2005 was the third year in a row of spectacular growth for Huawei, a blossoming competitor in the global telecommunications equipment market. As illustrated in Exhibit I, total revenues of US$8.2 billion were 47 percent over 2004 levels, following 46 percent and 43 percent annual increases in 2004 and 2003. Perhaps more significantly, international revenues grew 111 percent in 2005 over 2004 to 58 percent of total revenues, the first time in Huawei's 18-year history that the ex-China component has represented the majority revenue stream for the company.

Having famously settled a potentially disastrous intellectual property lawsuit with rival Cisco Systems in 2004, by the end of 2005 Huawei had achieved a significant presence in the global marketplace. The company ranked number one in NGN solutions for global VoIP, second in the global DSLAM market, first in the global Internet protocol (IP)-based DSLAM market, second in the global optical network market, and numerous similar market rankings (2005 Huawei Annual Report). In 2005, Huawei successfully passed strict authentication procedures from leading operators including British Telecom, Vodafone, France Telecom, and Telecom Italia, opening other doors for international growth. In 2006, the company further raised its international presence by signing a global deal for 3G handsets with Vodafone (Staff Writer, *Huawei lands global handset deal with Vodafone*, 2006),

Exhibit I   Huawei Annual Contract Sales (*Financial Highlights*, 2006; 2004 Huawei Annual Report; 2005 Huawei Annual Report; Kiran and Chaudhuri, 2004)

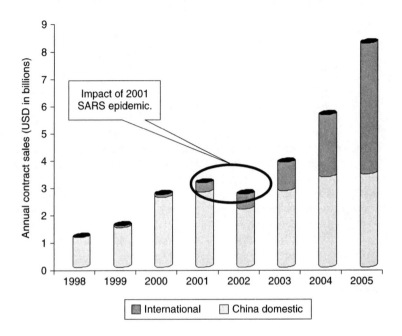

the world's largest mobile telecommunications company, and by winning its first 3G contract in the US market with Leap Wireless International (Matsumoto, 2006).

But it is not all smooth sailing for the upstart Chinese company, particularly in regard to attempts to enter the US market. In February 2006, a joint venture was inked with Nortel with great promise for targeting the global high-speed broadband access market and giving Huawei a strong expansion point into the North American market (Reuters, 2006). However, 4 months later, it was quietly announced that the agreement had been cancelled (Faultline, 2006). In addition, while the Leap Wireless deal establishes a foothold in the US market, Huawei is a long way from competing for the business of market leaders Verizon, Sprint, Cingular, and AT&T. This case study looks at how Huawei has grown to its current state and what issues exist for its future, particularly as they pertain to the US market.

Company history

Huawei was founded in Shenzen, China, in 1998 by Ren Zhengfei, a former officer in the People's Liberation Army (PLA). Ren served as director of the Information Engineering Academy, the research arm of the PLA, until 1984 when he retired in his 40s as a colonel. After retirement, he went to work just north of Hong Kong in Shenzen, China's first Special Economic Zone, for the state-owned Shenzen Electronics Corp. Four years later, Ren secured the support of 14 colleagues and a US$8.5 million loan from a state bank to found his company (Harper and White, 2004).

Initially targeting the domestic China market, international expansion began with the company's first globalization strategy in 1996 (2005 Huawei Annual Report). By the end of 2005, Huawei's products and solutions had been deployed in over 100 countries by 28 of the world's top 50 telecommunications operators, serving more than 1 billion users worldwide.

Product lines are grouped into Wireless Network, Fixed Network, Optical Network, Data Communications, Application & Software, and Wireless Terminals. Huawei's products and solutions cover a wide range of technologies and standards including HSDPA/WCDMA/EDGE/GPRS/GSM, CDMA2000 1X EVDO/CDMA2000 1X, WiMAX, IMS, Mobile Softswitch, NGN, FTTX, xDSL, Optical, and IN (2005 Huawei Annual Report). The roots of the company's success can be traced back to its first internally developed application-specific integrated circuit (ASIC) chip in 1992; this breakthrough enabled Huawei's first product line and provided the company significant internal control over quality and production costs (Park, 2006).

Fertile ground

Since President Deng Xiaoping first declared China's "Open Door" policy in 1978, China has followed a structured, rapid growth path that has been infused with foreign capital and technology. By 1999, the amount of foreign direct investment (FDI) into China had peaked in 1993 at US$111.4 billion with the greatest growth in the number and value of joint venture contracts. In fact, China's investment policies frequently included explicit provisions for technology transfers, and the majority of industry representatives interviewed for a US government study published in 1999 clearly stated that technology transfers are required to do business in China (US Department of Commerce, 1999). It was in this environment rich in FDI and foreign-transferred technology that Huawei was founded.

Establishing a domestic market

The first business of Huawei in 1988 was as a distributor importing telecommunications switches from Hong Kong to compete with the dominant suppliers from Europe and the United States in the mainland China market. This business soon became very competitive, with over 100 distributors operating in Shenzen alone (Shengjun, 2006).

In parallel with this activity, Chinese companies had begun to manufacture switches locally and by the start of the 1990s, there were 200 state-owned domestic telecom switch makers. These products were small in scale (2000 ports or less) and could only support small business internal phone networks; larger switches were still imported. In 1992, Huawei made a strategic decision to develop a 10,000-port switch suitable for use in cities. Using knowledge gleaned from the switching products they imported (Kiran and Chaudhuri, 2004) and their internal ASIC chip, Huawei launched the C&C08 digital switch by 1994. From there, other products were developed aimed at taking market share from global giants such as Nortel, Alcatel, and Ericsson (Shengjun, 2006).

Quickly benefiting from PLA contracts and significant financial and R&D favors from the Shenzen government (Kiran and Chaudhuri, 2004), Huawei launched a domestic expansion strategy that has been described as adopting Mao Tse-Tung's "using the countryside to encircle and finally capture the cities." By targeting smaller counties and cities largely ignored by multinationals, Huawei grew to capture 30 percent of the domestic China market by 2005 (Shengjun, 2006).

The importance of technology

As with any equipment manufacturer in telecommunications, technology is a critical component for Huawei's value and success, which includes not only the underlying technology and intellectual property rights (IPR) that go into their products, but also the range of international telecommunication technology standards they support. Initially, Huawei benefited from the Chinese government's policy of joint ventures and technology transfer within the telecommunications industry. When Huawei was founded in 1998, five of its future multinational competitors had established joint venture R&D and/or manufacturing centers within China – Motorola in 1992, Ericsson in 1993 (*Ericsson Sets up New Joint Venture in China*, 2000), and Lucent Technologies (*Lucent Technologies increases investment in Qingdao*, 2006), Nortel (*Asia Pacific*, 2006), and Nokia (*Joint Ventures*, 2006) in 1995. Huawei's close ties to the People's Liberation Army and Communist Party undoubtedly facilitated access to much of the available technology from these joint ventures.

Investment in R&D

Since the company's inception, keeping up with evolving technologies has been an essential element of Huawei's strategy, exhibited by continually investing over 10 percent of annual revenues into R&D, with 10 percent of that investment used for preresearch to stay at the forefront of new technologies (2005 Huawei Annual Report). Huawei's R&D is now carried out in global centers in the Netherlands, Sweden, India, Russia, including two in the United States and seven in China; 48 percent of Huawei's over 44,000 employees are dedicated to R&D (*Company Overview*, 2006). According to the Worldwatch Institute in Washington DC, Huawei was the top Chinese company in 2005 for patent applications to the World Intellectual Property Organization (WIPO), helping to push China for the first time into the international top ten (*Huawei is top patent applicant in China*, 2006).

The net result of this technology transfer jump-start and continued investment in R&D is that Huawei has a breadth of technological expertise that belies its relatively young age. The company participates in 70 international standards organizations including the ITU and 3GPP and holds 2000 authorized patents as of September 2006, including 5 percent of the world's 3GPP essential patents for 3G mobile communications (*Research & Development*, 2006). Products and solutions cover a wide range of technologies and standards, from Wireless Network (HSDPA/WCDMA/EDGE/GPRS/GSM, CDMA2000 1X EVDO/CDMA2000 1X, WiMAX), Fixed Network (IMS, Softswitch, NGN), Optical Network (FTTX, xDSL, Optical, Routers, LAN Switch), Application & Software (IN, mobile data service, Boss), and Wireless Terminals (UMTS/CDMA). Major products are based on Huawei's own ASIC chips versus incorporating chips with costly licensing fees from global leaders like Texas Instruments and Qualcomm.

In addition to its own research, Huawei continues to leverage joint ventures with other multinational companies to grow its technological expertise. In 1997 alone, joint R&D labs were established with Texas Instruments, Motorola, IBM, Intel, Agere Systems, Sun Microsystems, Altera, Qualcomm, Infineon, and Microsoft (*Milestones*, 2006). In November 2003, a joint venture was established with 3Com to sell networking equipment to Chinese business customers (Charny, 2003). A 2004 joint venture with Siemens continues to develop TD-SCDMA mobile technology for the China market (*Milestones*, 2006).

Tactics coming into question

Exactly how Huawei has achieved its rapid acquisition of technology has been questioned by the Western business world for many years. Concerns that the fast-growing Chinese company is "a little too close to the Chinese government, and a little too obsessed with acquiring advanced technology" (Simons, 2006) sum up the skepticism. This concern is hindering Huawei's expansion plans in China's national rival, India, where, according to press reports, "India's Intelligence Bureau suspects that Huawei has ties to China's intelligence apparatus and military, and even performs the debugging sweeps for the Chinese Embassy in India" (Simons, 2006).

The only substantiated case of intellectual property violations thus far arose in January 2003 when competitor Cisco Systems filed a lawsuit against Huawei and its US subsidiary alleging infringement against some of Cisco's software technology patents. In June 2003, a court injunction instructed Huawei to cease using the alleged illegal software components. By the end of July 2003, Cisco announced a closed settlement between the two companies and by July 2004, the lawsuit was formally terminated (Shengjun, 2006).

No matter what past or present IPR practices actually exist, Huawei and all Chinese companies have a significant R&D resource advantage over competitors from developed countries. Chinese universities churn out engineering graduates in huge numbers at starting salaries around US$8500 a year, much less than the typical US$20,000 in Japan (Simons, 2006) and even higher salaries in the United States and Western Europe.

International strategy

International revenues grew 111 percent in 2005 over 2004 to 58 percent of total revenues, the first time in Huawei's 18-year history that the ex-China component has represented the majority revenue stream for the company. Exhibit II lists many of the company's international market share achievements and rankings. Huawei is a key player in China's national ambitions to see domestic companies "go forth" into the international marketplace, an industrial policy first set out in China's 2001–2005 5-year plan (Staff Writer, *Huawei and ZTE: Going Forth, Can they Conquer?*, 2005). The company's first international contract in 1996 was from Hong Kong's Hutchison Telecommunications to provide fixed-line network products (*Milestones*, 2006). Though physically right next door to Huawei's Shenzen headquarters, Hong Kong was still fully a British holding, the handover to China would not occur until the next year. International expansion then paralleled the domestic approach; Huawei targeted customers in neighboring Asian countries where China had historically favorable relations and where competition from the large multinationals was limited (Kiran and Chaudhuri, 2004).

Exhibit II   Huawei Market Share Achievements and Rankings (2005 Huawei Annual Report)

- 19 UMTS commercial networks had been deployed by the end of 2005
- Huawei is the No. 1 NGN provider in the global VoIP market with 29.3 percent of market share in terms of port shipments (Dittberner, 3Q05)
- No. 2 in the global DSLAM market with 16.9 percent of market share
- No. 1 in the global IP DSLAM market with 32 percent market share (Infonetics, 3Q05)
- No. 1 provider in MSAN with 32.3 percent of market share in terms of port shipments (Infonetics, 3Q05)
- No. 2 in the global optical network market with 10.3 percent of market share (Ovum-RHK, 4Q04-3Q05)
- No. 1 in the global long-haul DWDM market with 15.9 percent of market share (Ovum-RHK, 4Q04š3Q05)
- No. 3 in the global carrier-router market (Gartner, 2Q05)
- No. 1 in terms of the number of users of intelligent network products with 21.6 percent of market share (Ovum-RHK)

Beyond Asia

Huawei was working in Russia as early as 1996, but in 1999, Huawei successfully expanded beyond Asia into Africa with the Ethiopian Telecommunications Corporation. Further African contracts followed with the company again targeting markets ignored by the multinational competition where Huawei's significantly lower pricing were very attractive. Typically, Huawei's products were of comparable or sometimes better quality but priced at least 25 percent below the American and European competition (Shengjun, 2006).

In 2000 and 2001, Huawei secured its first sizeable European contracts with Russian, East European, and second-tier West European companies (Kiran and Chaudhuri, 2004). Huawei passed a significant step in 2005 toward winning first-tier European business by passing strict authentication procedures from leading operators including British Telecom, Vodafone, France Telecom, and Telecom Italia. The first fruits of this achievement were realized with the 2005 selection as a preferred supplier by British Telecom to provide network access components and transmission equipment (*Milestones*, 2006), and with the 2006 global Vodafone deal for 3G handsets.

Market penetration in the Americas followed a similar route, with success in smaller markets and second-tier carriers. Huawei was selected in September 2006 to construct Latin America's first UMTS network by the leading telecom operator in Uruguay (*Latin America's First UMTS Network is Constructed by Huawei*, 2006). Additionally, a significant network expansion contract was announced in July 2006 with Columbia Movil (Parthajit, 2006).

> The most important single market remains, of course, the United States.... We can be successful on the global market only if we have a leading position in the US.
>
> Dr Heinrich v. Pierer, former President and
> Chief Executive Officer Siemens AG, 2004

The August 2006 award from second-tier carrier Leap Wireless is the first major award for Huawei in the United States. However, market growth in the United States in particular has been very slow. Huawei first made an entry in 2001, establishing a "FutureWei" subsidiary in Plano, Texas, in the heart of the Dallas telecom corridor (*About Us*, 2006). In January 2006, expectations were high for the company to win a nationwide 3G contract with T-Mobile USA (Duffy, 2006), but they ultimately lost out to incumbents Nokia and Ericsson. Market expansion plans were further frustrated by the rapid dissolution of the February 2006 Nortel joint venture. While the award from Leap Wireless is significant, Huawei is still a long way from competing for business from market leaders Verizon, Sprint, Cingular T-Mobile, and AT&T.

Asset deployment overseas

In terms of its employment and deployment strategy outside of China, approximately 10,000, or 22 percent, of Huawei global employees are located overseas. Huawei currently divides its international operations into eight regions: Europe, Commonwealth of Independent States (CIS), North America, Middle East and North Africa, Latin America, Sub-Sahara Africa, Asia Pacific, and East Pacific (*About Us*, 2006). Significant efforts have been made to localize these operations, staffing them with more than 60 percent local employees. From Huawei's view, these employees are provided with favorable career development paths and some are in upper-management-level positions in branch management, sales, and services (2005 Huawei Annual Report). It can be inferred from the company's employee statements that the majority of, if not all, international R&D employees remain Chinese expatriates.

Huawei supports its first international markets in the East Pacific region through its headquarters in Shenzhen. This region comprises Hong Kong, South Korea, and other South Pacific nations with representative offices and technical support offices (TSO) in Hong Kong and Seoul to handle project implementation, after-sales services, and training. In the Southeast Asian and Indian subcontinent, countries comprising Huawei's Asia Pacific region, there are now branch offices in 13 countries with 70 percent local employees. The R&D institute in Bangalore, India, joint R&D teams in Thailand and Pakistan, and a training center in Malaysia support this region. Technical support institutes were also established in 12 countries with 80 percent local staff (*Huawei in the World*, 2006).

For the CIS region, there are currently 14 branch offices in Moscow and other Russian towns and 8 others throughout the CIS, with 80 percent local employees. There are also seven regional customer service centers, two training centers, and an R&D center in Moscow. The European region R&D centers are in the Netherlands and Sweden, with branch offices in 26 European countries; there are several local training centers and a European TAC in the United Kingdom (*Huawei in the World*, 2006).

The Middle East and the North Africa region now have 20 representative offices and a headquarters in Egypt, with more than half the staff being locals. The Egyptian operation is home to a regional Technical Assistance Center (TAC) and a regional training center. The 39 countries of the Sub-Sahara Africa region are covered out of South Africa.

The Latin America region is headquartered in Sao Paulo, Brazil, with a network of 11 branch offices. As mentioned above, Huawei's North American subsidiary, FutureWei, was founded in 2001 in Plano, Texas, as a base for R&D, sales, service, and support. FutureWei has also established branch offices close to their North American customers (*Huawei in the World*, 2006).

International R&D strategy

In his 1995 study "*The R&D Activities of Foreign Firms in the United States*," John Dunning, Professor of International Business at Rutgers University's

Graduate School of Management, theorized that the extent and form of investment by multinational enterprises (MNEs) in foreign R&D facilities are likely to depend on four categories of R&D activities: (Dunning and Narula, 1995):

- Type 1: Product, material, or process improvements
- Type 2: Basic materials or product research
- Type 3: Rationalized R&D
- Type 4: Strategic asset-seeking R&D

Huawei has leveraged a combination of Types 1, 2, and 4 in its international R&D facilities. All centers perform Type 1 activities, which are intended to adapt and tailor products and/or processes to local market conditions. Centers in India, the United States, and Sweden are all located near major global technology centers, where they have access to clusters of local resources and competitors to facilitate Type 2 and Type 4 activities, basic product research and strategic asset-seeking research. Relative to Type 4 activities, Huawei has imitated the Japanese tactic of deliberately seeking foreign technology and scientific skills by investing in overseas R&D facilities (Dunning and Narula, 1995). In the case of India and North America, Huawei has attempted to leverage R&D presence into market presence, and has met with resistance in both markets.

In the United States, the Cisco lawsuit contributed to the company's slow start in that market. In India, applications for a US$60 million R&D expansion and a license to bid as a supplier for large-scale Indian telecom projects have been delayed and hampered by the Indian government (Simons, 2006).

Seeking expert advice

According to Huawei management, the company has spent more than US$500 million to develop "a Chinese company with a Western management system" (Simons, 2006). They have retained leading international consulting companies like IBM, KPMG, PriceWaterhouseCoopers, Mercer, Gallup, and the Hay Group to assist in the transformation of practically all of their business management practices. In terms of marketing management (MM), integrated product development (IPD), integrated supply chain (ISC), customer relationship management (CRM), human resources management, financial management and quality control, Huawei credits these firms' role in what it terms a comprehensive business process transformation including introduction of industry best practices and establishment of IT-supported management platforms (2005 Huawei Annual Report).

Looking to the future

In its 18-year history, Huawei has systematically become a larger and more significant competitor in the global telecommunications equipment marketplace. First establishing itself as a serious competitor to global market leaders in the domestic China market, it steadily expanded internationally, becoming a serious player in Asia, Europe, Africa, and South America. Despite this multinational success, significant penetration into the US market still proves to be elusive. As exhibited by the Cisco lawsuit of 2003, Huawei's aggressive growth and R&D tactics have hindered its success in this market.

The total US telecommunications market for equipment and software was US$165.7 billion in 2005, with Huawei's segment of wireless devices, network equipment, and network facilities accounting for just under US$36 billion (*Spending in US Telecommunications Industry Rises 8.9% in 2005 Reaching $856.9 Billion*, 2006) more than four times Huawei's global sales for the same year. Its top competitors for this market segment are formidable: Motorola, buoyed by mobile phone sales, leads the pack with 2004 global revenues of US$31 billion; the upcoming merger of Alcatel-Lucent had combined 2004 revenues of approximately US$23 billion; Cisco Systems' 2004 revenues were US$22 billion; Ericsson came in at US$20 billion; and Nortel is the closest to Huawei with US$10 billion (*Company Profiles*, 2006). All of these competitors are sizable incumbents with one or more of the US market leaders Verizon, Sprint, Cingular T-Mobile, and AT&T. Even with 2006 growth at 5.2 percent, it will continue to be difficult for Huawei to significantly penetrate this market.

Can Huawei succeed as a global company without succeeding in the US market? Or is success in this "most important single market" critical to the company's future, and therefore Huawei needs to redouble its efforts to stay relevant and growing?

Glossary

2G – Second-Generation mobile technologies – the family of digital mobile technologies that includes GSM, GPRS, EDGE, CDMA, and CDMA2000 1X.

3G – Third-Generation mobile technologies – the family of digital mobile technologies that includes UMTS, WCDMA, TD-SCDMA, WiMAX, and CDMA2000 1X EVDO.

3GPP – The 3rd Generation Partnership Project – a collaboration agreement that brings together a number of telecommunications standards bodies to produce globally applicable Technical Specifications and Technical Reports for a third-generation mobile system based on evolved GSM networks. The scope includes the maintenance and development of GSM Technical Specifications and Technical Reports including evolved radio access technologies.

ASIC – Application-Specific Integrated Circuit – an integrated circuit chip that has been designed specifically for one application, as differentiated from a general-purpose integrated circuit chip.

CMB – Cell Multimedia Broadcast – a simplified technology solution for 3G mobile multimedia services first put forth by Huawei as a precursor to the full UMTS standard Multimedia Broadcast Multicast Service (MBMS) technology (*Leading Edge – MBMS, the next hot topic?*, 2006).

CDMA – Code Division Multiple Access – a digital mobile air interface technology that is used in both 2G and 3G mobile standards, though more generally referring to the 2G technology branded cdmaOne and comprising standards IS-95A and IS-95B.

CDMA2000 1X – a 2G digital mobile technology evolution from cdmaOne that provides for packet data services.

CDMA2000 1X EVDO – 1x Evolution Data Only – a 3G digital mobile standard evolved from CDMA that provides for high-speed packet data services.

xDSL – Digital Subscriber Line – a technology enabling high-speed data traffic over ordinary telephone lines into the home or office. There are two main categories: asymmetric DSL (ADSL) where fast downstream is required, but slow upstream is acceptable and symmetric DSL (SDSL, HDSL, etc.) designed for connections that require high speed in both directions (Encyclopedia, 2006).

DSLAM – Digital Subscriber Line Access Multiplexer – an interface unit in a digital subscriber line (xDSL) system that enables high-speed data transmission over existing copper telephone lines. A DSLAM separates the voice-frequency signals from the high-speed data traffic and controls and routes traffic between the subscriber's end-user equipment (router, modem, or network interface card (NIC)) and the network service provider's network (Encyclopedia, 2006).

EDGE – Enhanced Data rates for GSM Evolution – a standard for delivering higher-rate packet data service over GSM mobile networks than GPRS provides.

FTTX – Fiber To The "X" – refers to all optical "fiber-to-the-wherever" technologies (Encyclopedia, 2006).

GPRS – General Packet Radio Service – the first standard for delivering packet data services over GSM mobile networks.

GSM – Global System for Mobile communication – the 2G digital mobile network standard developed in Europe and utilized worldwide.

HSDPA – High Speed Digital Packet Access – a technology evolution of UMTS that provides higher-speed packet data services.

IMS – IP Multimedia Subsystem – an international, recognized standard defining a generic architecture for offering Voice over IP (VoIP) and multimedia services. First specified by the Third Generation Partnership Project

(3GPP/3GPP2) and now being embraced by other standards bodies including ETSI/TISPAN; the standard supports multiple access types including GSM, WCDMA, CDMA2000, wireline broadband, and WLAN (Encyclopedia, 2006).

IN – Intelligent Network – the public switched telephone network architecture of the 1990s, developed by Bellcore (now Telcordia) and the ITU. It was created to provide a variety of advanced telephony services such as 800 number translation, local number portability (LNP), call forwarding, call screening, and wireless integration (Encyclopedia, 2006).

ITU – International Telecommunication Union – an international organization within the United Nations System where governments and the private sector coordinate global telecom networks and services.

IP – Internet Protocol – the data communications network layer standard that is implemented by all Internet-based communications links and systems.

LAN – Local Area Network – a communications network that serves users through a central server group within a confined geographical area (Encyclopedia, 2006).

NGN – Next Generation Networking – a general term capturing all efforts to continually evolve telecommunications networking technologies. The term also applies to products that are on the forefront of current networking technology.

Softswitch – an evolution of the telecommunications switch for Internet protocol (IP) packet-switched networks. Instead of a traditional special-purpose hardware device for communications switching, a softswitch is a high-performance software application running on a more generic computer platform.

TD-SCDMA – Time Division Synchronous CDMA – a wireless access technology proposed by China Wireless Telecommunication Standards group and approved by the ITU in 1999. The technology is being developed by the Chinese Academy of Telecommunications Technology and Siemens (*TD-SCDMA*, 2006).

UMTS – Universal Mobile Telecommunications System – the 3G wireless and network access standards for mobile communications put forth by the 3GPP.

VoIP – Voice over Internet Protocol – a technology for delivering digitized voice communications over IP networks.

WCDMA – Wideband Code-Division Multiple-Access – the wireless access technology utilized by the UMTS 3G mobile standard.

WiMAX – Worldwide Interoperability for Microwave Access – a broadband wireless access technology providing throughput of up to 40 Mbps per channel to distances of up to three kilometers.

References

2004 Huawei Annual Report.

2005 Huawei Annual Report.

"About Us" (2006) *Futurewei Corporate Website* [online]http://www.futurewei.com/aboutus.asp [cited September 2006].

"Asia Pacific" (2006) *Nortel Corporate Website* [online]http://www.nortel.com/corporate/global/asia/ [cited September 2006].

Charny, Ben (2003) "3Com and Huawei start China venture," *CNET News.com* [online] (18November) http://www.zdnetasia.com/news/hardware0,39042 972, 39158288,00.htm [cited September 2006].

"Company Overview" (2006) *Huawei Corporate Website*[online]http://huawei.com/about/info.do?cid=-1002&id=58[cited September 2006].

"Company Profiles" (2006) *Computer Business Review Online* [online] http://www.cbronline.com/[cited September 2006].

Duffy, Jim (2006) "Huawei about to land its first major U.S. contract," *Network World* [online] (24 January) http://www.networkworld.com/newsletters/viewedge/2006/0123edge1. html? fsrc=rss-wanservices[cited September 2006].

Dunning, John H and Narula, Rajneesh (1995) "The R&D Activities of Foreign Firms in the United States," *International Studies of Management & Organization* (Spring/Summer; 25, 1, 2), pp. 39–73.

"Encyclopedia," *PC Magazine.com* [online]http://www.pcmag.com/encyclopedia/ [cited September 2006].

"Ericsson Sets up New Joint Venture in China" (2000) *People's Daily* [online] (13 May) http://english.people.com.cn/english/200005/13/eng20000513_40738.html [cited September 2006].

Faultline (2006), "Nortel weakened by failure of Huawei venture," *The Register* [online] (16 June) http://www.theregister.co.uk/2006/06/16/nortel_huawei_failure/ [cited September 2006].

"Financial Highlights," *Huawei Corporate Website* [online] http://huawei.com/about/info.do?cid=-1002&id=64 [cited September 2006].

Harper, Sarah and White, Steven (2004) "Huawei and 3Com," *Insead*, Case Study 304-316-1.

Hennock, Mary (2005) "China IT giant eyes new horizons," *BBC News* [online] (31 January) http://news.bbc.co.uk/2/hi/business/4221889.stm [cited September 2006].

"Huawei in the World" (2006) *Huawei Corporate Website*[online]http://www.huawei.com/about/inworld.do [cited September 2006].

"Huawei is top patent applicant in China," *Huawei Corporate Website* [online] http://www.huawei.com/news/view.do?id=472&cid=43 [cited September 2006].

"Huawei's CMB Technology Helps PCCW Achieve World First in Real-time TV Broadcast over its 3G Network" (2006) *Huawei Corporate Website* [online] (8 June) http://www.huawei.com/news/view.do?id=1025&cid=42 [cited September 2006].

"Joint Ventures" (2006) *Nokia Corporate Website* [online]http://www.nokia.com/A4126373 [cited September 2006].

Kiran, V Bala and Chaudhuri, Sumit Kumar (2004) "Huawei Technologies: Growth Strategies," *ICFAI Business School*, Case Study 304-261-1.

"Latin America's First UMTS Network is Constructed by Huawei," *Futurewei Corporate Website*, [online] (4 September)http://www.futurewei.com/detail.asp?dt=news& id=113 [cited September 2006].

"Leading Edge–MBMS, the next hot topic?" (2006) *Huawei Corporate Website* [online]http://www.huawei.com/publications/view.do?id=318&cid=96&pid=61 [cited September 2006].

"Lucent Technologies increases investment in Qingdao" (2006) *Lucent Corporate Website* [online] http://www.lucent.com/press/1201/011225.coa.html [cited September 2006].

Matsumoto, Craig (2006) "Huawei Leaps Into US 3G," *Light Reading* [online] (15 August) http://www.lightreading.com/document.asp?doc_id=101523 [cited September 2006]

"Milestones," *Huawei Corporate Website* [online]http://huawei.com/about/info.do? cid=-1002&id=63 [cited September 2006].

"Huawei wins GSM expansion contract with Colombia Movil" (2006) *Huawei Corporate Website* [online](7 September)http://www.huawei.com/news/view.do? id=1825&cid=42 [cited September 2006].

"Research & Development," *Huawei Corporate Website* [online]http://huawei.com/ about/info.do?cid=-1002&id=67 [cited September 2006].

Reuters (2006), "Nortel, China's Huawei in joint venture," *ZDNet News*, [online] (1 February) http://news.zdnet.com/2100-1035_22-6033959.html [cited September 2006].

Shengjun, Liu (2006) "Huawei Technologies Co., Ltd.," *China Europe International Business School (CEIBS)*, Case Study CC-305-021.

Simons, Craig (2006) "The Huawei Way," *Newsweek International* [online] (16 January) http://www.msnbc.msn.com/id/10756804/site/newsweek/ [cited September 2006].

"Spending in U.S. Telecommunications Industry Rises 8.9% in 2005 Reaching $856.9 Billion" (2006) *Telecommunications Industry Association Newsletter* [online] (March) http://pulse.tiaonline.org/article.cfm?id=2295 [cited September 2006].

Staff Writer (2005) "Huawei and ZTE: Going Forth, Can they Conquer?" *BDA China, Ltd* (March).

Staff Writer (2006), "Huawei lands global handset deal with Vodafone," *Cellular Business Review* [online] (16 February) http://www.cbronline.com/article_feature. asp?guid=617A3C3F-DA07-43AF-88AE-3CFA8194DBAE [cited September 2006].

Park, Sam (2006) "Huawei's Strategic Review (A)," *Insead*, Case Study 306-154-1.

v. Pierer, Heinrich (2004) "Annual Shareholders' Meeting of Siemens AG" (22 January)

"TD-SCDMA," *UMTS World*, [online] http://www.umtsworld.com/technology/ tdscdma.htm [cited September 2006].

U.S. Department of Commerce (1999) "US Government Policies and Perspectives on Technology Transfer" [online] http://bxa.doc.gov/ DefenseIndustrialBase Programs/OSIES/DefMarketResearchRpts/techtransfer2prc.html [cited September 2006].

14

Internationalization Positioning of Wuliangye Distillery: China's Leading Manufacturer and Seller of Spirits and Wine

James P. Gilbert

Introduction

Wuliangye (pronounced woo-leeang-ye) distillery is located in Yibin, China. Yibin is a city of about 600,000 residents surrounded by tall mountains, bamboo forests, and orange groves. Industry in Yibin includes paper, silk, leather goods, electronics, food products, and the distillery/spirits industry. Yibin is the first city along the Yangtze River and the concourse of the Jinsa and Min rivers in Sichuan Province (Figure 14.1).

The Yibin factory covers 3.5 square kilometers and is famous for its garden-like grounds (Figure 14.2). The Fenjin Tower with its shining steel horse on top (symbolizing the enterprising "spirit" of the managers) is situated in the center of the factory and its workshops, lawns, pavilions, sculptures, and script stones, thus forming an integrated whole.[1] The Garden Factory is known for its enterprising sprit, good working conditions, and its history museum.

Wuliangye Yibin Co., Ltd, is also engaged in the printing, chemical, anti-forge, plastics, medical production, mineral water production, motorcycle parts, and shock-proof material businesses. In August 2006 the Comtex News Network reported that the Wuliangye Group is getting closer to their goal of manufacturing automobiles (2006a). Wuliangye has partnered with the Brilliance Group to obtain control of a subsidiary, Xinhua Combustion Engine, driving this company more into diversification. At this point, Wuliangye will not be producing automobiles but will enter the market as producers and sellers of automobile engines. To support this initiative, the Wuliangye Group received approval from the Sichuan Branch of the State-owned Assets Supervision and Administration Commission (SASAC) to transfer the $10.9 million state-owned net assets in the Sichuan Rubber Group. Wuliangye expects to invest $375 million into the rubber tire business to set up a new steel radial tire line (SinoCast, 2004a).

World Atlas

Yibin, Sichuan, China

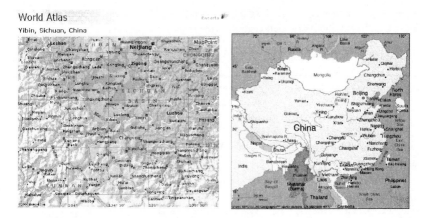

Figure 14.1 Map of Yibin, Sichuan, China area

Figure 14.2 The Fenjin Tower on the garden campus of Wuliangye Distillery

In early 2006 Wuliangye Yibin Co., Ltd, entered the wine business in a major way. The General Manager, Mr Fu Zhong, stated that the new high-quality fumet wine would be bottled in China (SinoCast, 2006). The firm invested $25 million to build a factory specializing in wine products under the name of Wuliangye Wine Co., Ltd (Comtex News Service (2006). The firm strives to drive annual sales of wine to $250 million within 5 years. This would put it in the top three wines makers in China (TMC Net, 2006). This strategy was aided by the reduction of China import tariffs after joining the World Trade Organization (WTO) in 2001. The work force numbers 15,000, with fixed assets of 2 billion yuan (RMB) and an annual liquor production capacity of 120,000 tons. Wuliangye Distillery posted the third quarter 2006 profit of $25.2 million, representing a 10.2 percent increase with approximately 4000 employees (Goliath, 2006). The firm's assets were valued in August 2006 at about $1.24 billion (Financial Times, 2006). The Wuliangye Group has an extensive distribution network of more than 2000 distributors.

The managing director is Mr Wang Guochun (picture) and the senior vice president is Mr Ye Weiquan. The Yibin plant manufacturers four types of distilled products in 25 varieties and 50 specifications of liquor with its primary brands including its preeminent Wuliangye Spirits (a full-bodied flavor and sweet-smelling liquor) along with Jianzhuang, Wuliang Spring, Wuliang Purity, Ampenas Whiskey, and fruit wines (Figure 14.3). Its products are sold throughout China and in 130 countries and regions  including the United States, Canada, the United Kingdom, France, the Netherlands, Italy, Spain, Australia, New Zealand, Japan, Korea, Myanmar, Laos, Thailand, and Taiwan.

Starting in 1915 with the Gold Prize at the Panama International Fair, Wuliangye Spirits have won 39 gold medals at more than 20 international fairs. In 1995 the distillery was named the "King of Chinese Liquor" at the 15th International Statistics Conference. Wuliangye Distillery was introduced to the US market when the firm sponsored the Chinese Sports Delegation to the 1996 Atlanta, Georgia, Olympic Games. The delegation included

Figure 14.3   Wuliangye Spirits

Figure 14.4 The 1996 Olympic Wuliangye Cheering Squad

the first Olympic cheering squad (Figure 14.4). In the 2006 *Wall Street Journal* Asia's reader survey of China's most admired companies placed Wuliangye Yibin Co. in seventh place (*The Wall Street Journal*, 2006). Customers give the firm strong marks for reputation and product quality.

The Wuliangye Distillery logo and flag use the red color of the product and a red circle representing the earth. The five lines represent the five major ingredients (broomcorn, glutinous rice, rice, wheat, and corn) while the two concentric circles represent the full cooperation and unity of purpose of the leaders and workforce of Wuliangye (Figure 14.5). Legends have built up around the power of these five grains of distillation.

Figure 14.5 Logo and flag of Wuliangye Distillery

Chinese wine/liquor industry

China has a long tradition of serving its strong sweet-smelling liquor in small shot glasses that are usually consumed in a single swallow at the dinner table. This is in line with the Chinese proverb: "Frequent drinking makes friends surrounding." Wuliangye is one of the two most famous brands for this "toasting" ritual along with competitor Maotai. These two brands are used almost exclusively at state banquets for distinguished guests. These toasts at formal state dinners are obligatory. The Chinese Ganbei (as in the toast "bottoms up") may go for several "rounds." This white liquor (called Baijiu (白酒) or shaojiu (烧酒)) is a potent Chinese distilled drink. The small glass of warm liquor is consumed in one gulp and once the bottle is opened it is impolite not to finish it. The alcohol content of these liquors is about 60 percent; Western spirits are typically around 40 percent.

Sales of alcoholic drinks in 2005 reached 416 billion RMB and 35 billion liters. This represented an 8 percent growth over 2003 (Euromonitor, 2006). Growth in 2005 was still strong at 6 percent over 2004. It appears that the growth is somewhat generated by the "upscale" drink purchases of urban consumers.

In the first six months of 2006, profit from white liquor sales has increased 30.13 percent, surpassing beer and wine markets, which grew at about 12 percent for the same period (Research China, 2006). The Chinese distilleries shifted to premium brands as a result of a 1991 tax that required manufacturers to pay according to both price and production volumes. In order to avoid this "double tax" many distillers shifted their focus to premium spirits. The tax drove the spirits sales volumes down 33.9 percent from 2000 to 2005 (Just-Drinks, 2006b:9). We see this brand shift in market share numbers for 2005 where premium spirits accounted for 14 percent of the more than 70 billion Yuan sales. For those, like Wuliangye, who were already positioned in the premium market this was a boon. Some foreign investors saw this as an opportunity to invest and purchased shares of major Chinese companies. Wuliangye did receive some of this foreign capital during this period (Research China, 2006).

As the purchasing power expands with the standard of living in China we can expect the alcoholic drink market to expand as well (Table 14.1 for a summary of China exports, imports, and investments for the past 3 years). Competition in the market has improved product quality, which also helps expand the market. It appears that there will be continued strong demand for upper-mid and high-end spirits for quality and image brands – strong points for Wuliangye Distilleries. This may lead to more industry consolidation and increased competition from non-Chinese brands.

Strategic moves have already been taken by Wuliangye to strengthen its worldwide market position (Financial Times, 2004). In November 2004 the

Table 14.1   Summary of past 3 years in China

GDP	2003	2003 Growth percent	2004	2004 Growth percent	2005	2005 Growth percent
	RMB 13.6 T	10.0 (real)	RMB 16.0 T	10.1 (real)	RMB T 18.2	9.9 (real)
Exports	US$438 B	34.6	US$ 593 B	35.4	US$762 B	28.4
Imports	US$413 B	39.9	US$ 561 B	36.0	US$660 B	17.6
Exchange Reserve	US$403 B	40.8	US$ 610 B	51.3	US$819 B	34.3
Tax Revenue	RMB 2.06 T	19.0	RMB 2.57 T	26.7	RMB 3.09 T	20.0
Resident Savings	RMB 11.1 T	17.4	RMB 12.6 T	14.0	RMB 14.7 T	16.5
Investment	RMB 6.67 T	27.7	RMB 7.01 T	26.8	RMB 8.86 T	26.7

Source: Adapted from: Wang, Jianmao (2006) "Next Five Years down the Road of China's Long March," presentation at the International Meeting of the Production & Operations Management Society (POMS), China Europe International Business School (CEIBS), Shanghai, the People's Republic of China, June.

firm reduced its brands from 26 to 18. This will better position Wuliangye to maintain its number 1 brand in China and consolidate for world market penetration. Wuliangye has now one world-famous brand, nine national brands, and eight regional brands. The 18 brands will be driven by customer popularity in various markets. This strategic move by Wuliangye may well be in response to the Chinese Liquor Commerce Association's encouragement of foreign wine enterprises and relevant industries to establish and develop grape and wine businesses in China (SinoCast China, 2002). The firm also has registered its trademark in Taiwan in order to enter outside mainland China markets (Asiainfo, 2002).

Industry consolidation

Increased competition, reduction in import tariffs along with high oil prices, and increased production costs continue to pose a threat to profitability for spirit manufacturers such as Wuliangye. This has led to some consolidation as distillers try to boost profitability and strengthen their competitive positions. This is evidenced by the brand share agreements of Wuliangye, Jian Nan Chun, Maotai, and Luzhou Lao Jiao. It is clear that brand and quality consciousness is increasing in China. This is a market trend that is

Table 14.2   Largest producers of distilled spirits: 2004 sales (million 9-liter cases)

Diageo	87
Hite	77
Pernod Ricard	76
UB	39
Bacardi-Martini	32
Beam	28
San Miguel	24
Muller de Bebidas	23
SPI	22
Wuliangye	19

Source: International Wine & Spirit Record (IWSR), 2005.

very favorable to Wuliangye as they have many upscale brands and a strong reputation.

Company organization

The Wuliangye Distillery was founded in 1957 and became the Wuliangye Group Co., Ltd, in 1985. The Wuliangye Group is the largest and most profitable distillery in China with an annual production of about 250,000 tons of liquor (Strategis, 2006). It is the tenth largest producer of distilled spirits worldwide (Table 14.2).

The Push Group Co., Ltd, was established in 1998 to identify and develop new markets for the Wuliangye Group Co., Ltd. This has been a most successful partnership. Sales in 2001 were 700 million RMB (Ubest, 2006). The key financial data for the firm are all strong (Table 14.3). Table 14.4 shows the main business indicators for the first half of 2006.

Competition for the Chinese market

World competitors in the spirit manufacturing industry are finding a firm foothold in China because of lowered tariffs and the huge sales potential of the market. Sales of non-Chinese brands have boomed in urban markets (Euromonitor, 2006). Non-Chinese distillers are also finding shelf space in supermarkets and hypermarkets, which are expanding rapidly inland in major cities. The domestic Chinese market for alcoholic drinks has increased 26.2 percent from 2000 to 2005 (Just-Drinks, 2006). The 2005 estimate for consumer expenditures on alcoholic drinks

Table 14.3 Wuliangye Yibin Co., Ltd Financials 2001–2005

Period End Date Auditor/Accountant	31-Dec.-2005 Sichuan Huaxin CPA	31-Dec.-2004 Sichuan Huaxin CPA	31-Dec.-2003 Sichuan Huaxin CPA	31-Dec.-2002 Sicherman (Irving) & Co.	31-Dec.-2001 Sichuan Huaxin CPA
Annual Income Statement: (CNY, In millions)					
Total Revenue	6,418.75	6,297.58	6,333.09	5,706.52	4,742.10
Cost of Revenue	4,005.09	3,831.87	4,161.86	3,972.34	3,100.90
Gross Profit	2,413.66	2,465.72	2,171.23	1,734.18	1,641.20
Selling, General and Administrative Expense	1,244.21	1,213.17	1,108.29	891.56	745.66
Interest Expense, Net Operating	(25.26)	(26.48)	(28.37)	(26.70)	(25.42)
Other Operating Expenses, Total	(5.66)	(3.83)	(3.69)	(3.83)	(2.19)
Total Operating Expense	5,218.38	5,014.72	5,238.09	4,833.38	3,818.95
Operating Income	1,200.37	1,282.86	1,095.01	873.14	923.15
Non-Operating Interest Income (Expense), Net	(3.92)	(0.13)	(0.55)	0.18	12.35
Other Non-Operating Income, Net	(0.54)	(11.57)	(7.21)	(4.25)	(2.40)
Income Before Tax	1,195.91	1,271.16	1,087.24	869.07	933.09
Income After Tax	799.01	829.76	703.79	618.98	816.32
Net Income	791.35	828.00	702.98	613.23	811.41

Table 14.3 (Continued)

Period End Date Auditor/Accountant	31-Dec.-2005 Sichuan Huaxin CPA	31-Dec.-2004 Sichuan Huaxin CPA	31-Dec.-2003 Sichuan Huaxin CPA	31-Dec.-2002 Sicherman (Irving) & Co.	31-Dec.-2001 Sichuan Huaxin CPA
Income Available to Common Excl. Extraordinary Items	791.35	828.00	702.98	613.23	811.41
Income Available to Common Incl. Extraordinary Items	791.35	828.00	702.98	613.23	811.41
Basic EPS excluding Extraordinary Items	0.29	0.31	0.26	0.23	0.30
Basic EPS including Extraordinary Items	0.29	0.31	0.26	0.23	0.30
Diluted EPS excluding Extraordinary Items	0.29	0.31	0.26	0.23	0.30
Diluted EPS including Extraordinary Items	0.29	0.31	0.26	0.23	0.30
Normalized Income Before Tax	1,195.91	1,271.16	1,087.24	869.07	933.09
Normalized Income After Taxes	799.01	829.76	703.79	618.98	816.32
Normalized Income Available To Common	791.35	828.00	702.98	613.23	811.41

Table 14.4 Main business indicators for the first half of 2006 (all values in yuan)

	First half of 2006/adjusted	First half of 2005/adjusted
Earnings per share	(0.302)	0.217
Net Assets per share	2.916	2.714
Return on net assets	10.36	8.22
Main operating turnover(in million yuan)	4,397	3,807
Net profit(in million yuan)	817	588

Source: Xinhua News Agency—Xinhua Economic News Service (2006) Wuliangye Yibin (August 9).

is $6.868 billion, representing a sales volume of 36.18 billion hectoliters (Just-Drinks, 2006b:5).

In 2006 Wuliangye was ranked number 1 in the Best Chinese Liquor category followed by Moutai at number 2 and Luzhou Laojiao at number 3 (Hurun Report, 2006). European brands won the majority of awards in 2006 but Wuliangye and Moutai stand out as stewards of Chinese culture and history in the industry.

Conclusion

The world's largest population is growing at a rate of approximately 0.70 percent per year, which means that by 2012 there may be 1.37 billion people living in China. Thus, the domestic and foreign alcoholic drinks markets will be fertile ground for the Wuliangye Group. It is clear that the Wuliangye Group has been a major success story in China's burgeoning internationalization strategy. No matter what market Wuliangye enters they enter with passion. Mr Guochun, Board Chairman of the Wuliangye Group, stated that they will enter markets only when they have the necessary core technology and funding. Wuliangye is strategically ambitious with an attitude of being the major brand in every industry it enters.

Clearly, Wuliangye is fine-tuning its business strategies on many fronts. On the intraorganizational level they are responding to global challenges quickly. At the interorganizational level the firm is working closely with the Chinese government and developing strategic alliances and partnerships outside of China (Figure 14.6). The firm has found that its rich cultural traditions, a customer-focused strategy, and sound investments in new technologies and product ventures will move it into the new age of the multinational enterprise.

Figure 14.6   Wuliangye's response within the holistic organizational management interface

Source: Adapted from Alon, Ilan, Theodore T. Herbert and J. Mark Muñoz (2006) "Performance Strategies for the Globalizing Chinese Business Enterprise: Resource and Capabilities-Based Insights from a Three-level Strategic Fit Model."

Note

1. Factory web site at: http://www.cbw.com/company/wuliangye/intro.html.

References

Alon, Ilan, Theodore T. Herbert, and J. Mark Muñoz (2006) *Performance Strategies for the Globalizing Chinese Business Enterprise: Resource and Capabilities-Based Insights from a Three-level Strategic Fit Model.*

Asianinfo Daily China News (2002) *Mainland Trademarks Registered in Taiwan*, 8 May:1.

Areddy, James T. (2006) "Chinese Consumer Firms Earn Praise," *The Wall Street Journal*, Wednesday, October 18, 2006: B2C.

China ip Express (2002) *News and Developments of Intellectual Property: Protection & Enforcement in the People's Republic of China*, [www document] http://www.iprights.com/publications/chinapexpress/ciex_121.asp.

COMTEX News Network, Inc. (2006a) "Brewster Wuliangye Nearing Auto Dream," LexisNexis, 14 August.

COMTEX News Network, Inc. (2006b) "Chinese Wineries Remain Upbeat," LexisNexis, 30 March.

Euromonitor (2006) *Alcoholic Drinks in China*, [www document]. http://www.eoromonitor.com/Alcoholic_Drinks_in_China.

Financial Times: Global News Wire—Asia Africa Intelligence Wire (2006a) "Wuliangye Yibin 1st-half Net Profit up 39.19 percent," [www document] http://web.lexis-nexis.com/universe/document?_m=0a760a313d7b412c0e2264fdea78abf.

Financial Times: Global News Wire—Asia Africa Intelligence Wire (2006b) "Wuliangye Brewing Ambitious Plan," [www document] http://web.lexis-nexis.com/universe/document?_m=ec25daf92c3151382113f790e85d260, 18 November.

Goliath Report (2006), "Sichuan Yibin Wuliangye Distillery, October 5," [www document] http://goliath.ecnext.com/free-scripts/documents_view_v3.pl?item_id.

Huron Report (2006) "2006 Best of the Best—Preferred Brands of China's Richest," [www document] http://www.hurun.net/bestdetailen18, region3.aspx.

Just-Drinks (2006a) "China: Wuliangye Quells Sale Talks," [www document] http://www.just-drinks.com/article.aspx?id-86918&lk-alrt3&amd=3076.

Just-Drinks (2006b) "China's Market for Alcoholic Drinks—Forecasts for 2012: The Domestic Market," ABI/INFORM Global:5.

National Bureau of Statistics, China Statistical Yearbook 2002.

Research China (2006) "Distilleries Taste Bigger Profits," [www document] http://www.researchchina.com/news/Beverage/200609/2127.html.

SinoCast China Business Daily News (2002) "China Encourages Foreign Investment in Wine Industry," 17 September:1.

SinoCast China Business Daily News (2004a) "Wuliangye Group Eyes on China's Rubber Tire Laeader," 14 May: 1.

SinoCast China Business Daily News (2006) "Wuliangye to Muscle into Wine Industry," 16 October: 1.

Strategis—Stat-USA Market Research Reports (2006) [www document] http://strategis.ic.gc.ca/epic/internet/inimr-ri3.nsf/en/gr-93115e.html.

TMC Net (2006) "Liquor Firm Building Wine Brand," [www document] http://www.tmcnet.com/usubmit/2006/10/15/1982628.htm.

Ubest (2006) "Push Group Co., Ltd.," [www document] http://www.ubest.net/ton/ton_en.asp?tonid=657.

U.S. Government Documents (2006) [www document] http://www.cia.gov/cia/publications/factbook/rankorder/2119rank.html.

Wang, Jianmao (2006) "Next Five Years down the Road of China's Long March," presentation at the International Meeting of the Production & Operations Management Society (POMS), China Europe International Business School (CEIBS), Shanghai, The People's Republic of China, June.

Xinhua News Agengy—Xinhua Economic News Service (2006b) 'Wuliangye Yibin,' (9 August) [www document] http://web.lexis-lexis.com/universe/document?_m=0a760a313d7b4120e2264fdea78abf.

15
Conclusion: Final Reflections

John R. McIntyre

The world has been coming to China since the days of Deng Xiaoping and the opening of this country's doors. This process of rediscovery has been ongoing for three decades, drawing over 500 billion dollars of foreign investment, driving China's export exploits. A rate of growth of 10% in gross domestic product (GDP) per annum is merely the proverbial "tip of the iceberg" of sea changes under way in the society and economy. In fact, other economies, in Asia, have experienced such a growth rate in the past. What is notable in the Chinese case is obviously China's population estimated at over 1.3 billion inhabitants. As the leading emerging economy, China is set to overtake both Japan and Germany within a time horizon of some 17 years and thereby become the second largest economy (Shenkar, 2006). At currently some 16% of world GDP, China is not far behind the United States or the European Union-27 (IMF, 2007). This process will culminate in the Beijing Olympics, marking China's full reinsertion and acceptance in the world economy. A parallel movement, equally significant and far-reaching, is the extension of Chinese economic influence in the rest of the world and outside of its traditional region of influence (Beraud and Changeur, 2006; Zeng and Williamson, 2007). The emergence of China as one of the new economic powers – not fully global yet and consolidating its role as Asia's central actor – is one of the defining features of the third decade of globalization.

While the debate rages on about the nature of this power shift, whether it is benign or portends deep fissures in the geopolitical architecture, most Chinese do not consider their reemerging economy as a fracture in the long cycles of history. A view supported by Angus Maddison (1998) in his classic work on the world economy and by Antoine van Agtmael (2007), arguing that China is likely to resume its natural role as the world's largest economy by 2015, regaining a position it had held until the early nineteenth century. The underlying question finds roots in a broader set of issues (Maddison, 2001). Will the emergence of China as a regional and global economic power, as manifest in its trade performance, its inward and now outward foreign investments, its military capabilities, and the creative energies of its work-force, represent a challenge to world order and stability? In other words, from global economics to geopolitics the gap is narrow.

China, the Kingdom of the Middle, has become a remarkably open eco-nomy with a trade-to-GDP ratio of 69% and a rising tide of foreign invest-ment (*The Economist*, 2007). It would also be misleading to focus exclusively and obsessively on Chinese low-cost manufacturing, export surpluses glob-ally, and capacity to attract and absorb inward foreign direct investment (FDI). The Economist Intelligence Unit, in a special report on *World Invest-ment Prospects to 2010: Boom or Backlash*, has noted that China's share of world FDI inflows is in fact above its share in world trade and in world GDP at market exchange rates – but not dramatically so. The same report noted that China's share of global FDI is, however, far below its share in world GDP at purchasing power parity (PPP). These figures are harbingers of a great growth potential in both inward and outward FDI. Chinese mul-tinational firms have been learning from joint ventures and best practices of overseas firms establishing roots in China. China's regional and increasingly global economic power derives not only from its export competitiveness but increasingly from its ability to import and invest outside its region and beyond. China's economic strength is being felt around the world through its growing overseas investment in a resource-seeking drive for strategic assets but also increasingly in markets and corporate acquisitions. China has acquired assets across Southeast Asia, Africa, and Central Asia and its outward FDI has more than quintupled in the period 2000–2005, rising to $11.3 billion that year (Economist Intelligence Unit). China's investment finds outlets increasingly in the advanced industrialized countries. In this learning and adaptation process, China has leveraged numerous assets and bridgeheads as it forges ahead in the regional and global economies: Hong Kong, Taiwan, Singapore as well as the Chinese Diaspora.

This book chose a focus that considers resource-based theory of the Chinese firm in understanding its outward FDI behavior; recognizes the unique institutional considerations that underlie Chinese firm interna-tionalization, with particular regard to state-owned enterprises; places the phenomenon in its proper regional context before considering its global implications; and illustrates the contributions made by a series of well-crafted case studies in seeking broad-ranging applicable analyses.

The achievement of a position of leadership for China in world mar-kets is being redefined not only because of the tremendous demand of the Chinese consumers and the growing Chinese economy but also because of the expansion of Chinese firms in foreign countries both developed and developing. The most recent internationalization initiatives such as the pur-chase of Schneider Electronics by TCL in 2002 or the purchase of IBM PC division by Lenovo in 2004, or the purchase of Rover by Nanjing Automotive Industry Corporations (NAICS) in 2005, to mention a few, bear witness to this ongoing process. A notable trend, underlined in a Deutsche Bank study, in matters of Chinese outward investment has been the gradual appearance of cross-border mergers and acquisitions (M&As) as a primary mode for China's direct investment abroad compared to other forms, including joint ventures and the establishment of overseas subsidiaries that have been prevalent in years past.

From 2004 to 2005, China's cross-border M&A purchases increased from $1.3 billion to $2.2 billion, or over 32 (Economist Intelligence Unit). Figures from China's Ministry of Commerce, however, have traditionally underestimated total outward FDI as they include only investments submitted for official approval. Interestingly, the so-called BRICs (Brazil, Russia, India, China), and certainly China remain far more integrated into international FDI inward flows rather than outward. These numbers must be tempered by the observation that the BRICs amount to about 2.4% of global cross-border M&As for 2005 (Sauvant, 2006). They must also be set against the background of what some economists believe to be "an increasing risk of crisis in its still immature financial system and capital markets" (Batson, 2007).

Using the Dunning classification for FDI determinants, Chinese firms investing outward are so far more focused on resource-seeking behavior (natural resource inputs), to achieve ownership rights to commodities such as energy resources and metals. There are some outward investments that are market-seeking investments in manufacturing operations outside China. Investing abroad is regarded as an additional way to keep and increase market shares abroad, particularly for emerging market economies' firms that have captured comparative and competitive advantages of export. Lower labor costs were, on average, the least important motive for emerging economies' firms investing abroad, reflected in the modest frequency of locating production units abroad at this stage in China's internationalization. But, for China, more than for other countries, the advantage of "leaping up the technology ladder" is also a clear motivation for outward investment (Kynge, 2006).

Buckley (2004) has applied the Dunning framework to the peculiarities of the China situation in the global system and has considered how the distortions of China's unique domestic system interact with the global strategies of its multinational enterprises. He concludes that Chinese multinational firms engage in suboptimal location decisions, excessively internalizing their activities within China. The Chinese government's "going out" policy has encouraged some overseas investment to lessen the dependency on the local market and achieve global brand status and reputational reach. In short, Chinese multinationals continue to grow in terms of both their size and global ambitions. Allied to a steady appreciation of the renminbi, their ability to engage in efficiency-seeking and asset-seeking acquisition patterns, like their more traditional Western sisters, can only grow.

Chinese firms that choose the path to global leadership will face the leading Western-based multinationals and their home markets. First attempts are under way such as Hair, the microwave manufacturer, which produces in the US market and sells through the Wal-Mart network. Chinese automotive company producers Brilliance and Chery are entering the European Union market. Other cases reviewed in our contributions include the Bank of China, China Telecom, Hua Wei, Lenovo, PetroChina, Sinpec, TCL International, and Tsingtao Beer. This is not a new phenomenon with firms from so-called third world countries. In fact, a literature developed in the 1980s with authors such as Kumar and McLeod (1981) and Wells (1983), among others, trying to find models with descriptive, explanatory, and predictive power. Third world multinationals are already competing with the largest multinationals in the world. They are already global firms and China is joining an existing trend that is well established. But the Chinese approach, precisely because of the systemic features of the Chinese economy and its paramount role in the region, yields different and largely unexplored patterns. In short, the external environment governing Chinese firms' decision making and implementation of outward FDI yield theoretically diverse explanations.

Zeng and Williamson (2004) evolved a fourfold typology of Chinese companies going international, in the wake of the Chinese government's open policy: national champions pursuing their advantage as domestic leaders to build global brands; dedicated exporters leveraging their economy of scale to penetrate foreign markets; competitive networks that bring together smaller, specialized companies operating closely together; and technology upstarts, using innovations of China's government-owned research institution to enter new emerging sectors. These are all budding multinationals whose behavior and whose environmental opportunities and constraints deserve deepening analysis.

Existing theoretical frameworks have partial applicability to the Chinese situation. John Dunning's eclectic paradigm model (1993) predicts that a firm has to possess firm-specific advantages to be able to invest abroad and that the foreign location should be better than the one at home, that internalization is the best mode for maximization for firm-specific advantages. Dunning's investment development path paradigm (1981) postulates that, before investing abroad, countries first host FDI and that investing abroad is a function of GDP per capita. It is also established that the changing net outward investment position of a country cannot be explained only by rising GDP but also by the changing configuration of a firm, location, and internalization advantages and macroorganizational policies. The new version of the investment development path model, as presented by Dunning and Narula, posits that in a globalized world outward FDI starts earlier and the amplitudes of the stages are shorter.

The Uppsala sequential internationalization process model predicts a "normal" sequential step-by-step learning process in the stages of internationalization (Johanson and Valhne, 1990). But critics are convinced that internationalization is not necessarily sequential and that knowledge gained from other firms may allow some leapfrogging – a process that is indeed seen in our authors' contributions. Many studies indicate that management is crucial in the internationalization of firms and that investing abroad is often influenced by risk-taking management willing to undertake risky operations in the early stage of a firm's development. Investing in Triad countries for Chinese-based firms may seem less risky but it is in fact fraught with perils for newcomers to the world of Triad M&As. Therefore, outward-bound FDI cannot be understood without looking into strategic management theories. In this sense, Chinese firms have much to learn in navigating globalization of their firms' operations to gain effective corporate governance structure and strengthen their financial base as they reach out of boundaries.

Wells (1983) observed that "the theories have done little to answer why firms from developing countries invest abroad" and data are lacking to confirm the relevance of some of the existing body of internationalization theory. Matheus concluded that most of the leading theories of multinational firm internationalization, growth, and expansion are somewhat inadequate and proposed a "process-oriented account of dragon multinationals' transnationalization in which three key elements are emphasized: outward orientation, leverage through building linkages and achieving organizational efficiency through integration" (2002). Nolan and Zhang, in a growing body of work, have noted that fast-growing, late-industrializing countries that it is realistic to hope "that Chinese large enterprise would be able to 'catch' rapidly with the world's leading firms" (2002).

This work has sought to open new pathways on the nascent and expanding phenomenon of the internationalization of Chinese firms, building on a scant but growing body of thought (Child and Rodrigues, 2005). Both China scholars and business managers will derive from this collective research work a deeper understanding and more insightful strategic choices as Chinese firms reach out of boundaries. This process will change the operating rules of the multinational game in both anticipated and unexpected ways.

References

Batson, A. (2007) "Why China isn't cheering its GDP," *The Wall Street Journal*, April 20, p A2.

Beraud, P. and Changeur, S. (eds.) (2006) *La Chine dans la Mondialisation: Marches et Stratégies*, Maisonneuve & Larose: Paris.

Buckley, P. (2004) "The Role of China in the Global Strategy of Multinational Enterprises," *Journal of Chinese Economic and Business Studies*, January (2): 1–25.

Child, J. and Rodrigues, S. (2005) "The Internationalization of Chinese Firms: A Case for Theoretical Extension," *Management and Organization Review* 1 (3): 381–410.

Deutsche Bank. (2005) *Global Champions in Waiting: Perspectives on China's Overseas Direct Investment*, August 2006.

Dunning, J.H. (1981) "Explaining Outward Direct Investment of Developing Countries: In Support of the Eclectic Theory of International Production," in Kumar, K. and McLeod, M.C. (eds) *Multinationals from Developing Countries*, Lexington Books: Lexington, Kentucky.

Dunning, J.H. (1993) *Multinational Enterprises and the Global Economy*, Addison Wesley Publishing Company: Workingham.

Dunning, J.H., and Narula, R. (1996) "The Investment Development Path Revisited: Some Emerging Issues," *Foreign Direct Investment and Governments, Catalyst for Economic Restructuring*, Routledge: London.

The Economist. (2007) "Reaching for a Renaissance: A Special Report on China and its Region," *The Economist*, 31 March 2007, pp. 3–18.

Economist Intelligence Unit and the Colombia Program on International Investment. (2006) *World Investment Prospects to 2010: Boom or Backlash?*

International Monetary Fund. (2007) *World Economic Outlook 2007: Spillovers and cycles in the Global Economy*, International Monetary Fund: Washington, DC.

Johanson, J. and Vahlne, J.E. (1990) "The Mechanisms of Internationalization," *International Marketing Review* 7: 11–24.

Kumar, K. and McLeod, M.G. (1981) *Multinationals from Developing Countries*, Lexington Books: Lexington, Kentucky.

Kynge, J. (2006) *China Shake the World: A Titan's Rise and Troubled Future—and the Challenge for America*, Houghton Mifflin Company: New York.

Maddison, A. (1998) *Chinese Economic Performance in the Long Run*, OECD Publishing: Paris.

Maddison, A. (2001) *The World Economy: A Millennial Perspective*, OECD Publishing: Paris.

Matheus, A.J. (2002) *Dragon Multinationals: A New Model for Global Growth*, Oxford University Press: New York.

Nolan, P. and Zhang, J. (2002) *The Challenge of Globalization for Large Chinese Firms*, UNCTAD Paper No. 162, July 2002, UNCTAD: Geneva.

Sauvant, K.P. (2006) "Inward and outward FDI and the BRICs," in Jain, S. (ed.) *Competing with the BRICs*, Edward Elgar: Cheltenham.

Shenkar, O. (2006) *The Chinese Century: The Rising Chinese Economy and its Impact on the Global Economy, the Balance of Power, and Your Job*, Wharton School Publishing.

van Agtmael, A. (2007) *The Emerging Markets Century: How a New Breed of World-Class Companies is Overtaking the World*, Simon & Schuster: New York.

Wells, L. Jr. (1983) *Third World Multinationals: The Rise of Foreign Investment from Developing Countries*, MIT Press: Cambridge, MA.

Zeng, M. and Williamson, P.J. (2004) "The Hidden Dragons," *Harvard Business Review on Doing Business in China*, Harvard Business School Publishing Corporation: Boston, MA, pp. 57–78.

Zeng, M. and Williamson, P.J. (2007) *Dragons at Your Door: How Chinese Cost Innovation is Disrupting Global Competition*, Harvard Business School Press: Cambridge, MA.

Author Index

Subject Index

Non-textual references, such as Figures or Tables, are in *italic* print